THE
NEEDLECRAFT
SHOP
PRESENTS

Afghan Romance™

Editorial Director: *Donna Robertson*
Product Development Manager: *Fran Rohus*
Production/Photography Director: *Ange Van Arman*

Editorial
Senior Editor/Story Author: *Jennifer Christiansen McClain*
Editor: *Sharon Lothrop*
Associate Editors: *Lyne Pickens, Jana Robertson, Trudy Atteberry*
Copy Editor: *Salway Sabri*

Production
Production Manager: *Cathy Mullins*
Book Design: *Greg Smith*
Color Specialist: *Betty Holmes*
Production Coordinator: *Glenda Chamberlain*

Photography
Photography Manager: *Scott Campbell*
Photographers: *Russell Chaffin, Keith Godfrey*
Photography Coordinator/Stylist: *Ruth Whitaker*

Product Design
Design Coordinator: *Tonya Flynn*

Business
CEO: *John Robinson*
Vice President/Marketing: *Greg Deily*

Dear Friends,

Romance is as much a part of our day-to-day lives as the rising and setting sun. All around us, people search for and participate in romance of all sorts. What does romance have to do with afghans? As you read this letter, you are holding in your hands a unique new addition to the craft industry. A unique new twist on an ages-old craft, this book is the first of its kind. Never before has anyone presented crochet patterns in this way — intertwined with a charming love story.

When Fran Rohus and Donna Robertson first approached me about doing a book such as this, we were both a little apprehensive. We had never attempted a creation such as this, and even though the idea seemed feasible, we knew we were breaking new ground. As I began working on the story, the book began to take shape and soon, we were on a roll. It turned out to truly be an adventure in creativity and teamwork.

I hope you enjoy the short story we have wound around this gorgeous selection of afghans. As always, these are never-before-published designs from extremely talented people who are also in love with crochet. After reading the story, perhaps you can incorporate some of our heroine's ideology into your own life by using crochet to spread love to all those around you.

Here's to romance,

Jennifer

Credits

Sincerest thanks to all the designers, manufacturers and other professionals whose dedication has made this book possible.

Library of Congress Cataloging-in-Publication Data
ISBN: 1-57367-108-8
First Printing 1999
Library of Congress Catalog Card Number: 99-74316
Published and Distributed by:
The Needlecraft Shop, LLC, Big Sandy, Texas 75755
www.needlecraftshop.com
Printed in the United States of America.

The story included in this book is a work of fiction. Names, characters, places and incidents are products of the author's imagination or are used fictitiously. Any resemblance to actual events or locales or persons, living or dead, is entirely coincidental.

Contents

Comforting Country

Antique Treasures

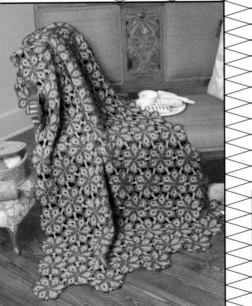

City Sophistication

Everyday Delights

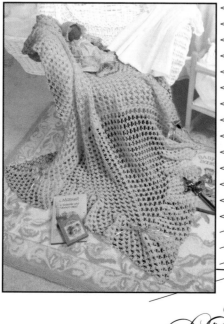

Dear Ashley

Corinne awoke with a start. Heart pounding, she lay motionless, staring off into the dark room. Hemi, her cat, still lay peacefully curled in a silky blue-gray ball, obviously untroubled by whatever Corinne had heard. Suddenly, a brilliant light pierced the room, followed by a loud crack of thunder. Relieved, she closed her eyes, realizing that must have been what had awakened her. Rolling over, she reached down and pulled the afghan up from the foot of the bed. As she lay there listening to the storm brewing in the distance, she couldn't help but be reminded of Steven. Oh, how they had loved to snuggle together when it stormed. The thunderstorms of early spring in Colorado could be quite spectacular, and growing up, Corinne had dreaded them. But nestled safe within Steven's strong, loving arms, she was never scared. It was one of the many magical times of her four short years with him. So much magic, so little time.

The next morning dawned as sunny as ever, the landscape rinsed clean by its pre-dawn shower. As the coffee brewed in the kitchen, Corinne finished brushing her shoulder-length chestnut hair. Opening the dresser drawer, she picked up the flannel shirt and jeans she'd folded just yesterday and carried them to the kitchen. Glaring at her from his perch atop the window seat, Hemi meowed impatiently, thoroughly confused as to why his morning meal wasn't in his dish yet. "Oh, Hemingway," she mused aloud, "we go through this every morning. Why is it that you think the food should just be waiting there for you when you know darn good and well I have to open the can?" Her query fell on disinterested ears, as Hemi proceeded to perform the ritualistic dance he did each day, weaving in and out between her legs, while she went about carefully emptying the contents of the can into his dish. Purring loudly, Hemi voraciously dove face-first into the tidbits and gravy served him and began to gulp it down as if it were to be his last. "Will you ever learn, you silly thing," Corinne chided the gluttonous tom. "I know you used to have to scrounge for food, but those days are gone. Remember," she patted his head, "I promised that you'd never go hungry again. Judging from the size of your tummy, I shouldn't feed you but once a day anyhow. Oh, well! I guess everyone is allowed to hang onto a little baggage, even cats."

With Hemi contentedly licking his whiskers, Corinne poured a cup of coffee and set about toasting a bagel for her breakfast. Sunday was her favorite day. A time to recharge before launching herself into another tightly scheduled week. She walked over to the window and gazed out at the pristine scenery that surrounded her home. Nestled in the rolling foothills of the Rocky Mountains southwest of Denver, Morningside Ranch was a unique blend of raw beauty and manicured luxury. Purchased by her grandfather decades ago with funds from the sale of his West Virginia farm, the ranch now spanned more than twice its original thousand acres. Corinne's father, Eustace "Milt" Hamilton, had inherited the operation when he was just twenty-one and despite some trying times in the early years, eventually transformed it into a grand showplace. The quaint house Corinne called home had been built by her father when he first married. Today, Milt and Clarice lived in the restored Victorian home that had been his father's. The huge rooms and high ceilings served as the perfect setting for Clarice's antique collection.

As she munched a banana and leafed through yesterday's mail, Corinne's eye fell on a thick, pale blue envelope addressed in an all-too-familiar handwriting. Conspicuously missing, however, was the trademark heart-shaped happy face her childhood friend, Ashley Cunningham, normally penned in the upper right corner. "How odd," Corinne thought as she opened the back and extracted the letter. "What on earth could Ashley possibly have to say that would take this much paper?" Scooting Hemi out of the way, she sat down on the window seat and wrapped an afghan around her legs. She took a sip of coffee and began to read. Twenty minutes later, the now-cold bagel still untouched in the toaster, a teary-eyed Corinne looked up and heaved a sigh of sympathy. She had known Ashley since they were four, and when the wedding invitation had arrived two months ago, she'd tried to be happy for her friend. On the surface, Doug had seemed nice enough, but when Corinne had met him once while in Kansas City, she had felt distinctly uneasy about the cavalier way he approached the upcoming nuptials. "Poor Ashley," she said aloud. Hemi looked up from where he lay curled at her feet and she scratched his ear lovingly. "I guess not everyone can find their knight-in-shining-armor like I did."

At that moment a little light went on in Corinne's head. "You know Hemi, with five great matches to my credit, maybe I should be the one to choose Ashley's next guy. She obviously needs a little help, and since I seem to be able to pick them, I'll just do it for her. Actually," she smiled as she reached to lift Hemi off the afghan, "I think I already know who'd be the perfect match. You just watch, Hemi," she announced, "Corinne Hamilton Thornburg, matchmaker par excellence will strike again."

Mountain Sunrise

Designed by Maggie Weldon

SIZE: 42" x 62".

MATERIALS: Worsted-weight yarn — 30 oz. off-white and 23 oz. variegated; tapestry needle; J crochet hook or size needed to obtain gauge.

GAUGE: 6 sts = 2"; rnds 1-2 = 2½" across. Each Block is 6¾" square.

SKILL LEVEL: ☆☆ Average

BLOCK (make 54)

Rnd 1: With off-white, ch 3, sl st in first ch to form ring, ch 3, 2 dc in ring, ch 2, (3 dc in ring, ch 2) 3 times, join with sl st in top of ch-3, fasten off (12 dc, 4 corner ch-2 sps).

Rnd 2: Join variegated with sc in st before one corner ch sp, 3 sc in next ch sp, sc in next st, ch 10, skip next st, (sc in next st, 3 sc in next ch sp, sc in next st, ch 10, skip next st) around, join with sl st in first sc, fasten off (20 sc, 4 ch-10 lps).

Rnd 3: Join off-white with sl st in center st of any 3-sc group, ch 3, (dc, ch 2, 2 dc) in same st, *[dc in each of next 2 sts; working behind next ch-10 sp, dc in skipped st on rnd before last, dc in each of next 2 sts on last rnd], (2 dc, ch 2, 2 dc) in next st; repeat from * 2 more times; repeat between [ ], join with sl st in top of ch-3, fasten off (36 dc, 4 ch sps).

Rnd 4: Join variegated with sc in any corner ch sp, 2 sc in same sp, *[sc in each of next 2 sts, (ch 10, skip next st, sc in next st) 3 times, sc in next st], 3 sc in next corner ch sp; repeat from * 2 more times; repeat between [ ], join with sl st in first sc, fasten off (36 sc, 12 ch-10 lps).

Rnd 5: Join off-white with sl st in any center corner st, ch 5, dc in same st, *[dc in each of next 3 sts; working behind ch-10 sps, (dc in next skipped st on rnd before last, dc in next st on last rnd) 3 times, dc in each of next 2 sts], (dc, ch 2, dc) in next center corner st; repeat from * 2 more times; repeat between [ ], join with sl st in 3rd ch of ch-5 (13 dc on each side between corner ch sps).

Continued on page 135

Dearest Ashley

I know I should have called when I got your letter, but I figured we'd just end up crying. Besides, what could I possibly say at this time that would make you feel better? You know I believe everything happens for a purpose and if your marriage to Doug wasn't meant to be, then I'm glad you found out now. What a louse! I can't believe he'd be so stupid as to get caught in your apartment with another woman! Did you really throw a lamp at him? You should have used a chair! Oh, Ashley, I know it's hard to keep your chin up, but look — you have your entire life still ahead of you and there ARE lots of great guys around. You'll soon find someone to help you over the hump, and I may know just the guy to do it. I haven't ever said much to you about Tyler, our ranch manager, but maybe now's a good time. He's tall, dark, handsome and I know he's a gentleman. Oohhh! I still see red every time I think about what Doug did to you!!

How are you handling work with Doug right down the hall? I know what you need — a vacation. Why don't you come to Morningside? You haven't been out in ages and you haven't seen my cat, Hemi, either. Hemi is short for Hemingway. Remember, I told you I was teaching that adult reading program? One night as I was leaving the library, I heard the most pitiful meows. I walked over to a nearby dumpster and called. Then, here comes the mangiest little gray cat I'd ever seen. You know me! I couldn't resist, so I took him home. Little did I realize that I had found a truly intelligent cat with immaculate manners, except where eating is concerned, but that's another letter entirely. Trust me, you'll be impressed. You should see him now. It's very difficult to write a letter with a cat in your lap. Unfortunately, he seems to think the sofa is his, especially when the fireplace is going.

Now, back to the issue of your visit. Please think about it seriously. I'd love to have you, and you know how wonderfully peaceful it is here. You can't let this Doug thing get to you, okay? I know it hurts now, and it will keep on hurting for quite a while, any loss does. You know how I was after Steven died. I didn't think I'd ever get better, but I have, and you will, too. Write again soon!

All my love, C—

Reflections

Designed by Jennifer Christiansen McClain

SIZE: 55" x 67" not including Fringe.

MATERIALS: Chunky yarn — 55 oz. pastel variegated; mohair sport yarn — 19 oz. off-white; J and K crochet hooks or sizes needed to obtain gauges.

GAUGE: With **J hook and chunky yarn,** 5 dc = 2"; 3 dc rows = 2". With **K hook and 2 strands mohair sport yarn held together,** 2 sc = ¾"; 2 rows = ¾".

SKILL LEVEL: ☆☆ Average

AFGHAN

NOTES: *Leave 7" end when joining and fastening off to be worked in Fringe later.*

Do not *turn at ends of rows unless otherwise stated.*

Use J hook with chunky yarn and K hook with mohair yarn throughout.

Ch-3 at beginning of rows is used and counted as first st.

*For **2-tr cluster (cl)**, yo 2 times, insert hook in next ch-1 sp, yo, draw lp through, (yo, draw through 2 lps on hook) 2 times, yo 2 times, insert hook in same ch-1 sp, yo, draw lp through, (yo, draw through 2 lps on hook) 2 times, yo, draw through all 3 lps on hook.*

Row 1: With chunky yarn, ch 169, dc in 4th ch from hook, dc in each ch across, fasten off (167 dc).

Rows 2-3: Join chunky yarn with sl st in first st, ch 3, dc in same st, 2 dc in each of next 2 sts across, fasten off.

Row 4: With 2 strands mohair yarn held together, join with sc in first st, (ch 1, skip next st, sc in each of next 2 sts) across to last st, sc in last st, **turn.**

Row 5: For **cable row,** ch 1, sc in first st, (skip next 2 sts, cl in next ch-1 sp; holding cl to back, sc in each of last 2 skipped sts) across to last st, sc in last st, **turn,** fasten off.

Rows 6-8: Join chunky yarn with sl st in first st, ch 3, dc in each st across, fasten off.

Rows 9-10: Repeat rows 4 and 5.

Rows 11-15: Join chunky yarn with sl st in first st, ch 3, dc in each st across, fasten off.

Rows 16-96: Repeat rows 4-15 consecutively, ending with row 13. At end of last row, fasten off.

FRINGE

For **each Fringe,** cut 2 strands each 15" long of each color; holding all 4 strands together, fold in half; insert hook in end of row, draw fold through, draw all loose ends through fold including 7" end, tighten. Trim ends.

Work Fringe in each dc row and in each cable row across short ends of Afghan.❦

Dear Journal,

What a beautiful day. Had dinner with Mom and Dad. Juanita outdid herself, as usual, with a scrumptious chicken dish. I don't know what we'd do with out her, or Ben for that matter. We'd be hard-pressed to find a couple that would work as well for the ranch as they do. After dinner, I told them about Ashley's news and that I'd invited her to visit. They agreed wholeheartedly.

Preston must be swamped! I haven't heard from him for two days. You'd think once a girl gets a diamond ring, at least she'd get a ring on the phone occasionally. I shouldn't complain. Preston's business has been so successful the last few months, I know it's all for the best. Once he's established among the architectural community in Chicago, life will be much easier for him. Then maybe he won't have to work 16-hour days and we can have some time together.

I must get my stitching done tonight. The guild is having another meeting tomorrow to plan our "Great Afghan Give-Away." We have over four hundred afghans so far to hand out to needy families. We're going to go to the Mile-High Faith Center downtown and "auction" the afghans Chinese style. Each family that signs up will take a number. When their number is called, they will go up and choose an afghan or two, depending on the size of their family. Any afghans that are left will go to the West Denver Homeless Shelter so Brother Dan can give them out to anyone who comes in. It's such a great feeling to help others. I guess that's why I do it. I've had so much all my life that I can't imagine what it would be like not having clothes, food or blankets. Preston says I'm a sucker for a sad face, but I say he's wrong. God intended those of us with plenty to help those in need, and I fully intend to keep it up.

Faithful Friends

Designed by Maggie Weldon

SIZE: 46" x 67".

MATERIALS: Worsted-weight yarn — 24½ oz. white, 17½ oz. gray, 14 oz. pink and small amount black; 60 black ⁹⁄₁₆" flat buttons; craft glue or hot glue gun; black sewing thread; sewing and tapestry needles; H crochet hook or size needed to obtain gauge.

GAUGE: 7 sts = 2"; 4 sc rows = 1". Each Block is 9" x 11".

SKILL LEVEL: ☆☆ Average

BLOCK (make 30)

NOTES: *When changing colors (see page 159), always drop yarn to wrong side of work. Use a separate skein or ball of yarn for each color section. **Do not** carry yarn across from one section to another. Fasten off colors at end of each color section.*

Work odd-numbered graph rows from right to left and even-numbered rows from left to right.

Each square on graph equals one sc.

Row 1: With white, ch 25, sc in 2nd ch from hook, sc in each ch across, turn (24 sc).

Row 2: Ch 1, sc in each st across, turn.

Row 3: For **row 3 of Graph** (see page 135), ch 1, sc in each of first 2 sts changing to pink in last st made, sc in next 16 sts changing to gray in last st made, sc in next 4 sts changing to white in last st made, sc in each of last 2 sts, turn.

Rows 4-36: Ch 1, sc in each st across changing colors according to Graph, turn. At end of last row, **do not** fasten off.

Rnd 37: Working in rnds around outer edge, in sts and in ends of rows, ch 3, (dc, ch 2, 2 dc) in same st, dc in next 22 sts, (2 dc, ch 2, 2 dc) in next st, *skip first row, (dc in next 6 rows, skip next row) 5 times*; working in starting ch on opposite side of row 1, (2 dc, ch 2, 2 dc) in first ch, dc in next 22 chs, (2 dc, ch 2, 2 dc) in last ch; repeat between **, join with sl st in top of ch-3, fasten off (26 sts across each short end between corner ch sps; 34 sts across each long edge between corner ch sps).

NOTE: *For cross stitch (cr st), skip next st, dc in next st; working over dc just made, dc in skipped st.*

Rnd 38: Join pink with sl st in corner ch sp before one short end, ch 3, (dc, ch 2, 2 dc) in same sp, **cross st** around with (2 dc, ch 2, 2 dc) in each corner ch sp, join, fasten off (13 cross sts and 4 dc across each short end between corner ch sps; 17 cross sts and 4 dc across each long edge between corner ch sps).

Continued on page 135

Dear Ashley,

Hello! Got your letter. It certainly sounded a lot more upbeat than the last, but based on what you said, you still need to get away. You can't spend your life eating Hagendaz on the sofa wrapped in an afghan, even if it is one I gave you! I know it must be depressing having to deal with Doug at work, but you know, you could look for another job. You're one of the best corporate lawyers around, and I'm sure there's another firm in Kansas City that would love to have you! I'd bet if Abernathy & Yost thought they might lose you, they'd probably fire Doug. Wouldn't that be revenge! What did you see in that rat anyway? Yeah, he's handsome, rich and charming, but what good is that if he doesn't know how to treat a lady. Now take Tyler for instance. He's always a gentleman. I know it's been years since you've seen him, so let me refresh your memory. He's very charming, very handsome and looks great in a pair of Wranglers. I can't wait to introduce you two again. He can only remember you as a giggling teenager who wore braces and talked too much. I told him that I was positive he'd have a very different opinion now.

I've been horribly busy helping the guild plan our "Great Afghan Give-Away." It's a charity event to supply needy families with free afghans. It's been really fun, but very tiring. I've crocheted till bedtime every night for weeks. Hemi gets very impatient if I stitch too much. He prefers that I read so he can lay in my lap.

Well, better close for now. Write soon so we can discuss when you're going to take that vacation.

Love, C—

Tropical Evening

Designed by Geneva Boggs

SIZE: 48" x 71".

MATERIALS: Worsted-weight yarn — 20 oz. blue, 15 oz. green, 10 oz. each variegated and mauve; G and H crochet hooks or sizes needed to obtain gauges.

GAUGES: With **H hook,** lg shell = 1¾"; 6 lg shell rows = 5". With **G hook,** 7 dc = 2"; 3 dc rows = 2". Each Strip is 5¾" wide.

SKILL LEVEL: ☆☆ Average

STRIP (make 8)
NOTES: *For **small shell (sm shell),** (2 dc, ch 1, 2 dc) in next st or ch sp.*

*For **beginning large shell (beg lg shell),** ch 3, (2 dc, ch 1, 3 dc) in same st or ch sp.*

*For **large shell (lg shell),** (3 dc, ch 1, 3 dc) in next st or ch sp.*

Ch-3 at beginning of each row is used and counted as first st.

Row 1: With H hook and variegated, ch 6, sl st in first ch to form ring, beg shell in ring, turn (1 lg shell).

Rows 2-78: Ch 3, lg shell in ch sp of next shell, dc in last dc, turn. At end of last row, fasten off (1 lg shell, 2 dc).

NOTE: *Use G hook for remainder of pattern.*

Rnd 79: Working in rnds around outer edge, in sts and in ends of rows, join mauve with sl st in ring at base of lg shell on row 1; beg lg shell, ch 1, skip first row, sm shell in next row, 3 dc in each of next 75 rows, sm shell in last row, ch 1; lg shell in next lg shell, sm shell in first row, 3 dc in each of next 75 rows, sm shell in next row, skip last row, join with sl st in top of ch-3, **turn,** fasten off.

Rnd 80: Join green with sl st in first lg shell, beg lg shell, *3 dc in next ch sp, sm shell in next sm shell, 3 dc in sp between same sm shell and next 3-dc group, 3 dc in each sp between 3-dc groups across to next sm shell, 3-dc in sp between last 3-dc group and next sm shell, sm shell in next sm shell, 3 dc in next ch sp*, lg shell in next lg shell; repeat between **, join, **turn,** fasten off.

Rnd 81: Join blue with sl st in first lg shell, beg lg shell, *3 dc in sp between same lg shell and next 3-dc group, 3 dc in sp between 3-dc group and next sm shell, sm shell in next sm shell, 3 dc in sp between same sm shell and next 3-dc group, 3 dc in each sp between 3-dc groups across to next sm shell, 3 dc in sp between last 3-dc group and next sm shell, sm shell in next sm shell, 3 dc in sp between same sm shell and next 3-dc group, 3 dc in sp between 3-dc group and next lg shell*, lg shell in

Continued on page 135

My dearest Preston,

Got your message today, thanks for calling! I've tried to call you a hundred times over the last couple weeks and all I get is your answering machine. I know this Anderson project must have you totally exhausted. Maybe when our schedules slow down a little we can get away for awhile. I hear New Zealand is great this time of year. Think about it, love. It's been ages since we seen each other. Promise me you'll at least think about it, okay?

I hadn't told you about Ashley yet, had I. Well, the prince-charming she was engaged to turned out to be a real toad! She came home from a seminar in Tampa several weeks ago and found Doug and another woman involved in some very interpersonal communication in her apartment. Turns out the woman, who had on a brass-studded black leather teddy and cape outfit, was Ashley's new next-door neighbor. Now, not only does she have to work with "Doug the Slug," but she has to live down the hall from "Vampirella." I told her she needed a vacation and suggested she come to Morningside. A couple weeks of fresh Colorado air would really do her good.

We're only a week away from the "Great Afghan Give-Away," the fund-raiser I've been helping with. I just finished my fourth afghan in as many weeks. At last count we had 548 afghans that had been donated. It's so heart-warming to see how eager people are to help those less fortunate than themselves. It's late, so I better finish. It really was great to hear from you, Sweetheart. Call again as soon as you can.

Love, C—

Spring Melody

Designed by Melissa Leapman

SIZE: 46" x 67" not including Fringe.

MATERIALS: Worsted-weight yarn — 18 oz. lt. rust, 14 oz. each dk. rust and peach, 7 oz. each brown and off-white; H crochet hook or size needed to obtain gauge.

GAUGE: Three 3-dc groups = 2½"; 5 rows worked in pattern = 3".

SKILL LEVEL: ☆☆ Average

AFGHAN

Row 1: With lt. rust, ch 217, 3 dc in 7th ch from hook, (skip next 2 chs, 3 dc in next ch) 4 times, skip next 5 chs, (3 dc in next ch, skip next 2 chs) 4 times, *(3 dc, ch 3, 3 dc) in next ch, (skip next 2 chs, 3 dc in next ch) 4 times, skip next 5 chs, (3 dc in next ch, skip next 2 chs) 4 times; repeat from * across to last ch, (3 dc, ch 3, dc) in last ch, turn (70 3-dc groups, 8 ch sps).

NOTE: *Work remainder of pattern in ch sps and in sps between 3-dc groups.*

Row 2: Ch 6, 3 dc in first ch sp, 3 dc in next 4 sps, skip next sp, 3 dc in next 4 sps, *(3 dc, ch 2, 3 dc) in next ch sp, 3 dc in next 4 sps, skip next sp, 3 dc in next 4 sps; repeat from * across to last ch sp, (3 dc, ch 3, dc) in last ch sp, turn, fasten off.

Row 3: Join dk. rust with sl st in first st, ch 6, 3 dc in next ch sp, 3 dc in next 4 sps, skip next sp, 3 dc in next 4 sps, *(3 dc, ch 2, 3 dc) in next ch sp, 3 dc in next 4 sps, skip next sp, 3 dc in next 4 sps; repeat from * across to last ch sp, (3 dc, ch 3, dc) in last ch sp, turn.

Rows 4-90: Repeat rows 2 and 3 alternately, working in color sequence of brown, dk. rust, lt. rusk, peach, off-white, peach, lt. rust, dk. rust, ending with row 2 and lt. rust.

FRINGE

For **each Fringe,** cut 20 strands lt. rust each 21" long. With all 20 strands held together, fold in half, insert hook in ch sp of point, draw fold through, draw all loose ends through fold, tighten. Trim ends.

Fringe in each point on each short end of Afghan.

Grandma's Favorite

Designed by Darla J. Fanton

SIZE: 53½" x 75½".

MATERIALS: Worsted-weight yarn — 37½ oz. med. blue, 20 oz. scrap yarn in assorted colors; K crochet hook or size needed to obtain gauge.

GAUGE: Rnds 1-5 of each Motif = 4" across.

SKILL LEVEL: ☆☆ Average

MOTIFS (make 140)

Rnd 1: With desired color scrap yarn, ch 4, sl st in first ch to form ring, ch 1, 8 sc in ring, join with sl st in first sc, fasten off (8 sc).

Rnd 2: Join next color scrap yarn with sl st in any sc, ch 3, hdc in next st, ch 2, (hdc in next st, ch 1, hdc in next st, ch 2) around, join with sl st in 2nd ch of ch-3, fasten off (8 ch sps).

Rnd 3: Join scrap yarn with sl st in any ch-2 sp, ch 3, (dc, ch 2, 2 dc) in same sp, ch 1, skip next ch-1 sp, *(2 dc, ch 2, 2 dc) in next ch-2 sp, ch 1, skip next ch-1 sp; repeat from * around, join with sl st in top of ch-3, fasten off (16 dc, 8 ch sps).

Rnd 4: Join next color scrap yarn with sl st in any corner ch-2 sp, ch 4, (dc, ch 2, dc, ch 1, dc) in same sp, *[ch 1, dc next 2 sts tog, ch 1; working over ch-1 sp on last rnd, dc in ch-1 sp on rnd before last, ch 1, dc next 2 sts tog, ch 1], (dc, ch 1, dc, ch 2, dc, ch 1, dc, ch 1) in next corner ch-2 sp; repeat from * 2 more times; repeat between [ ], join with sl st in 3rd ch of ch-4, fasten off (6 ch-1 sps across each side between corner ch-2 sps).

Rnd 5: Join med. blue with sl st in any corner ch-2 sp, ch 3, (dc, ch 2, 2 dc) in same sp, *[dc in each ch-1 sp across to next corner ch-2 sp skipping sts in between], (2 dc, ch 2, 2 dc) in next sp; repeat from * 2 more times; repeat between [ ]; join with sl st in top of ch-3 (10 dc across each side between corner ch-2 sps).

Rnd 6: Ch 1, skip first st, sc in next st, *[sl st in next corner ch sp, ch 12, sc in same sp], (ch 12, skip next st, sc in next st) 5 times; repeat from * 2 more times; repeat between [ ], ch 12, skip next st, (sc in next st, ch 12, skip next st) 4 times, join with sl st in first sc, fasten off (24 ch-12 lps).

ASSEMBLY

NOTE: *When beginnning to lace Motifs or Motif rows together, always begin with Motif on left.*

To **lace ch-12 lps between Motifs together,** lay 2 Motifs side by side on flat surface, beginning on left Motif, insert hook from bottom to top in bottom corner ch lp on this Motif and from top to bottom in bottom corner ch lp on right Motif at same time, draw 2nd lp through *(lp twists automatically when you pick up next ch-12 lp)*; *insert hook from bottom to top in next lp on left Motif, draw lp through, insert hook from top to bottom in next lp on right Motif, draw lp through; repeat from * 5 more times; secure last lp with safety pin to use when lacing Motif rows.

Working on opposite side of last joined Motif, lace Motifs together, making 10 strips of 14 Motifs each.

Continued on page 136

Corinne still loved to fly, a tribute to her determination not to let Steven's death ruin her life. Ever since she learned his Cessna had crashed in a mountainous region of South America, she'd vowed to go on living. Steven would have wanted it that way. As a doctor, he was devoted to helping others live, and if he could have said goodbye to Corinne, he'd have wrung that promise from her with those loving brown eyes just as surely as he'd stolen her heart.

Beneath them the countryside shouted, "Spring has sprung!" Holding Hemi on her lap, she leaned against the window to get a better view. Fields in various shades of green and brown formed an intricate crazy-quilt design on the earth below. Some pieces were neatly shaped, perfectly edged by ribbons of gray or brown. Some were worn and appeared to be stitched together along tattered edges by black-green tree rows and silvery rivers. Shimmery lakes and ponds added the finishing touch, like glistening sequins in the mid-day sun.

The finished piece reminded her of the journey of her life. Born in possession of a diamond-studded version of the proverbial silver-spoon, she'd never lacked for anything. Never, that is, until the sudden demise of her beloved Steven. Then, for long, sorrowful months, she struggled with the reason for life itself. Slowly, with the help of family and friends, and by throwing herself into her charity work, she found purpose again by helping others. That's when she'd learned to truly love crochet. The steady intertwining of yarn to build stitch upon stitch seemed the perfect way to slowly weave together the strands of her shattered life. Today, she still found solace most through her hooks and yarn.

It was brilliantly sunny when the Hamilton's jet landed at Logan International Airport in Boston. By the time Phillip, the family's pilot of ten years, had the plane in the hanger and the girls' luggage unloaded, the rented Toyota 4-Runner had already arrived. As the girls began packing their cargo, Ashley commented, "You have such astounding taste, Corinne. Only you would think to rent an S. U. V. to spend a week at a B & B." Corinne laughed just as Hemi meowed loudly, pronouncing his dislike of small, cramped spaces. Picking up his carrier, Ashley smiled and Corinne cooed liltingly in an attempt to placate the squalling feline. "Just a few more hours, baby," Corinne promised, "then you can get out."

With the last of the luggage in place, the girls climbed into the plush vehicle, waved goodbye to Phillip and drove away. Later, traveling along the winding highways outside Boston, Corinne couldn't help but appreciate the scenery. She felt carelessly free in the country and thoughtfully wondered if Ashley could enjoy it the same way. The nimble vehicle glided effortlessly along the narrow curves as the two old friends chatted about childhood adventures and future dreams. As always, the talk eventually turned to marriage, and Ashley prodded Corinne. "When are you and Preston going to set a date? You've been engaged for over a year now and you haven't even begun to plan the wedding." Ashley rolled her eyes in mock disgust, then grinned slyly. "Maybe my experience with 'Mr. Right' has left you a little gun-shy," she quipped.

"Never, and you know it," Corinne retorted. "I know Preston better than you think, and I know he'd never take up with some surgically-altered blond wanna-be. He appreciates a woman with brains as well as beauty. And besides, you forget, I believe in true love. I know it exists for everyone, you just have to look for it." Ashley turned and looked her straight in the eye and said very slowly, "Then, pray tell, my dear friend, how do you explain the situation between you and Preston." Corinne shot her an exasperated glance. "There's nothing wrong with our so-called situation, as you put it. We're just extremely busy people."

"I'm not convinced," said Ashley. "I knew you when you were married to Steven, and you two couldn't get enough of each other. You spent every free second doing something together and never spent a night apart except when he went off on his relief missions to South America. You and Preston, on the other hand, rarely see each other. You converse by phone, or worse, by mail, displaying no apparent urgency to change the arrangements. I don't get it."

"Oh, Ashley, you just don't understand," moaned Corinne. "Love isn't always fireworks and sweat. Sometimes it comes about from a deep abiding respect for a person and their values. Preston is a wonderful man with good solid principles. You won't find a more scrupulous guy. That's why we're perfectly content being so far apart right now. I trust him and he trusts me. When the time is right, we'll be together." On that note a comfortable silence fell between the friends. "Speaking of trust," Corinne interjected after a few minutes, "Tyler is a guy you could really trust. I've known him since I was four, so I speak from experience."

"Don't start that again," Ashley whined. "Trust *me* — I'd be reluctant to get within spitting distance of any variation of the male species right now, except for Hemi of course." Corinne laughed, tossing a quick look at Hemi curled up cozily in his carrier. "Yeah," Ashley noted, "if guys were more like cats, we'd be much better off."

Roses & Lace

Designed by Maggie Weldon

SIZE: 45" x 63".

MATERIALS: Worsted-weight yarn — 35 oz. rose, 3½ oz. each green and burgundy; tapestry needle; I crochet hook or size needed to obtain gauge.

GAUGE: Rnds 1 and 2 of Motif = 2" across. Each Motif is 9" across.

SKILL LEVEL: ☆☆ Average

FIRST ROW
First Large Motif

Rnd 1: With rose, ch 2, 8 sc in 2nd ch from hook, join with sl st in first sc (8 sc).

Rnd 2: Ch 5, dc in next st, ch 2, (dc in next st, ch 2) around, join with sl st in 3rd ch of ch-5 (8 dc, 8 ch-2 sps).

NOTES: *For beginning popcorn (beg pc), ch 3, 4 dc in same sp, drop lp from hook, insert hook in top of ch-3, draw dropped lp through.*

For popcorn (pc), 5 dc in next ch sp, drop lp from hook, insert hook in first st of 5-dc group, draw dropped lp through.

Rnd 3: Sl st in next ch sp, beg pc, ch 3, pc in next ch sp, ch 3, dc in next st, ch 3, *(pc in next ch sp, ch 3) 2 times, dc in next st, ch 3; repeat from * around, join with sl st in top of beg pc (12 ch-3 sps, 8 pc, 4 dc).

Rnd 4: Sl st in next ch sp, beg pc, (*ch 3, dc in next ch sp, ch 3, dc in next st, ch 3, dc in next ch sp, ch 3*, pc in next ch sp) 3 times; repeat between **, join (16 ch-3 sps, 12 dc, 4 pc).

Rnd 5: Sl st in next ch sp, ch 3, 2 dc in same sp, 4 dc in each of next 3 ch sps, (3 dc in next ch sp, 4 dc in each of next 3 ch sps) around, join with sl st in top of ch-3 (60 dc).

Rnd 6: Ch 5, skip next st, (dc in next st, ch 2, skip next st) around, join with sl st in 3rd ch of ch-5 (30 dc, 30 ch-2 sps).

Rnd 7: Sl st in next ch sp, ch 3, 3 dc in same sp, 3 dc in each of next 4 ch sps, (4 dc in next ch sp, 3 dc in each of next 4 ch sps) around, join with sl st in top of ch-3 (96 dc).

Rnd 8: Ch 1, sc in first st, ch 5, skip next 2 sts, (sc in next st, ch 5, skip next 2 sts) around, join with sl st in first sc, fasten off (32 ch-5 sps).

Second Large Motif

Rnds 1-7: Repeat same rnds of First Large Motif.

Rnd 8: Ch 1, sc in first st; joining to side of last Large Motif, (ch 2, sl st in 3rd ch of corresponding ch sp on other Motif—see Joining Diagram on page 136, ch 2, skip next 2 sts on this Motif, sc in next st) 4 times, ch 5, skip next 2 sts, (sc in next st, ch 5, skip next 2 sts) around, join with sl st in first sc, fasten off.

Repeat Second Large Motif 3 more times for a total of 5 Motifs.

SECOND ROW
First Large Motif

Joining to bottom of First Large Motif on last row, work

Continued on page 136

Dear Journal,

Arrived at the Four Seasons Inn yesterday. What a fantastic place! The approach to the house is up a narrow winding drive that appears to have seen more horse-drawn carriages than cars. As you round the final curve, you are greeted by a majestic Greek Revival-style home with massive columns that flank the front veranda. Flower beds line the flagstone path up to the house, shaded by hundred-year-old chestnut trees. The house, which sits atop a hill overlooking a valley of sugar maples, was originally built as a two-family dwelling but was renovated before it became the Four Seasons. Made from hand-hewn timbers, it is three stories and has twenty-two rooms, some of which are so large you could get lost in them. The furnishings are an awe-inspiring collection of antiques of all kinds. The room I'm in is done in a Victorian theme with roses and lace. Plus, I must admit Grandma Alice's taste is impeccable — there's at least one afghan in every room. I will presented her with the one I brought after dinner tonight, and have already seen the perfect spot for it. The meals here are just as impressive as the house with every gourmet course being hand-raised and home-made. No wonder it is one of the most frequented inns in the area. Tomorrow we plan to go sight-seeing. Alice says there's a wonderful yarn shop in the village. I'm sure I'll find something there. It will give Ashley and me some time together to relax and talk about important things, like her visit to Morningside to meet Ty.

Wildflowers

Designed by Ruth Owens

SIZE: 50" x 62".

MATERIALS: Worsted-weight yarn — 14 oz. white, 5 oz. each dk. green, brown and variegated green, 2½ oz. each yellow, peach, lavender, pink and lt. blue (flower colors); I crochet hook or size needed to obtain gauge.

GAUGE: Rnds 1 and 2 of each Motif = 2¾" across. Each Motif is 12" square.

SKILL LEVEL: ☆☆☆ Advanced

FIRST ROW
First Motif

Rnd 1: With white, ch 7, sl st in first ch to form ring, ch 1, 12 sc in ring, join with sl st in first sc (12 sc).

NOTES: *For beginning dc cluster (beg dc-cl), ch 3, (yo, insert hook in same st or sp, yo, draw lp through, yo, draw through 2 lps on hook) 2 times, yo, draw through all 3 lps on hook.*

For dc cluster (dc-cl), yo, insert hook in next st or ch sp, yo, draw lp through, yo, draw through 2 lps on hook, (yo, insert hook in same st or sp, yo, draw lp through, yo, draw through 2 lps on hook) 2 times, yo, draw through all 4 lps on hook.

Rnd 2: Beg dc-cl, ch 5, dc-cl in same st, ch 2, skip next 2 sts, *(dc-cl, ch 5, dc-cl) in next st, ch 2, skip next 2 sts; repeat from * around, join with sl st in top of beg dc-cl (8 dc-cls, 4 ch-5 sps, 4 ch-2 sps).

Rnd 3: Sl st in next ch-5 sp, beg dc-cl, ch 5, dc-cl in same sp, ch 3, dc in next ch-2 sp, ch 3, *(dc-cl, ch 5, dc-cl) in next ch-5 sp, ch 3, dc in next ch-2 sp, ch 3; repeat from * around, join, fasten off.

NOTE: *For popcorn (pc), 5 dc in next st, drop lp from hook, insert hook in first st of 5-dc group, draw dropped lp through.*

Rnd 4: Join brown with sc in first dc-cl, (*ch 5, pc in next ch-5 sp, ch 5, sc in next dc-cl, ch 5, sc in next dc, ch 5*, sc in next dc-cl) 3 times; repeat between **, join with sl st in first sc, fasten off (16 ch-5 sps, 12 sc, 4 pc).

NOTES: *For beginning tr cluster (beg tr-cl), ch 4, *yo 2 times, insert hook in same st or sp, yo, draw lp through, (yo, draw through 2 lps on hook) 2 times; repeat from *, yo, draw through all 3 lps on hook.*

*For tr cluster (tr-cl), yo 2 times, insert hook in next st or ch sp, yo, draw lp through, (yo, draw through 2 lps on hook) 2 times, *yo 2 times, insert hook in same st or sp, yo, draw lp through, (yo, draw through 2 lps on hook) 2 times; repeat*

Continued on page 136

Dear Tyler,

Meanwhile, back at the ranch...how's it going? Thought I'd drop you a note and let you in on a little secret. I'm having the time of my life with an amazing friend. Ashley and I went to the village today and browsed through the antique shops. I picked up a little something for you, too. But I'm not going to tell you what it is. I just know you'll love it! At lunch, we stopped at this quaint cottage tea room that specializes in soups of all kinds. I had the creamed chicken and portabello and Ashley ordered lentil and leek. The soups are served with a plate of assorted cheeses and homemade rolls.

After lunch, we strolled along this sidewalk that was built before the Civil War next to the Mystic River. Now it is a public garden. You should have seen us! We spent about two hours sitting on benches beneath colossal oak trees with at least ten shopping bags full of stuff stacked around our feet while I tried to teach Ashley to crochet. She finally got the hang of it, I think, and I was able to finish the afghan I was stitching on the flight over. It was so relaxing. I guess I really should get away more often.

Now, back to the reason I'm writing. I really want you to seriously think about what I talked to you about. I think you and Ashley would make a great couple if you'd give it a chance. Ashley is just the type of girl you'd like. She's witty, intelligent, financially secure, pretty and kind to small animals. What more could you want? Not to mention, she's one of the best corporate lawyers there is. Just think about it. You'd never have to hire an attorney again! I'll be home in about a week and we can talk more then.

Love, C—

Midnight Mosaic

Designed by Tammy Hildebrand

SIZE: 45" x 69" not including Tassels.

MATERIALS: Worsted-weight yarn — 35 oz. assorted scrap colors and 31 oz. black; J crochet hook or size needed to obtain gauge.

GAUGE: Each Flower on Flower Strip = 1¾" across. Each Strip is 4½" wide.

SKILL LEVEL: ☆☆ Average

FIRST STRIP

First Flower

NOTES: *For beginning cluster (beg cl), ch 3, (yo, insert hook in same sp, yo, draw lp through, yo, draw through 2 lps on hook) 2 times, yo, draw through all 3 lps on hook.*

For cluster (cl), yo, insert hook in next ch sp, yo, draw lp through, yo, draw through 2 lps on hook, (yo, insert hook in same sp, yo, draw lp through, yo, draw through 2 lps on hook) 2 times, yo, draw through all 4 lps on hook.

With any color scrap yarn, ch 3, sl st in first ch to form ring, beg cl in ring, ch 1, (cl in ring, ch 1) 7 times, join with sl st in top of beg cl, fasten off (8 cls, 8 ch-1 sps).

Next Flower

With any color scrap yarn, ch 3, sl st in first ch to form ring, beg cl in ring, drop lp from hook, insert hook in center bottom ch on last Flower, draw dropped lp through, (cl in ring on this Flower, ch 1) 7 times, join with sl st in top of beg cl, fasten off.

Repeat Next Flower 28 more times for a total of 30 Flowers in strip.

Border

Rnd 1: Working around outer edge of Flower strip, join black with sl st in ch-1 sp on either end of Flower strip, ch 3, (2 dc, ch 3, 3 dc) in same sp, ◊*[(hdc, ch 1, hdc) in next ch-1 sp, (sc, ch 1, sc) in next ch-1 sp, (hdc, ch 1, hdc) in next ch-1 sp], tr in next joining seam; repeat from * 28 more times; repeat between [ ]◊, (3 dc, ch 3, 3 dc) in next ch-1 sp; repeat between ◊◊, join with sl st in top of ch-3 (90 ch-3 sps and 29 tr across each long edge between end ch-3 sps).

Rnd 2: Sl st in each of next 2 sts, sl st in next ch-3 sp, ch 3, (2 dc, ch 2, 3 dc) in same sp, [(2 dc, ch 1, 2 dc) in next ch-1 sp, (3 dc, ch 3, 3 dc) in next ch-1 sp, *skip next ch-1 sp, dc in next tr, skip next ch-1 sp, (3 dc, ch 3, 3 dc) in next ch-1 sp; repeat from * 28 more times, (2 dc, ch 1, 2 dc) in next ch-1 sp], (3 dc, ch 2, 3 dc) in next ch-3 sp;

Continued on page 137

Dearest Preston,

Hi, darling! Sorry I missed you the day before we flew out. I talked to your foreman and he said you'd already left to go out to the site, so I knew better than to wait. Have they gotten past that easement problem yet? I'm sure the lawyers will work it out soon. Then maybe you'll have more time on your hands, or should I say your calender, and we could finalize some of our plans. I think the Four Seasons would be a great place to take our honeymoon. It's not the typical B&B. The rooms are massive, the food terrific and what a view! Out on the porch this evening, I looked up at the stars and they all seemed to be a different color. Definitely not like Chicago!

Ashley and I are having a terrific visit. Of course, her grandmother Alice is treating us like royalty, but that's okay with us. I've also had plenty of time to get Ashley used to the idea of meeting Tyler. I think they'd be a great match. Now, now, I can hear you already. But look, I know two peas in a pod when I see them, and I really believe Ashley and Tyler would work well together. You went to school with Ty. You know almost as much about him as I do. Once you meet Ashley and get to know her, you'll agree, I'm sure. More to come on that subject.

I'd better go. We have a full schedule again today. We're going down to Mystic Seaport, a shipbuilding village dating back to the 17th century that is now a living museum. Take care of yourself and don't work too hard. I'll phone again when I get back home.

Love, C—

Eternal Blooms

Designed by Maggie Weldon

SIZE: 44" x 66".

MATERIALS: Worsted-weight yarn — 24½ oz. lt. peach and 17½ oz. dk. peach; H crochet hook or size needed to obtain gauge.

GAUGE: Rnds 1 and 2 = 2¾" across. Each Motif is 5½" across.

SKILL LEVEL: ☆☆☆☆ Challenging

FIRST ROW
First Motif

Rnd 1: With lt. peach, ch 4, sl st in first ch to form ring, ch 5, (dc in ring, ch 2) 5 times, join with sl st in 3rd ch of ch-5 (6 ch-2 sps).

Rnd 2: Ch 4, dc in same st, ch 2, skip next ch sp, *(dc, ch 1, dc) in next st, ch 2, skip next ch sp; repeat from * around, join with sl st in 3rd ch of ch-4 (12 dc, 6 ch-2 sps, 6 ch-1 sps).

Rnd 3: Ch 3, dc in same st, ch 1, skip next ch-1 sp, 2 dc in next st, ch 2, skip next ch-2 sp, (2 dc in next st, ch 1, skip next ch-1 sp, 2 dc in next st, ch 2, skip next ch-2 sp) around, join with sl st in top of ch-3 (24 dc, 6 ch-2 sps, 6 ch-1 sps).

Rnd 4: Sl st in next st, sl st in next ch-1 sp, ch 4, dc in same sp, (ch 1, dc in same sp) 3 times, (sl st, ch 5, sl st) in next ch-2 sp, *dc in next ch-1 sp, (ch 1, dc in same sp) 4 times, (sl st, ch 5, sl st) in next ch-2 sp; repeat from * around, join with sl st in 3rd ch of ch-4, fasten off (24 ch-1 sps, 6 ch-5 sps).

Rnd 5: Working over top of rnds 1-4, join dk. peach with sl st in ch-2 sp of rnd 3 before any (sl st, ch 5, sl st) group on last rnd, *[ch 3, (sl st in next ch-2 sp on next rnd, ch 3) 2 times, sl st in ring between next 2 dc on rnd 1, ch 3, (sl st in same ch-2 sp on next rnd, ch 3) 2 times, sl st in same ch-2 sp on next rnd after same (sl st, ch 5, sl st) group, ch 1, sc in next ch-1 sp on last rnd, (ch 3, sc in next ch-1 sp) 3 times, ch 1], sl st in next ch-2 sp on rnd 3 before next (sl st, ch 5, sl st) group; repeat from * 4 more times; repeat between [ ], join with sl st in first sl st, fasten off.

Second Motif

Rnds 1-3: Repeat same rnds of First Motif.

Rnd 4: Sl st in next st, sl st in next ch-1 sp, ch 4, dc in same sp, (ch 1, dc in same sp) 3 times, sl st in next ch-2 sp; joining to last Motif (see Joining Diagram on page 52), ch 2, sl st in 3rd ch of center bottom ch-5 sp on last Motif, ch 2, sl st in same sp on this Motif, *dc in next ch-1 sp, (ch 1, dc in same sp) 4 times, (sl st, ch 5, sl st) in next ch-2 sp; repeat from * around, join with sl st in 3rd ch of ch-4, fasten off.

Rnd 5: Working over top of rnds 1-4, join dk. peach with sl st in ch-2 sp of rnd 3 before last (sl st, ch 5, sl st) group on last rnd, *ch 3, (sl st in next ch-2 sp on next rnd, ch 3) 2 times, sl st in ring between next 2 dc on rnd 1, ch 3, (sl st in same ch-2 sp on next rnd, ch 3) 2 times, sl st in same ch-2

Continued on page 138

Dear Journal,

Ashley and I had a wonderful day today at Mystic Seaport. The antique ships were breathtaking and the crafts were fascinating. Throughout the village there were people recreating the different aspects of life in the 19th century. Couldn't help but think of Steven, though, and the year we went to New York while he attended that convention. Can't remember exactly, something to do with the effect of disease on third world countries I think. There were so many of those things that Steven dealt with, they all run together now.

That was such a wonderful trip. We practically had that quaint little resort outside Lake Placid to ourselves. It was so romantic. We'd eat breakfast on our balcony every morning, then in the afternoon when Steven got back, we'd go for long walks around the gardens. At night, we'd go down for awhile and listen to that little jazz band in the bistro, then go back to the room and order dessert. Steven couldn't get enough of those wonderful pastries they served. Sitting by the fireplace sharing that time was so special. Steven was so special. I can't believe it's been almost four years since I lost him. I can still see him sitting on that antique loveseat beside me reading while I crocheted. He used to love to watch me crochet, it fascinated him how I could turn a strand of yarn into something as beautiful as an afghan. It took someone as beautiful as Steven to recognize beauty in everything around him.

Tailor's Fancy

Designed by Maggie Weldon

SIZE: 54½" x 69".

MATERIALS: Worsted-weight yarn — 35 oz. off-white, 21 oz. taupe, 4 yds. scrap color each for 112 spools; tapestry needle; I crochet hook or size needed to obtain gauge.

GAUGE: 3 sc = 1"; 16 sc rows = 5".

SKILL LEVEL: ☆☆ Average

STRIP (make 8)

Row 1: With off-white, ch 17, sc in 2nd ch from hook, sc in each ch across, turn (16 sc). *Front of row 1 is right side of work.*

Row 2: Ch 1, sc in each st across, turn.

NOTES: *When changing colors (see page 159), always drop yarn to wrong side of work. Use a separate ball of yarn for each color section.* **Do not** *carry yarn across from one section to another. Fasten off colors at end of each color section.*

At beginning of each scrap color section, leave 5" end on **right side** *of work.* **Do not** *hide this end (see photo).*

Always change to next color in last st of last color used.

Row 3: Ch 1, sc in each of first 2 sts; with taupe, sc in next 12 sts; with off-white, sc in each of last 2 sts, turn.

Row 4: Ch 1, sc in each of first 3 sts; with taupe, sc in next 10 sts; with off-white, sc in each of last 3 sts, turn.

Row 5: Ch 1, sc in first 4 sts; with taupe, sc in next 8 sts; with off-white, sc in last 4 sts, turn.

Row 6: Ch 1, sc in first 5 sts; with any scrap color, sc in next 6 sts; with off-white, sc in last 5 sts, turn.

Rows 7-11: Ch 1, sc in first 5 sts; with same scrap color, sc in next 6 sts; with off-white, sc in last 5 sts, turn.

Rows 12-14: Repeat rows 5, 4 and 3.

Rows 15-17: Repeat row 2.

Rows 18-211: Repeat rows 3-17 consecutively, ending with row 16. At end of last row, do not fasten off.

Rnd 212: Working around outer edge, ch 1, 3 sc in first st, skipping first and last rows, sc in each st and in end of each row around with 3 sc in each corner st, join with sl st in first sc, turn, fasten off (458 sc).

Rnd 213: Join taupe with sc in any st, sc in each st around with 3 sc in each center corner st, join, fasten off (466).

Holding Strips wrong sides together, matching sts, with taupe, sew together through **back lps** leaving 18 sts on each end unsewn.

EDGING

Rnd 1: Working around entire outer edge, join off-white with sl st in any center corner st, ch 3, (dc, ch 2, 2 dc) in same st, dc in each st and in each seam around with (2 dc, ch 2, 2 dc) in each center corner st, join with sl st in top of ch-3, fasten off (155 dc across each short end between corner ch-2 sps, 215 dc across each long edge between corner ch-2 sps).

Rnd 2: Join taupe with sc in any corner ch sp, ch 3, sc in same sp, *[ch 3, skip next st, (sc in next st, ch 3, skip next st) across] to next corner ch sp, (sc, ch 3, sc) in next corner ch sp; repeat from * 2 more times; repeat between [ ], join with sl st in first sc, fasten off.❦

Dear Mother,

Hello! Sorry I haven't written sooner, but we've been going ninety or nothing since we got here. You'd love it! Ashley's grandmother is the sweetest thing. The Four Seasons Inn is a showplace and the village is a shopper's dream. I hate to admit it, but I've spent almost $300 on yarn already. There's one shop that makes its own hand-dyed wool yarn. I couldn't resist. And, to make matters "worse," they had another room filled with stitched pieces that were for sale as well as antique needlework tools. I did manage to find three "new" hooks for my collection and a silver case.

The weather has been super. Cool evenings, sunny days. You still need a sweater, but it's been quite pleasant. There are so many things to see and do, we can't possibly get it all done before we leave. Ashley has to get back before too long. Something about a hearing she's supposed to attend. She seems to be warming up to the idea of meeting Ty. I've talked him up big time ever since we got here. Well, nothing that's not true anyway. You know what a great guy Ty is. It isn't hard to come up with things to say. Plus, it's not like they don't actually know each other. She spent many a weekend at our place when we were kids. It's just at that time, since Ty was so much older, she never paid any attention to him. Maybe it's time she did.

This is short, I know, but I'll be home soon and I can fill you in on all the details then. Take care and give Daddy a hug and kiss for me.

Love, C—

Anticipation

Designed by Melissa Leapman

SIZE: 50" x 59" not including Tassels.

MATERIALS: Worsted-weight yarn — 42 oz. variegated and 34 oz. green; tapestry needle; H crochet hook or size needed to obtain gauge.

GAUGE: Rnds 1 and 2 of each Motif = 2¾" across. Each Motif is 4½" across.

SKILL LEVEL: ☆☆ Average

MOTIF (make 158)

Rnd 1: With variegated, ch 4, sl st in first ch to form ring, ch 3, 11 dc in ring, join with sl st in top of ch-3 (12 dc).

Rnd 2: Ch 3, (dc, ch 2, 2 dc) in same st, skip next st, *(2 dc, ch 2, 2 dc) in next st, skip next st; repeat from * around, join (24 dc, 6 ch-2 sps).

Rnd 3: Sl st in next st, sl st in next ch sp, ch 3, 8 dc in same sp, 9 dc in each ch sp around, join, fasten off (54 dc).

NOTE: *For **long double crochet (ldc),** yo, insert hook in next skipped st on rnd 1, yo, draw up long lp, (yo, draw through 2 lps on hook) 2 times.*

Rnd 4: Join green with sc in 5th st, sc in each of next 2 sts, skip next 2 sts, 2 ldc in next skipped st on rnd 1, skip next 2 sts of next 9-dc group on last rnd, (sc in next 5 sts, skip next 2 sts, 2 ldc in next skipped st on rnd 1, skip next

2 sts of next 9-dc group on last rnd) around to last 2 sts, sc in each of last 2 sts, join with sl st in first sc (30 sc, 12 ldc).

Rnd 5: Ch 1, 2 sc in first st, sc in next 6 sts, (2 sc in next st, sc in next 6 sts) around, join, fasten off (48 sc).

Holding Motifs wrong sides together, matching corners, with green, sew together through **back lps** according to Assembly Diagram on page 140.

EDGING

Working around outer edge, join green with sc in any st, *(sc in each st and 2 sc in each st of each 2-sc group at each corner) across to 2 sts before next indentation, (sc next 2 sts tog) 2 times; repeat from * around, sc in each st across, join with sl st in first sc, fasten off.

TASSEL (make 22)

Cut 42 strands green each 12" long. Tie separate strand green tightly around middle of all strands; fold strands in half. Wrap another strand 2 or 3 times around folded strands 1¼" from top of fold; secure and hide ends inside Tassel. Trim ends even.

Tie one Tassel to each point on each short end of Afghan.❧

Dear Journal,

Ashley and I must leave tomorrow. Talked to Mother this morning when I called to have the jet sent out. She said everything at the ranch was going great. The weather is warming up nicely so the pastures are really coming on. They'll be able to cut hay by next month if this keeps up. She's also on a tangent again about why I don't spend more time with Preston. She thinks I should have planned a vacation in Chicago, not Connecticut. She doesn't realize that if I had gone to Chicago, with the Anderson project under way right now, Preston couldn't have gotten away anyway. She thinks I'm dragging my feet again about getting married. I'm not dragging my feet, it just hasn't been really convenient yet. What with Preston's hectic schedule as well as my own, we just haven't been able to settle on when and where to have it. Mom wants us to have the ceremony in Denver, but Preston would prefer Chicago. This afternoon while Ashley and I were out, I found some bridal magazines. One has a stunning gown on the cover that would be perfect for me. I also finished that afghan Mom has been wanting for the sun room. Between the two, maybe I can get out of the dog house.

I guess I don't really see why everyone thinks we have to get married right now. Preston and I are perfectly happy with the arrangements just as they are. With us both being so involved with outside interests, it wouldn't really be fair to each other anyway. Preston can't possibly move now, and with all the things I've got going in Denver, I couldn't live in Chicago either. So, we'll just have to wait.

I'll close for now. Must finish packing.

"Are you sure you have everything, dear?," asked Clarice Hamilton as she examined her daughter's luggage. "It looks like you're taking more afghans than clothes. I've never seen you pack this light." Corinne sniffed, "Oh, come on, Mom. I told you I planned to do some serious shopping while I'm in Chicago." Clarice leafed through the suit bag containing her daughter's outfits again, shaking her head. "Well, I hope so. The selection in this bag is rather slim if you ask me. You can't expect to impress your fiance in any of this old stuff. Your wardrobe is getting as dated as your decor. You really should do something about that."

"You worry too much, Mother," Corinne snapped as she zipped her suitcase. "Steven and I fixed this house up just like we wanted. It's perfect for my antiques and I've never seen the need to change it. As for my clothes, Preston doesn't have to be impressed, he already knows me." Clarice reached down to pick up Hemi who had sauntered into the room. "I know," she said with a somewhat concerned look, "but you really should think about updating. You need to let go. And, it's been so long since you and Preston spent any real time together that I just feel like you should try to rekindle some of that old spark."

Corinne laughed as she brushed Hemi away and sat down beside her mother. "Preston and I are best friends. You know we never went through that 'sparkling' stage. Our relationship is based on shared values and goals. We're comfortable with what we have, and neither of us feels we have to rush to get married. Besides that, we're both adults, and I know establishing his career is important to him. Please don't worry. Everything is going to work out just fine."

Corinne reached for her purse. "Try not to spoil Hemi too much while I'm gone. I wanted to take him, but you know Preston is allergic to cats." Clarice embraced her daughter. "I love you, Corinne, and I don't mean to be such a busy-body, but, I just don't want to see you unhappy. When you were married to Steven, you were always on cloud nine. I'd hate to see you settle for less."

"I'm not settling, Mom. Preston is a great guy. He's handsome, intelligent, wealthy, comes from an excellent family...what more could you ask for in a son-in-law." Corinne dropped a kiss on her mother's cheek and picked up her bags. "I'm so glad Ty was going to Denver today. I sure don't feel like driving in this rain," When Corinne got downstairs, Tyler was already waiting and quickly came over to help with her luggage. "Go on out and get in," he said as she struggled with her umbrella. "I'll get the rest of your bags." Corinne climbed into Ty's new Chevy Tahoe, trying not to get too much water on the seats. He was right behind her and quickly shut his door. Dropping his hat onto the back floorboard, he leaned over and pulled a hand towel from under his seat and handed it to Corinne. "This will help you dry off a little," he said, starting the engine. "I'm glad you brought this and not your old truck," she said, smiling, "but I sure hated to get your new seats all wet." "Me too," Ty admitted. "I've been saving for years to get this Tahoe, and the week I buy it, it rains buckets. But I don't mind. I wouldn't have made you ride in the old truck anyway." As he drove along the winding road leading to the highway, Corinne studied his hands on the wheel. Dressed in starched jeans, crisp western shirt and his ever-present boots, Ty was a strikingly good-looking man. About two inches over six feet tall, his broad shoulders and muscular arms were the perfect emphasis for his narrow waist and long legs. "He always did know how to dress," Corinne thought to herself, glancing at him through lowered lashes. "But then again," she thought with a slight pang of guilt, "he looks good even when he's been out working cattle all day."

"So tell me," Ty suddenly said, causing Corinne to jump, "just what is this Ashley-person really like." Given an opportunity to indulge in one of her best occupations, that of matchmaker, Corinne was happy to spend the rest of the trip to Denver giving Ty a glowing account of Ashley's best attributes. As she rambled on in her animated discourse, Tyler watched her green eyes sparkle and wondered if he'd always compare every other woman he met to Corinne. Ever since he'd come to live with the Hamiltons at the age of twelve after his parents were killed in a boating accident, Corinne, who was only four at the time, had treated him more like a brother than a hired-hand. Milt and Clarice had given him a good home and a permanent position on the ranch. When he turned twenty-one, Milt made him foreman, and through the years, the relationship had worked remarkably well. Ty rarely saw Corinne these days, except at family functions and on the rare occasions when she had time to ride. He did however, keep track of her through Clarice and Milt, always aware of her actions and whereabouts, with a brotherly sort of interest. Her parents were very anxious to see her married to Preston, but Ty had his doubts. None of which he'd ever voice to Corinne.

It was still raining lightly when he pulled into the private hanger at Denver's airport. Phillip was waiting and soon, Corinne was safely on board and the jet was taxiing out to take its place on the runway. "Best of luck, kiddo," Ty said to no one in particular as he closed his door and drove off.

Sculpted Sapphires

Designed by Zelda Workman

SIZE: 41" x 61½" not including Fringe.

MATERIALS: Worsted-weight yarn — 40. oz. dk. blue and 24 oz. lt. blue; I crochet hook or size needed to obtain gauge.

GAUGE: 3 sc = 1"; 4 sc rows = 1".

SKILL LEVEL: ☆☆ Average

AFGHAN

Row 1: With dk. blue, ch 185, sc in 2nd ch from hook, sc in each ch across, turn (184 sc).

Row 2: Ch 1, sc in each of first 3 sts, ch 3, (sc in each of next 2 sts, ch 3) across to last 3 sts, sc in each of last 3 sts, turn (184 sc, 89 ch sps). Front of row 2 is right side of work.

Row 3: Ch 1, sc in each st across skipping ch sps, turn.

Row 4: Ch 1, sc in each st across, turn.

Row 5: Ch 1, sc in first 4 sts, ch 3, (sc in each of next 2 sts, ch 3) across to last 4 sts, sc in last 4 sts, turn.

Row 6: Ch 1, sc in each st across skipping ch sps, turn.

Row 7: Ch 1, sc in each st across, turn.

Row 8: Repeat row 2.

Row 9: Ch 1, sc in each st across skipping ch sps, turn.

Row 10: Ch 1, sc in each st across, turn, fasten off.

Row 11: Join lt. blue with sc in first st, sc in each st across, turn.

Rows 12-13: Ch 1, sc in each st across, turn.

NOTE: *For **front post (fp,** see page 159), yo 2 times, insert hook around next st 3 rows below, yo, draw lp through, (yo, draw through 2 lps on hook) 3 times. Skip next st on last row.*

Row 14: Ch 1, sc in each of first 2 sts, fp around 4th st on row 3 rows below, (sc in next st on last row, skip next st on row 3 rows below, fp around next st) across to last 3 sts on last row, sc in each of last 3 sts, turn.

Row 15: Ch 1, sc in each st across, turn, fasten off.

Row 16: Join dk. blue with sc in first st, sc in each st across, turn.

Row 17: Ch 1, sc in each st across, turn.

Row 18: Repeat row 2.

Row 19: Ch 1, sc in each st across skipping ch sps, turn.

Row 20: Repeat row 5.

Row 21: Ch 1, sc in each st across skipping ch sps, turn.

Continued on page 140

Dear Journal,

Whew! What a day. I thought I led an active life, but Preston's puts mine to shame! We had breakfast with about fifty other people from the firm Preston works for, including Michael Benedict their C.E.O. Benedict, Darnell & Monk has good reason to celebrate the completion of the Anderson project. They are receiving rave reviews from across the nation because of the innovative design of this building. It is being touted as the most modern, state-of-the-art, high-tech medical research center of its kind. There's even going to be a write-up in Business Architecture Today, featuring, of course, Preston, the brilliant architect who master-minded the entire project. He's been waiting years to put some of these ideas to use, and this was the perfect opportunity.

Lunch was a quieter, more private affair with only about twenty people in attendance. There, I met Stanley Darnell and Thaddius Monk and their wives, as well as the executive committee of the Anderson Research Center. Later that afternoon they had the formal ribbon-cutting with live television coverage. After that, we had just enough time to rush back to the condo and change before meeting the Benedicts and Monks at Ché LeMondé for dinner.

I thought the day would never end, but we finally got home around eleven. Preston was acting just like a kid with a new toy the entire night. I couldn't get a word in edge-wise. He had my favorite chablis' already iced down at the condo and while he poured it, I got out the afghan I'd made for him. He was so pleased. It went great with his new furniture. After a glass of wine, we finally relaxed and kicked off our shoes. Then, he proceeded to tell me about the contract he's already got in the works for a high-rise apartment building for handicapped residents that the city has proposed. Guess he won't get a break now after all.

Didn't realize it was so late. It's after two, I'd better turn in.

Inlaid Amythest

Designed by Ellen Anderson

SIZE: 45" x 66".

MATERIALS: Worsted-weight yarn — 30 oz. purple/fuchsia/green variegated, 12½ oz. green, 8½ oz. purple and 6 oz. fuchsia; H crochet hook or size needed to obtain gauge.

GAUGE: 7 sc = 2"; 4 sc rows = 1".

SKILL LEVEL: ☆☆ Average

AFGHAN

Row 1: With purple, ch 231, sc in 2nd ch from hook, sc in next 12 chs, 3 sc in next ch, sc in next 13 chs, (skip next 2 chs, sc in next 13 chs, 3 sc in next ch, sc in next 13 chs) across, turn (232 sc).

Row 2: Ch 1, skip first st, sc in next 13 sts, 3 sc in next st, sc in next 13 sts, (skip next 2 sts, sc in next 13 sts, 3 sc in next st, sc in next 13 sts) across to last st, skip last st, turn.

NOTE: *For front post (fp, see page 159), yo, insert hook from front to back around post of next st on row before last, yo, draw lp through, (yo, draw through 2 lps on hook) 2 times. Skip next st on last row.*

Row 3: Ch 1, skip first st, sc in each of next 3 sts, fp around 6th st on row before last, *[(sc in each of next 3 sts on last row, skip next 3 sts on row before last, fp around next st) 2 times, sc in next st on last row, 3 sc in next st, sc in next st, skip next st on row before last, fp around next st, sc in each of next 3 sts on last row, (skip next 3 sts on row before last, fp around next st, sc in each of next 3 sts on last row) 2 times], skip next 2 sts on last row, sc in each of next 3 sts, skip next 10 sts on row before last, fp around next st; repeat from * 6 more times; repeat between [ ], skip last st, turn.

Row 4: Repeat row 2.

Row 5: Ch 1, skip first st, *[sc in next st, (fp around next fp on row before last, sc in each of next 3 sts on last row) 3 times, 3 sc in next st, (sc in each of next 3 sts, fp around next fp on row before last) 3 times, sc in next st], skip next 2 sts; repeat from * 6 more times; repeat between [ ], skip last st, **do not** turn, fasten off.

Row 6: Working this row in **back lps** only, join variegated with sc in 2nd st, sc in next 12 sts, 3 sc in next st, sc in next 13 sts, (skip next 2 sts, sc in next 13 sts, 3 sc in next st, sc in next 13 sts) across to last st, skip last st, turn.

Rows 7-165: Working in color sequence of green, variegated, fuchsia, variegated, repeat rows 2-6 consecutively, ending with row 5.❧

Grandiloquence

Designed by Eleanor Albano-Miles

SIZE: 49" x 64".

MATERIALS: Worsted-weight yarn — 72 oz. pink; I crochet hook or size needed to obtain gauge.

GAUGE: 3 sc = 1"; 4 sc rows = 1".

SKILL LEVEL: ☆☆ Average

AFGHAN

Row 1: Ch 136, sc in 2nd ch from hook, sc in each ch across, turn (135 sc).

Row 2: Ch 1, sc in each st across, turn.

NOTES: *For* **front post (fp,** *see page 159), yo, insert hook from front to back around post of next st on row before last, yo, draw lp through, (yo, draw through 2 lps on hook) 2 times. Skip next st on last row.*

For **puff stitch (puff st),** *yo, insert hook in next st, yo, draw up long lp, (yo, insert hook in same st, yo, draw up long lp) 3 times, yo, draw through all 8 lps on hook, yo, draw through 2 lps on hook.*

Row 3: Ch 1, sc in each of first 2 sts, fp, (sc in next st, fp) 2 times, *sc in next 4 sts, puff st, sc in next 4 sts, fp, (sc in next st, fp) 2 times; repeat from * across to last 2 sts, sc in each of last 2 sts, turn (96 sc, 30 fp, 9 puff sts).

Row 4: Ch 1, sc in each st across, turn.

Row 5: Ch 1, sc in each of first 2 sts, fp around next fp on row before last, (sc in next st, fp around next fp on row before last) 2 times, *sc in each of next 2 sts, puff st, (sc in next st, puff st) 2 times, sc in each of next 2 sts, fp around next fp on row before last, (sc in next st, fp around next fp on row before last) 2 times; repeat from * across to last 2 sts, sc in each of last 2 sts, turn.

Row 6: Ch 1, sc in each st across, turn.

Row 7: Repeat row 3.

Rows 8-10: Ch 1, sc in each st across, turn.

Rows 11-240: Repeat rows 3-10 consecutively, ending with row 8. At end of last row, fasten off.

BORDER

Rnd 1: Working around outer edge, with right side facing you, join with sc in first st, (ch 2, sc) in same st, sc in each st across to last st, (sc, ch 2, sc) in last st; *working in ends of rows, skip first row, sc in each of next 3 rows, (skip next 2 rows, sc in next 4 rows), across to last 2 rows, skip last 2 rows*; working in starting ch on opposite side of row

Continued on page 140

Dear Journal,

Had dinner this evening with Preston's Uncle Foster and Aunt Faye. They are such a sweet couple, and if it hadn't been for them, Preston wouldn't be where he is now. I never knew Uncle Foster had known Thaddius Monk for decades and sold him on Preston as soon as he earned his degree. According to Uncle Foster, prior to their hiring Preston, Benedict, Darnell & Monk had never hired anyone who didn't have at least ten years experience. I guess Preston really is lucky there.

I swear Foster and Faye's home gets bigger and more ostentatious every time I'm there. It's beautiful, I must admit, from the Monet in the grand foyer with the marble spiral staircase right down to the matching his and hers master baths with black marble jaccuzis. I guess it goes to show that even a good thing can be carried a little too far. Unfortunately, Preston seemed inspired by all the glitz and glamour and got off on a kick about "our" house. It seems he's already selected a building site in a newly opened, very prestigious new development. He's never really mentioned building a house yet, and I guess I never thought about it either. Now, all of a sudden, he seems to be on a mission.

After we got back to his condo this evening, he pulled out a stack of house plan books and some blue-prints and started showing me his plans for our house. I guess I was a little taken aback since he'd never said anything to me before about this. He apologized for not including me, but out hit and miss communications aren't really conducive to my helping with the decisions. At least that's what he said.

We're to go to Faye and Foster's again tomorrow, as Preston wants to show them the house plans and get some more information from Aunt Faye about the decorator she used. He also asked me to make an afghan for their parlor and was surprised to find I'd already brought one. At least I was a step ahead on one thing.

Carved Ivory

Designed by Hazel Osborn Jones

SIZE: 44" x 64" not including fringe.

MATERIALS: Worsted-weight yarn — 31 oz. soft white and 23 oz. rose/yellow/blue/ green variegated; H crochet hook or size needed to obtain gauge.

GAUGE: 7 sc = 2"; 7 cr sts worked in pattern = 4"; 6 sc rows worked in **back lps,** one cr st row and one puff st row = 3½".

NOTES: For **puff stitch (puff st),** yo, insert hook in next st, yo, draw up long lp, (yo, insert hook in same st, yo, draw up long lp) 3 times, yo, draw through 8 lps on hook, yo, draw through 2 lps on hook.

For **cross stitch (cr st),** skip next st, dc in next st; working over dc just made, dc in skipped st.

Do not turn at end of each row unless otherwise stated. Leave 6" end at beginning and end of each row.

SKILL LEVEL: ☆☆ Average

AFGHAN

Row 1: With soft white, ch 226, sc in 2nd ch from hook, sc in each ch across, fasten off (225 sc).

Rows 2-7: Working these rows in **back lps** only, join soft white with sc in first st, sc in each st across, fasten off. At end of last row, **turn.**

Row 8: Working in **both lps,** join variegated with sl st in first st, ch 3, dc in next st, puff st in next st, (ch 1, skip next st, puff st in next st) across to last 2 sts, dc in each of last 2 sts, **turn,** fasten off (111 puff sts, 110 ch sps, 4 dc).

Row 9: Join soft white with sc in first st, in each st and in each ch across, fasten off (225 sc).

Rows 10-11: Working these rows in **back lps** only, join soft white with sc in first st, sc in each st across, fasten off.

Row 12: Join soft white with sl st in first st, ch 3, dc in

Continued on page 140

Dear Ashley,

I spoke to Ty yesterday when I called Mom. He just happened to be up at the house talking to Daddy. He said he had gotten your letter and picture and was duly impressed, just as I'd told him he'd be. Ty has always preferred girls with both beauty and brains. Of course, he grew up around me so why wouldn't he? Ha!

Seriously, having been with Ty through some pretty tough times, I can say first-hand that he's a first-rate guy. Did I ever tell you about the time Stormy, that blue roan mare I had, got colic. Ty was exhausted when he found her. He'd been out in the Clear Creek area pulling a calf that he then had to carry two miles back to the truck. Once he got back to the stables and found Stormy, he never left her. Ben offered to stay up with her after the vet left, but Ty wouldn't have it. Then there was the time when Maxie decided to have her puppies in the hay barn in a blizzard. Ty knew the puppies couldn't stand that much cold, so he carried Maxie back to his place and put her on an old blanket in his den. He sat all day with that old dog, feeding her little scraps of meat and giving her water on a spoon. She was so old, he was afraid she wouldn't make it through the delivery. Thanks to him, all seven pups survived just fine. You know, Ty's not just good to animals. He treats everyone with kindness and respect. For someone who went through the loss of his parents at age twelve, you'd think he wouldn't have such a good attitude about life, but he does. I'm telling you, this is one great guy!

I have been in over-drive since arriving in Chicago, and it's really beginning to get old. I haven't worn my jeans since I've been here and I think I starting to have symptoms of withdrawal. I have gotten to go shopping a few days, so the trip hasn't been totally wasted. Yesterday was especially pleasant. Went to a luncheon at the home of Dottie Bealle, a former client of Preston's. She's a music professor at the university and the fourth-year students gave a recital afterwards. I was quite surprised that somehow she found out I hold a Master's Degree in music and insisted I play. I didn't mind, as she has the most exquisite grand piano. One thing that didn't surprise me though was that she had a beautiful crocheted afghan in her music room. Preston seems to have everyone in Chicago believing that afghans are "the" thing to have.

This letter has gotten entirely too long. I'd better close, and you'd better start planning that trip to Morningside!

Love, C—

Contradiction

Designed by Maggie Weldon

SIZE: 52" x 70" not including Fringe.

MATERIALS: Worsted-weight yarn — 21 oz. green, 14 oz. each rose and off-white; J crochet hook or size needed to obtain gauge.

GAUGE: 13 dc = 4"; 3 dc rows and 3 shells rows = 4¼".

SKILL LEVEL: ☆☆ Average

AFGHAN

NOTES: *Ch-5 at beginning of row 1 counts as first dc and ch sp.*

For **shell,** *(3 dc, ch 1, 3 dc) in next st.*

Row 1: With green, ch 172, dc in 6th ch from hook, (ch 1, skip next ch, dc in next ch) across, turn (85 dc, 84 ch sps).

Row 2: Ch 3, dc in each ch sp and in each st across, turn (169 dc).

Row 3: Ch 4, skip next st, dc in next st, (ch 1, skip next st, dc in next st) across, **do not** turn, fasten off.

Row 4: Join rose with sc in 3rd ch of first ch-4, (skip next dc, shell in next dc, skip next dc, sc in next dc) across, **do not** turn, fasten off (22 sc, 21 shells).

Row 5: Join off-white with sl st in first sc, ch 3, 3 dc in same st, sc in ch sp of next shell, (shell in next sc, sc in ch sp of next shell) across to last sc, 4 dc in last sc, **do not** turn, fasten off (21 sc, 20 shells, 8 dc).

Row 6: Join rose with sc in top of ch-3, shell in next sc, (sc in next shell, shell in next sc) across to last 4 dc, skip next 3 dc, sc in last dc, **do not** turn, fasten off (22 sc, 21 shells).

Row 7: Join green with sl st in first sc, ch 4, skip next dc, *[dc in next dc, ch 1, skip next dc, dc in next ch sp, ch 1, skip next dc, dc in next dc, ch 1, skip next dc, dc in next sc], ch 1, skip next dc; repeat from * 19 more times; repeat between [ ], **turn** (85 dc, 84 ch sps).

Rows 8-99: Repeat rows 2-7 consecutively, ending with row 3.

FRINGE

For **each Fringe,** cut 4 strands off-white each 12" long. Holding all 4 strands together, fold in half, insert hook in ch sp, draw fold through, draw all loose ends through fold, tighten. Trim ends.

Fringe in each ch sp across each short end of Afghan.

Dear Journal,

I have to confess, this has been one weird day! While we were at the reception today for the new *Loggins & Lybrant Law Firm* building that was designed by Preston, who should show up — Ashley. I was shocked. She hadn't said anything to me before about being there, but I guess her story sounded plausible enough. She's taking my advise about looking for a new job, and *Loggins & Lybrant* is wooing her to come to Chicago. I guess the thing that bugs me is that Preston, for some reason, felt compelled to introduce her to all the lawyers there, leaving me to fend for myself. Not that I can't, it's just that he seemed unnaturally intent on helping her establish her presence. If you ask me, she didn't need any help getting attention. That custom-fitted teal-green suit she was wearing took care of all that. Oh, listen to me. I'm just being catty because Preston left me standing on the sideline while he gave Ashley the royal treatment. I can't believe I'm sitting here feeling upset by that. Preston is the type of guy who would always help another professional out if he felt they deserved it, and maybe he just felt sorry for Ashley, having been dumped so unceremoniously by Doug. It's just that he really appeared a little too eager when it came to seeing her get set up in Chicago.

I don't understand why I feel so put-out by all this. Ashley's story of why she was there is believable, and Preston is the type to help the underdog. Since I know Preston has the tendency, and I'm secure in our relationship, and, I know Ashley would never dream of attempting to come between Preston and me, why am I compelled to spend so much time crocheting so fast my fingers hurt and eating creme sandwich cookies and washing them down with a gallon of milk? Why do I feel like I'm the one who was missing something? Preston just laughed when I mentioned to him that I felt slighted by him leaving me on my own to fend off all those pompous old goats who were flocking around the punch bowl. He said I was being too dramatic and asked if I had PMS. I can't believe he even thought that! He knows I'm not given to mood swings, and it's not like him to even suggest such a thing. I guess the best thing to do is to talk to him again tomorrow and let him know how I feel. Then we'll be able to work through this just like we always do. Meanwhile, my crochet hook is calling me to finishing that afghan I started.

City Lights

Designed by Tammy Hildebrand

SIZE: 47" x 62".

MATERIALS: Worsted-weight yarn — 23 oz. black, 15 oz. assorted scrap colors; I crochet hook or size needed to obtain gauge.

GAUGE: Rnd 1 of Motif = 1¼" across. Each Motif is 5" across.

SKILL LEVEL: ☆☆ Average

FIRST ROW

First Motif

Rnd 1: With any scrap color, ch 3, sl st in first ch to form ring, ch 3, 11 dc in ring, join with sl st in top of ch-3, fasten off (12 dc).

NOTES: *For beginning shell (beg shell), ch 3, (2 dc, ch 3, 3 dc) in same st.*

For shell, (3 dc, ch 3, 3 dc) in next st.

Rnd 2: Working this rnd in **back lps** only, join black with sl st in first st, beg shell, skip next 2 sts, (shell in next st, skip next 2 sts) around, join, fasten off (4 shells).

Rnd 3: Join any scrap color with sl st in ch sp of first shell, beg shell, (2 dc, ch 2, 2 dc) in sp between last shell and next shell, *shell in ch sp of next shell, (2 dc, ch 2, 2 dc) in sp between last shell and next shell; repeat from * around, join, fasten off (4 shells, 4 ch-2 sps).

Rnd 4: Join black with sl st in first shell, ch 3, (4 dc, ch 3, 5 dc) in same sp, *[skip next 3 sts of same shell, sc in sp between last skipped st and next st, (3 sc, ch 1, 3 sc) in next ch-2 sp, skip next 2 sts, sc in sp between last skipped st and next st], (5 dc, ch 3, 5 dc) in next shell; repeat from * 2 more times; repeat between [ ], join, fasten off.

Second Motif

Rnds 1-3: Repeat same rnds of First Motif.

Rnd 4: Join black with sl st in first shell, ch 3, 4 dc in same sp; joining to side of last Motif made (see Joining Diagram on page 141), ch 1, drop lp from hook, insert hook in center ch of corresponding ch-3 sp on other Motif, draw dropped lp through, ch 1, 5 dc in same sp on this Motif, skip next 3 sts, sc in sp between last skipped st and next st, 3 sc in next ch-2 sp, drop lp from hook, insert hook in next ch-1 sp on other Motif, draw dropped lp through, 3 sc in same sp

Continued on page 140

Dear Journal,

Mom called this morning just full of news. Apparently Diane Riggs has been frantically trying to reach me for help with the next fundraiser. Hemi appears to have a thorn embedded in his paw and has been limping badly. Ty is headed to Chicago to check out a prize Hereford bull Daddy wants to get and the jet needs to go in for service. With all that in mind, she thought I'd better come home tomorrow rather than wait until Saturday. I think she's right. Preston took me to dinner tonight at a quaint Italian restaurant downtown. The food was wonderful, the atmosphere warm and the service first class. They even had a dance floor, although Preston never asked me to dance. I thought when he suggested we go out, it would be a great chance for us to talk and solidify some of our plans, but all Preston wanted to discuss was work. Primarily how impressed everyone was with Ashley. Apparently, Michael Benedict wants to meet her now, so Preston is to take her to his office tomorrow morning. Wonder what she'll wear for that. There I go again! I should be ashamed of myself. I guess it really is time for me to get back to Morningside and clear my head. All this smog in the city has left me without any reason. I'm the one who suggested Ashley look for another job since she was having trouble working with Doug, and now I'm upset because she seems to have taken my advice. I guess I just didn't expect her to show up in Chicago looking so gorgeously needy. The problem is, Ashley is anything but needy. She's beautiful, capable and unstoppable, and she needs Preston's help like she needs a hole in her head. Okay, Corinne, snap out of it and be a big girl! Insecurity isn't your thing. All you need is some good fresh Colorado air to make you feel all better. Ty will be here tomorrow and will have you acting like your old self soon enough. He always knows how to make you laugh. This huge city has just gotten you down, and you'll be fine once you're back at Morningside.

Corinne finished an arrangement of fresh flowers, then carried the flo-blue vase over and set it down on the antique side table. "Perfect," she said aloud, "that's just what the room needed." She reached up and straightened a blue willow plate on the wall, then turned to plump the pillows on the sofa. Hemi, who was sleeping spread-eagle over the back, looked up at the thumping noise, twitching his ears back and adopting that "how-dare-you-bother-me" look he was so good at. "Don't you look at me in that tone of voice, young man," Corinne chided the cat, "or you'll find yourself lounging in the great outdoors." The handsome cat's ears softened and he stretched languorously, repositioning himself for another nap.

"Knock-knock! Anyone home?" Corinne turned as the front door opened and her mother walked in, carrying what appeared to be a pie. "Hi, Mom!" Corinne said, taking the pie before hugging her mother tightly. "Hello, darling," said Clarice. "Gosh, I missed you! You'd think as often as you travel, I'd get used to your being gone, but I just never have. I never can wait till you get home."

Corinne smiled warmly and reached to take the pie. Placing it on the counter, she opened the drawer and extracted a knife as Clarice pulled two coffee mugs off the rack. "You'd think," she said dryly, "as often as I travel, I'd get used to it!" Both women laughed. "But then again," Corinne said, "I've never found any place I liked being as well as I do here. Guess that's why I prefer coming home to traveling."

"Tell me about Chicago," Clarice probed, handing Corinne two small plates. "Did you and Preston finalize any plans? You said something about a house? What was that about?" Corinne put her hand up as if to fend off her mother's barrage of questions. "Whoa now, one question at a time!" She sliced through the center of the fresh apple pie, still warm from the oven, and transferred two generous pieces to the waiting plates. Handing one to her mother, she walked to the window seat, sat down and quickly dug into her pie. "This is heavenly, Mom," she mumbled through pursed lips, "which is more than I can say for Chicago."

Seated beside her, Clarice took a dainty bite and turned concerned eyes toward her only child. Despite her small frame and petite height, Corinne was much tougher than her stature implied, something Clarice had learned first-hand during the months after Steven's death. But Clarice also knew when Corinne was keeping something from her and pried gently, hoping to get to the bottom of Corinne's uncharacteristic moodiness. "Okay, so Chicago isn't heaven. You knew that before you left. What makes you seem so disappointed by the realization?" Corinne hesitated, "I guess I just got a really good taste this time of what being Mrs. Preston Richards would be like, and I'm a little scared."

Clarice chewed a bite of pie then reached for her coffee. Examining the mug thoughtfully, she asked, "Just exactly what part of that scares you? Surely you didn't encounter any social or personal situation in Chicago you haven't lived through before?" Corinne scooted an apple slice around on her plate, "Oh, I don't know, Mom. I'm not sure what I expected when I went, but I just can't shake this let-down feeling. Preston was his usual wonderful self, so I don't think it was that. You know him, always the gentleman, always willing to listen, always ready to do anything I ask."

Corinne leaned back, gazing out the window at the flowers and trees, lost in her thoughts. After a moment, she sighed tiredly and straightened up. "I do know of a few things that will have to change once Preston and I are married, though," she said, turning back toward Clarice. "For one, Preston isn't going to work seventy hours or more a week. I told him that's ridiculous. And two, the ladies social circles in Chicago are going to have to start *doing* something. Don't get me wrong, they are wonderful women, and it's not that they don't have things to do. It's just that what they do doesn't seem to be any real accomplishment. Nothing for the betterment of human-kind. Know what I mean?"

Clarice smiled lovingly at her daughter. "Yes, I know what you mean," she said. "But you have to remember, dear, not everyone shares your belief that each of us holds a certain responsibility toward helping others around us attain happiness." Corinne frowned. "That's not it, Mother. It's just that I think we should spend our time and energy making the world a better place to be, regardless of how we do it. Those women in Chicago just didn't get it. Being in the positions they are, they could do so much!" Clarice stood up and carried her plate to the sink. "That's what I said, Corinne," she chuckled, "not everyone shares your idealistic views."

Corinne drained her cup. "Well," she said, "I guess it's time they learned that charity isn't charity unless it serves to improve the world. And, speaking of charity," she laughed, "you've got to come see that afghan I told you I was working on for the upcoming event. I know you'll love it!"

Circles of Love

Designed by Maggie Weldon

SIZE: 49" x 67" without Fringe.

MATERIALS: Worsted-weight yarn — 28 oz. navy, 18 oz. green, 11 oz. each med. blue and pink; tapestry needle; I crochet hook or size needed to obtain gauge.

GAUGE: Rnds 1-3 of Block = 4½" across. Each Block is 6¾" square.

SKILL LEVEL: ☆☆ Average

BLOCK (make 63)

NOTES: *For beginning cluster (beg cl), ch 4, *yo 2 times, insert hook in ring, yo, draw lp through, (yo, draw through 2 lps on hook) 2 times; repeat from *, yo, draw through all 3 lps on hook.*

*For cluster (cl), *yo 2 times, insert hook in ring, yo, draw lp through, (yo, draw through 2 lps on hook) 2 times; repeat from * 2 more times, yo, draw through all 4 lps on hook.*

Rnd 1: With med. blue, ch 4, sl st in first ch to form ring, beg cl in ring, ch 3, (cl in ring, ch 3) 7 times, join with sl st in top of beg cl, fasten off (8 cls, 8 ch sps).

Rnd 2: Join pink with sc in any ch sp, 5 sc in same sp, 6 sc in each ch sp around, join with sl st in first sc, fasten off (48 sc).

Rnd 3: Join green with sc in 4th sc of any 6-sc group, 2 sc in same st, ch 2, (3 dc, ch 2, 3 dc) in 4th sc of next 6-sc group, ch 2, *3 sc in 4th sc of next 6-sc group, ch 2, (3 dc, ch 2, 3 dc) in 4th sc of next 6-sc group, ch 2; repeat fom * around, join with sl st in first sc, fasten off (24 dc, 12 sc, 12 ch sps).

Rnd 4: Join navy with sl st in any corner ch sp, ch 3, (dc, ch 2, 2 dc) in same sp, dc in each of next 3 sts, (2 dc in next ch sp, dc in each of next 3 sts) 2 times, *(2 dc, ch 2, 2 dc) in next ch sp, dc in each of next 3 sts, (2 dc in next ch sp, dc in each of next 3 sts) 2 times; repeat from * around, join with sl st in top of ch-3 (17 dc across each side between corner ch sps).

Rnd 5: Ch 3, dc in each st around with (2 dc, ch 2, 2 dc) in corner ch sp, join, fasten off (21 dc across each side between corner ch sps).

Holding Blocks wrong sides together, matching sts, with navy, sew together through **back lps** in 7 rows of 9 Blocks each.

BORDER

Working around outer edge, join navy with sl st in any corner ch sp, ch 3, (dc, ch 2, 2 dc) in same sp, dc in each st, in each ch sp on each side of seams and in each seam

Continued on page 141

Dear Journal,

I can't wait! Everyone is so excited about our "Afghan Extravaganza." What a great way to help those less fortunate. There was a big article on the society page of the paper today showing all the guild members, including the three men who joined last month, at Debra Gibson's home stitching on their various afghans. I love to get together like that with everyone and stitch. Crochet is just good for the soul. I don't care what anyone says. This is just the beginning! Hopefully with enough publicity, we'll get a great supply of afghans to be auctioned. I've talked with several of my piano students about the proposed youth-center and they can't wait either. They have had some great ideas, too, about different things we can have in the center. This will really be something super for the kids. Right now there's no place for them to go when school isn't on, and they need a place they can call their own. If everything goes as planned, we'll be able to raise enough to build the center and pay the salary of the staff for the first two years. I even got a call today from Curtis Hicks saying he wanted to relocate his 24-hour teen crisis intervention staff to the center as soon as it is completed. Yesterday, I talked to Peter Bertinelli who is looking into opening a burger franchise at the center that would allow kids to exchange volunteer work at the center for free meals. I can hardly believe the amount of support we're garnering from every avenue. Even Tyler agreed to help. I nearly fell over! He never goes near most social events, but said he'd be happy to coordinate the set-up crew. He already has a list of his buddies he's going to hit-up about helping. He says he has a fool-proof plan to get them there. The sun is almost down, so I'd better get busy if I'm going to finish this afghan before I go to bed!

Picture Perfect

Designed by Melissa Leapman

SIZE: 45" x 65".

MATERIALS: Worsted-weight yarn — 53 oz. country blue; F crochet hook or size needed to obtain gauge.

GAUGE: 9 sc = 2"; 9 sc rows = 2".

SKILL LEVEL: ☆☆ Average

AFGHAN

Row 1: Ch 252, 3 sc in 2nd ch from hook, sc in next 11 chs, skip next 2 chs, sc in next 11 chs, (5 sc in next ch, sc in next 11 chs, skip next 2 chs, sc in next 11 chs) across to last ch, 3 sc in last ch, turn (271 sc).

Rows 2-5: Working these rows in **back lps** only, ch 1, 2 sc in first st, sc in next 12 sts, skip next 2 sts, sc in next 12 sts, (3 sc in next st, sc in next 12 sts, skip next 2 sts, sc in next 12 sts) across to last st, 2 sc in last st, turn.

Row 6: Ch 4, skip next st, dc in next st, (ch 1, skip next st, dc in next st) 5 times, ch 1, skip next 2 sts, dc in next st, *(ch 1, skip next st, dc in next st) 12 times, ch 1, skip next 2 sts, dc in next st; repeat from * across to last 12 sts, (ch 1, skip next st, dc in next st) 6 times, turn (131 dc, 130 ch sps).

Row 7: Ch 1, 3 sc in first st, sc in next ch sp, (sc in next st, sc in next ch sp) 5 times, skip next 2 sts and one ch sp, sc in next ch sp, (sc in next st, sc in next ch sp) 5 times, *5 sc in next st, sc in next ch sp, (sc in next st, sc in next ch sp) 5 times, skip next 2 sts and one ch sp, sc in next ch sp, (sc in next st, sc in next ch sp) 5 times; repeat from * across to last st, 3 sc in last st, turn (271 sc).

Rows 8-191: Repeat rows 2-7 consecutively, ending with row 5. At end of last row, fasten off.

EDGING

Row 1: Working across one long edge, join with sc in first row, sc in each sc row and 2 sc in each dc row, across, turn.

Row 2: Ch 1, sc in each st across, fasten off.

Repeat on other long edge of Afghan.❦

Dear Ashley,

Hi! Got your letter. Yes! Labor Day weekend would be a great time for you to come out. We always have a big bar-be-cue that weekend, and everyone for miles around will be here. As a matter of fact, there will probably be quite a few people here that you'd remember from your days in Colorado. I saw a couple at the Cattle Baron's Gala last week. Tyler had to go to talk to someone about another hereford bull since he and Dad decided not to get the one in Chicago, so I went with him in hopes of drumming up more support for our "Afghan Extravaganza" to be held in July. The crochet guild I'm involved with is planning to auction off as many donated afghans as we can in order to raise money to build a youth center downtown. Tyler is helping with it as well by coordinating the set-up crew. You should have seen him, Ashley! It was black tie, of course, so Tyler rented this wonderful western-style tux with tails. He certainly caught the eye of every live woman in the ballroom. Even old Miss Greer, the teacher we had in first grade, fawned over him. Trust me, you would never be ashamed to be seen on that man's arm. I've enclosed some pictures for you, one of which is of Ty and his new horse, Comanche. The others are just of the rance and Mom and Dad's house. They should whet your appetite sufficiently to have you packing in no time. By Labor Day things will be a little quieter around the ranch, so Ty will be able to socialize more then, too.

I've spent almost every spare minute lately crocheting afghans for this event. I've gotten six done so far, and hope to do at least twelve more if my wrists hold out. I just had the greatest idea! I'm going to take pictures of all the afghans to be auctioned as we get them in to compile a directory of sorts. That way people would know exactly the order in which the afghans will be auctioned. I'm going to close now, because I want to go call Debra and tell her about my idea.

More later! Love, C —

Musical Days

Designed by Darla Fanton

SIZE: 52" x 78".

MATERIALS: Worsted-weight yarn — 17 oz. dk. purple, 15 oz. each med. purple and lt. purple, 5½ oz. green; H crochet hook or size needed to obtain gauge.

GAUGE: One petal cluster is ¾" tall. Each Strip is 2¼" wide.

SKILL LEVEL: ☆☆ Average

FIRST STRIP

NOTE: *For **petal cluster (petal cl)**, *yo 2 times, insert hook in st, yo, draw lp through, (yo, draw through 2 lps on hook) 2 times; repeat from * in same st, yo, draw through all 3 lps on hook.*

Row 1: With dk. purple, (ch 5, petal cl in 5th ch from hook) 57 times, **do not** turn (57 petal cls).

Rnd 2: Working in rnds, ch 6, petal cl in 5th ch from hook, ch 2, *(petal cl, ch 4, sl st, ch 4, petal cl) in base of next petal cl, ch 2*; repeat between ** across; working on opposite side of cls, repeat between ** across, (petal cl, ch 4, sl st) in base of first petal cl made on this rnd, fasten off.

NEXT STRIP

Row 1: With med. purple, (ch 5, petal cl in 5th ch from hook) 57 times, **do not** turn (57 petal cls).

Rnd 2: Working in rnds, ch 6, petal cl in 5th ch from hook; joining to side of last Strip made, ch 1, sl st in corresponding ch-2 sp on other Strip, ch 1, *(petal cl, ch 4, sl st, ch 4, petal cl) in base of next petal cl on this Strip, ch 1, sl st in next ch-2 sp on other Strip, ch 1*; repeat between ** across to end petal cl, (petal cl, ch 4, sl st, ch 4, petal cl) in base of end petal cl, ch 2; working on opposite side of cls, [(petal cl, ch 4, sl st, ch 4, petal cl) in base of next petal cl, ch 2]; repeat between [ ] across, (petal cl, ch 4, sl st) in base of first petal cl made on this rnd, fasten off.

Working in color sequence of lt. purple, dk. purple,

Continued on page 141

My dear Preston,

It was good to hear your voice the other night. Wish you could have talked longer, but I understand. And yes, I agree. If we're going to get married this year, it looks like we're going to have to just pick a date that's open and then make everything else on the calender fit around it. My calendar is just as full as yours, but it wouldn't be that hard to change. If you'll just look at yours and figure out the best time for you, I'll work with whatever you come up with. The only request I have is that we do it before it gets too horribly cold.

Let me know about Labor Day just as soon as you possibly can, okay? I know you don't like leaving when you've got a project going, but you need a break. You can't work constantly. It's not healthy or productive. You make everyone else look lazy by comparison, and they won't thank you for that. Ashley will be here that weekend as well, and I need to start planning now if you're both coming at the same time. I sent her some new pictures of Tyler a while back and they've been conversing on the phone since. Now she can't wait to come meet him in person. I know you don't think they'll hit it off, but I knew once I got them started in the right direction they'd come around to my way of thinking. You will too, just hide and watch.

One of my piano students graduated from high-school this week and received a full scholarship to Juliard so I threw her a big going-away party. I gave her an afghan to take to her dorm. It was just a simple lacy one in shades of purple, but she loved it. She said it reminded her of one she had as a child that her grandmother had given her. I was touched. She has been one of my best students, and I'll really miss her. I guess I've done my part though.

I'd better close for now, Hemi is asking for out. Let me know about Labor Day soon, and also about which date you think will work best for the wedding, then I'll start hunting for a contractor to do the addition on my bungalow like we talked about.

Take care and don't forget to get some sleep!

Love, C —

Country Communion

Designed by Maggie Weldon

SIZE: 58" x 62".

MATERIALS: Worsted-weight yarn — 42 oz. navy, 19 oz. off-white and 15 oz. maroon; tapestry needle; I crochet hook or size needed to obtain gauge.

GAUGE: 13 sc = 4"; 7 sc rows = 2". Each Block is 10" x 11¼".

SKILL LEVEL: ☆☆ Average

BLOCK (make 30)

NOTES: *When changing colors (see page __), always drop yarn to wrong side of work. Use a separate skein or ball of yarn for each color section.* **Do not** *carry yarn across from one section to another. Fasten off colors at end of each color section.*

Each square on graph equals one sc.

Work odd-numbered graph rows from right to left and even-numbered rows from left to right.

Row 1: With navy, ch 29, sc in 2nd ch from hook, sc in each ch across, turn (28 sc).

Row 2: For **row 2 of graph (see page 142)**, ch 1, sc in first 8 sts changing to off-white in last st made, sc in next st changing to navy, sc in next 10 sts changing to maroon, sc in next st changing to navy, sc in last 8 sts, turn.

Rows 3-26: Ch 1, sc in each st across changing colors according to graph, turn.

Rnd 27: Working around outer edge, ch 1, sc in each st and in end of each row around with 3 sc in each center corner st, join with sl st in first sc, fasten off.

Rnd 28: Join off-white with sc in any st, sc in each st around with 3 sc in each center corner st, join, fasten off.

Rnd 29: Join navy with sl st in any st, ch 3, dc in each st around with (2 dc, ch 2, 2 dc) in each center corner st, join with sl st in top of ch-3, fasten off.

Holding Blocks wrong sides together, matching sts, with navy, sew together through **back lps** in 5 rows of 6 Blocks each.

EDGING

Working around entire outer edge, join navy with sl st in corner ch sp before one short end, ch 3, (dc, ch 2, 2 dc) in same sp, dc in each st around with dc ch sps on each side of seams tog and (2 dc, ch 2, 2 dc) in each corner ch sp, join with sl st in top of ch-3, fasten off.

CENTER (make 30)

With maroon, ch 4, 9 dc in 4th ch from hook, join with sl st in top of ch-3, fasten off.

Sew one Center to center of star on each Block. ❧

Love's Devotion

Designed by Maggie Weldon

SIZE: 45¾" x 63¼".

MATERIALS: Worsted-weight yarn — 22 oz. white, 15 oz. purple and 8 oz. green; tapestry needle; H crochet hook or size needed to obtain gauge.

GAUGE: 7 sc = 2"; 7 sc rows = 2". Each Block is 8¾" square.

SKILL LEVEL: ☆☆ Average

AFGHAN
BLOCK (make 35)

NOTES: *When changing colors (see page _), always drop yarn to wrong side of work. Use a separate skein or ball of yarn for each color section.* **Do not** *carry yarn across from one section to another. Fasten off colors at end of each color section.*

Each square on graph equals 1 sc.

Work odd-numbered graph rows from right to left and even-numbered rows from left to right.

Row 1: With white, ch 26, sc in 2nd ch from hook, sc in each ch across, turn (25 sc).

Row 2: Ch 1, sc in each st across, turn.

Row 3: For **row 3 of graph (see page 142),** ch 1, sc in first 5 sts changing to purple in last st made, (sc in next st changing to white, sc in next 4 sts changing to purple in last st made, sc in next st changing to white), sc in each of next 3 sts changing to purple in last st made; repeat between ( ), sc in last 5 sts, turn.

Rows 4-25: Ch 1, sc in each st across changing colors according to graph, turn. At end of last row, **do not** turn.

Rnd 26: Working in sts and in ends of rows, ch 1, skip first row, sc in next 23 rows, skip last row; working in starting ch on opposite side of row 1, 3 sc in first ch, sc in each

Continued on page 141

Dear Ashley,

So sorry to hear you can't make it Labor Day. I hope your trip to Chicago is worth what you'll be missing out on here! But, I'm sure it will be in the end if you can find another position. I was surprised that Preston agreed to let you use his condo while he's here. He's very particular about letting anyone stay there since he has so many collectibles, especially when he's not around. But, you'll certainly be more than comfortable, he's got a great place. I'm sure you'll love it. He has very eclectic taste. As a matter of fact, when I think about it, he seems to like a lot of the same type things you do. Anyway, best of luck on the interview.

Ty and I helped one of our mares foal the other night. You should have seen this man, Ashley. He is so rugged, so strong and so manly, yet when he's helping an animal in need, he's a totally different guy. He sat with that horse for six hours straight and he never left her. Despite the fact that he had to get up early and go to Denver to check out things at the convention center where we're holding the "Afghan Extravaganza." He really is a special man, Ashley. He's helped me so much with this event, not to mention he's smart, funny, practical, and most of all, he's always kind to everyone. I know you'll recognize all of this when you meet him face to face.

Remember my Granny Mac? Last week was her 85th birthday, so we threw her a party. She is so outrageously funny for someone her age. You never know what she's going to do. I crocheted a lovely afghan for her and when she took it out of the box and unfolded it she asked, "Where's the man?" I didn't know what she meant, but then she said, "An afghan to snuggle in isn't any fun if you don't have a man to snuggle with you!" Everyone laughed so hard we practically cried. She soon had a couple volunteers from the group at her retirement community. Granny has certainly had fun "playing the field" these last few years since Grandpa died. She was totally devoted to that man, and took care of him night and day that last year he was sick. Now she says she's waiting to find someone who'll pamper her. Sounds like a good idea to me, but I'm afraid at her age she'd better look for a younger man!

I'd better sign off for now, but I'll write again soon. I'm sorry you can't make it. We would have loved to have you, but I understand your need to get away from where you're at. Let me know if you hear anything!

Love, C—

Rave Reviews

Designed by Maggie Weldon

SIZE: 48" x 67".

MATERIALS: Worsted-weight yarn — 24 oz. off-white, 16 oz. each burgundy fleck and navy fleck; I crochet hook or size needed to obtain gauge.

GAUGE: Rows 1-3 of Strip = 2" tall x 3" wide. Each Strip is 6½" wide.

SKILL LEVEL: ☆☆ Average

STRIP

Row 1: With white, ch 16, sc in 10th ch from hook, ch 3, skip next ch, sc in next ch, ch 3, skip next 3 chs, dc in last ch, turn (3 ch sps, 2 dc, 2 sc).

Row 2: Ch 5, sc in first ch sp, ch 1, 5 dc in next ch sp, ch 1, sc in next ch sp, ch 2, dc in 6th ch of ch-9, turn (7 dc, 2 ch-2 sps, 2 ch-1 sps).

NOTE: *For **cluster (cl),** yo, insert hook in next ch sp, yo, draw lp through, yo, draw through 2 lps on hook, (yo, insert hook in same sp, yo, draw lp through, yo, draw through 2 lps on hook) 3 times, yo, draw through all 5 lps on hook.*

Row 3: Ch 5, skip next ch-2 sp, skip next sc, skip next ch-1 sp, cl in next dc, (ch 3, skip next dc, cl in next dc) 2 times, ch 2, skip next ch-1 sp, skip next sc, dc in 3rd ch of ch-5, turn (3 cls, 2 dc, 2 ch-3 sps, 2 ch-2 sps).

Row 4: Ch 6, skip next ch-2 sp, (sc in next ch-3 sp, ch 3) 2 times, dc in 3rd ch of ch-5, turn.

Row 5: Ch 5, sc in first ch-3 sp, ch 1, 5 dc in next ch-3 sp, ch 1, sc in next ch-3 sp, ch 2, dc in 3rd ch of ch-6, turn.

Rows 6-94: Repeat rows 3-5 consecutively, ending with row 4. At end of last row, fasten off.

Rnd 95: Working in rnds, join burgundy with sl st in first st of last row, ch 3, (dc, ch 2, 2 dc) in same st, dc in each of next 3 chs, dc in next st, dc in next ch sp, dc in next st, dc in each of next 3 chs, (2 dc, ch 2, 2 dc) in next st; *working in ends of rows, dc in first row, 2 dc in each row across to last row, dc in last row*; working in starting ch on opposite side of row 1, (2 dc, ch 2, 2 dc) in first ch, dc in next 4 chs, dc in next ch sp, dc in next 4 chs, (2 dc, ch 2, 2 dc) in last ch; repeat between **, join with sl st in top of ch-3, fasten off (13 dc across each short end between corner ch sps, 190 dc across each long edge between corner ch sps).

Rnd 96: Join off-white with sc in first ch sp, (ch 3, sc) in

Continued on page 142

Dear Journal,

Well, it's all over. "Afghan Extravaganza" that is. And what a huge success. The auction went off without a hitch, mostly thanks to Ty's efforts at organizing the set-up crew. Everything was ready on time and functioned perfectly. I still can't quite fathom what made Ty decide to help with this. It's not that he doesn't enjoy helping, he just doesn't like the big "to-dos" as he calls them. Ty is first and foremost a country boy, but you sure couldn't tell the other night. He looked right at home in a suit and tie ushering all those people around and shouting directions to the crew. You'd have thought he did it all the time. Maybe herding cattle all the time isn't really all that different!

The director for the new youth center is to be announced next month and they say the building should be done by next summer. One of the first things we want to do when it opens is to organize daily craft, music and art classes to give the youth something to do during the summer. We also want to get a group of volunteers together that will do tutoring. It will also have an olympic-sized pool, fully-equipped gym, video arcade and a Burger Palace right under the same roof. I can't wait.

Maggie Smith has been bugging me for several months to come to London and help her get her crochet guild started, so it looks like now would be a great time. I've got some time between now and Labor Day and London should be beautiful this time of year. Guess I'll write her tomorrow and let her know. She'll be thrilled.

Preston called today to say he got the Inverness project. I'm really happy for him. He is on cloud nine, but also seemed a little tired. Hope he's not working too hard, but I can't say anything. He wouldn't slow down anyway unless you tied him to his chair. I can't really talk — some people say the same thing about me!

"Are you sure you have *everything*," asked Ty dryly as he surveyed the mountainous heap of luggage Corinne had piled by the door. "You're going to England, right? Not Tibet!" Corinne playfully smacked him with her purse as she walked past, headed toward the kitchen for one last check before they left. "Yes, I do have everything, thank you," she retorted in mock anger. "Everything that is but Hemi. He hates to sit in his carrier any longer than he has to. While you load the car, I'll load him." Ty turned and looked at her with an exasperated expression. "You expect me to carry all this stuff out to the car for you while you mess with a cat?" Corinne smiled sweetly and batted her lashes at him, playing the vixen. "Of course I do. What are big strong men for if not to help us little ol' girls with our luggage?" Ty snorted then hoisted several of the suitcases at once and struggled to the door. "At least you could help me open it," he said over his shoulder. Corinne gladly rushed over to help with the latch and couldn't help but notice he was wearing cologne. "Strange," she thought to herself. "Ty doesn't normally wear cologne just to drive me to the airport." This little tidbit of information left Corinne feeling quite unnerved, and not sure why.

"Tell me again why you're going to London," Tyler said as he turned out of the drive. "Well, I don't know if you've ever heard me talk about Maggie Smith. We both studied for our Masters at Juliard. She is originally from England, and now lives just outside London. She's also into needlecraft and has been bugging me to come over and help her get a guild started. I had a bit of breathing room in my calender so I took her up on the offer." Tyler turned and glanced at Corinne digging in her bag of yarn. "Is she sure London's ready for the likes of you? Maybe I should call ahead and warn someone," he said reaching to switch programs on the CD. Corinne slapped at him good-naturedly without comment then turned to her crochet.

"I'm really sorry Ashley isn't going to make it out for Labor Day,," Corinne said out of the blue. "What brought that up," asked Ty who had been enjoying the peaceful silence between the two of them. Corinne had been quietly stitching ever since they left the ranch. "Oh, I just happened to think about it," Corinne fibbed. She'd been thinking about it since before they got in the car. "Well, I guess I'm not as disappointed as you are," Ty stated flatly. "Labor Day is always a big weekend around the ranch and I'm not sure how I'd be able to coordinate my responsibilities for the annual bash your dad throws and spend time waiting hand and foot on some city-slicker female." Corinne turned to face him, raising one gracefully arched eyebrow. "Since when did

you start referring to Ashley as a city-slicker? You never had that opinion before now that I knew of."

"Look, no offense intended, Bugsy, I just know how it is when you have company and you're trying to do three things at once." Corinne winced inwardly at his use of the childhood nickname he gave her during her pesky years. "Can-it with the 'Bugsy' routine, buddy, or I'll have to hurt you," Corinne barked. Ty laughed out loud then, and Corinne had to follow suit. "If it's all the same to you," Ty said breathlessly after they both calmed down, "I'm not exactly in a tremendous hurry to get hitched, if you know what I mean. I like my life just the way it is right now. Not that Ashley doesn't seem like a wonderful lady, but I'm pretty fond of the country life, and I don't know how she'd take to living way out here rather than in the city."

Having composed herself sufficiently to talk again, Corinne waited a moment before replying. "I don't know how she'd feel now, Ty. She used to love the country when she was young, but she's grown quite accustomed to the fast lane now it seems. If all works out, she'll be out at Christmas so we'll find out then. I'm not worried. No one can resist Colorado at Christmas time!"

The rest of the trip was spent in companionable silence. Corinne stitching, Ty humming softly to his favorite country songs playing on the stereo. At the airport, Ty quickly transferred Corinne's luggage to the cargo hold of the waiting jet then stepped inside to say goodbye. Corinne was talking to Phillip about the estimated departure and arrival times when she felt a strong hand grip her arm. "I guess I'll be going," Ty said. "You take care of this gal, Phillip, you hear?" Phillip chuckled, "As if there's anyone or anything she can't handle," he laughed. "You know our Miss Corinne. She may be small, but so is dynamite." At that, Ty turned and gave Corinne a brotherly hug. "Don't forget where you live," he shouted as he climbed out.

As Phillip headed toward the cockpit, Corinne turned her attention to Hemi, seeing to it that the seat belt was snug against the carrier. The yellow eyes gleamed at her from within the cage holding her spellbound for a moment. "You look like you're up to something, Hemingway," she remarked, reaching in to stroke his ear. "What's going on in that little mind of yours, I wonder." Hemi merely swished his tail and proceeded to groom himself, indicating in his feline way that even if he could talk, he probably wouldn't say what he was thinking anyway. "You're just like someone else I know," Corinne said as she picked up her hook and glanced out the window to see Ty standing by the hanger, intently watching the plane.

Royal Bows

Designed by Maggie Weldon

SIZE: 55" x 76".

MATERIALS: Worsted-weight yarn — 28 oz. white, 21 oz. dk. blue and 7 oz. lt. blue; tapestry needle; I crochet hook or size needed to obtain gauge.

GAUGE: 3 sc = 1"; 3 sc rows = 1". Each Block is 10½" square.

SKILL LEVEL: ☆☆ Average

BLOCK (make 35)

Row 1: With white, ch 26, sc in 2nd ch from hook, sc in each ch across, turn (25 sc).

Row 2: Ch 1, sc in each st across, turn.

*NOTES: When changing colors (see page 159), always drop yarn to wrong side of work. Use a separate skein or ball of yarn for each color section. **Do not** carry yarn across from one section to another. Fasten off colors at end of each color section.*

Work odd-numbered graph rows from right to left and even-numbered rows from left to right.

Each square on graph equals one sc.

Row 3: For **row 3 of graph (see page 142),** ch 1, sc in each of first 2 sts changing to dk. blue in last st made, sc in next st changing to white, sc in next 19 sts changing to dk. blue in last st made, sc in next st changing to white, sc in each of last 2 sts, turn.

Rows 4-25: Ch 1, sc in each st across changing colors according to graph, turn.

Rnd 26: Working around outer edge, ch 1, 3 sc in first st, sc in each st across with 3 sc in last st; (working in ends of rows, skip first row, sc in each row across to last row, skip last row); working in starting ch on opposite side of row 1, 3 sc in first ch, sc in each ch across with 3 sc in last ch; repeat between ( ), join with sl st in first sc, **turn,** fasten off (25 sc across each side between corner sc).

Rnd 27: With right side facing you, join dk. blue with sl st in any center corner st, ch 3, (dc, ch 2, 2 dc) in same st, dc in each st around with (2 dc, ch 2, 2 dc) in each center corner st, join with sl st in top of ch-3, fasten off (29 dc across each side between ch sps).

Holding Blocks wrong sides together, matching sts, with dk. blue, sew together through **back lps** in 5 rows of 7 Blocks each.

BORDER

Rnd 1: Working around entire outer edge, with right side facing you, join dk. blue with sl st in any corner ch sp, ch 3, (dc, ch 2, 2 dc) in same sp, dc in each st and in each seam

Continued on page 142

Dear Journal,

Arrived in London today, you wouldn't believe the sights. This place is just like something out of a storybook. Maggie picked me up at Heathrow and we traveled by car back to her home. She lives on a magnificent estate just outside London that has been in her family for centuries. Everything is so, well, English! I know that sounds corny, but I just wasn't prepared to be so in awe of the surroundings here. Compared to the States, this is like one big, living museum. There are gardens everywhere and the architecture is positively breath-taking. We drove past a few of the sights, Buckingham Palace and Westminster Abbey, but plan to do some serious sight-seeing later. The wing she put me in overlooks a manicured rose garden and a fountain. It is furnished with Queen Anne style antiques, including a massive four-poster bed that's so high off the floor you have to have a step-stool to reach it. The walls, bed linens, curtains — everything — are done in a rose motif. It's perfect for the setting. There is even an adjoining bath on one side and a sitting room on the other. I've been in hotel suites at some very posh hotels that didn't compare to this. I could get used to this real quick! Maggie already has at least two weeks of events planned that we're supposed to squeeze into one. Hope I can keep up. We're to meet with her group of friends tomorrow to discuss organizing the guild. She's so excited. I've told her about some of the things we've been able to accomplish in Denver and they're really anxious to get going. Enough for now, have to get up early!

Picot Paradox

Designed by Rosetta Harshman

SIZE: 52½" x 67½".

MATERIALS: Worsted-weight yarn — 21 oz. white, 17 oz. green/rose/white variegated and 10 oz. green; G crochet hook or size needed to obtain gauge.

GAUGE: Rnds 1-3 of Large Motif = 3" across. Each Large Motif is 7½" across.

SKILL LEVEL: ☆☆ Average

FIRST ROW

First Large Motif

Rnd 1: With green, ch 7, sl st in first ch to form ring, ch 1, 12 sc in ring, join with sl st in first sc (12 sc).

Rnd 2: Ch 5, (dc in next st, ch 2) around, join with sl st in 3rd ch of ch-5 (12 dc, 12 ch sps).

Rnd 3: Sl st in first ch sp, ch 1, 3 sc in same sp, 3 sc in each ch sp around, join with sl st in first sc, fasten off (36 sc).

Rnd 4: Join variegated with sl st in first st, ch 7, skip next 4 sts, (sc in next 5 sts, ch 7, skip next 4 sts) around to last 4 sts, sc in last 4 sts, sc in same st as first sl st, **do not** join (20 sc, 4 ch sps).

Rnd 5: Sl st in first ch sp, ch 3, (7 tr, dc) in same sp, sc in next 5 sts, *(dc, 7 tr, dc) in next ch sp, sc in next 5 sts; repeat from * around, join with sl st in top of ch-3, fasten off (56 sts).

Rnd 6: Join white with sl st in first st, ch 5, dc in next st, (ch 2, dc in next st) 7 times, ch 3, skip next 2 sts, sc in next st, ch 3, skip next 2 sts, *dc in next st, (ch 2, dc in next st) 8 times, ch 3, skip next 2 sts, sc in next st, ch 3, skip next 2 sts; repeat from * around, join with sl st in 3rd ch of ch-5 (32 ch-2 sps, 8 ch-3 sps).

NOTE: *For picot, ch 3, sl st in top of last st made.*

Rnd 7: Ch 6, sl st in 3rd ch from hook (first picot made), (ch 2, dc in next dc, picot) 8 times, ch 3, skip next 2 ch-3 sps, *dc in next dc, picot, (ch 2, dc in next dc, picot) 8 times, ch 3, skip next 2 ch-3 sps; repeat from * around, join with sl st

Continued on page 143

Dear Preston

Was good to hear from you today. This time difference is really hard to work around, isn't it. That's why I opted to write rather than call. I'll get Maggie's husband to fax this to your office, that way you'll get it quicker than if I mailed it. I was glad to hear the Inverness project is going as planned, and the house as well. "Our" house, I guess I should say. It's just hard to refer to something as yours that you've never even seen.

About the wedding, I know I said for you to just pick a date and I'd work with it, but, I'm just not crazy about the idea of getting married in December. Colorado is great in the winter if you like to sky or sit by the fire, but a wedding would be really hard to do the way we want to at that time of year. And, Chicago wouldn't be any better. I really had my heart set on being a June bride. The dress I had picked out isn't suitable for cold weather, and we couldn't have the ceremony outdoors like I had hoped, either, if we get married in December. Please think about it, will you. Can we wait until June? We can go ahead and plan everything now, that way we'll have time to get properly organized. Plus, you said yourself that you wouldn't be able to get away for a honeymoon if we get married then, but maybe you could in June. I know this may seem like I'm dragging my feet, but I'm not. I just want the wedding to be everything we had hoped for, and rushing to get it done in December would be almost impossible. Let me know what you think about what I've said and we'll talk again.

I'm having a "jolly good time" here with Maggie, I got to see the changing of the guard today, as well as Big Ben. You'd love it here as the building are all so beautifully made. It certainly is charming. I'd better close this now, I'm getting a little too relaxed curled up in this chair, and I still have to help Maggie draft her guild's charter. We have another meeting tomorrow and I think they'll be finished with it then. Talk to you soon!

Love, C —

Petunia Potluck

Designed by Ellen Anderson

SIZE: 51" x 68".

MATERIALS: Worsted-weight yarn — 33 oz. assorted scrap colors (*Each Motif requires approximately 5 yds. of 2 scrap colors*), 28 oz. lt. green, and 3 oz. med. green; H crochet hook or size needed to obtain gauge.

GAUGE: Rnds 1-2 of Motif = 2¼" across. Each Motif is 4¼" across.

SKILL LEVEL: ☆☆ Average

FIRST ROW

First Motif

NOTES: For **beginning popcorn (beg pc)**, ch 3, 4 dc in same st, drop lp from hook, insert hook in top of ch-3, draw dropped lp through.

For **popcorn (pc)**, 5 dc in next st, drop lp from hook, insert hook in first st of 5-dc group, draw dropped lp through.

For **beginning dc cluster (beg dc-cl)**, ch 3, (yo, insert hook in same sp, yo, draw lp through, yo, draw through 2 lps on hook) 2 times, yo, draw through all 3 lps on hook.

For **dc cluster (dc-cl)**, yo, insert hook in next ch sp, yo, draw lp through, yo, draw through 2 lps on hook, (yo, insert hook in same sp, yo, draw lp through, yo, draw through 2 lps on hook) 2 times, yo, draw through all 4 lps on hook.

For **treble crochet cluster (tr-cl)**, yo 2 times, insert hook in next ch sp, yo, draw lp through, (yo, draw through 2 lps on hook) 2 times, *yo 2 times, insert hook in same sp, yo, draw lp through, (yo, draw through 2 lps on hook) 2 times; repeat from * , yo, draw through all 4 lps on hook.

Rnd 1: With first scrap color, ch 2, 6 sc in 2nd ch from hook, join with sl st in first sc (6 sc).

Rnd 2: Beg pc, ch 3, (pc in next st, ch 3) around, join with sl st in top of beg pc, fasten off (6 pc, 6 ch sps).

Rnd 3: Join next scrap color with sl st in any ch sp, beg dc-cl, (ch 3, dc-cl) in same sp, ch 3, *(dc-cl, ch 3, dc-cl) in next ch sp, ch 3; repeat from * around, join with sl st in top of beg dc-cl, fasten off (12 dc-cls, 12 ch sps).

Rnd 4: Join lt. green with sl st in 2nd ch sp, beg dc-cl, (ch 3, tr-cl, ch 3, dc-cl) in same sp, ch 1, dc in next ch sp, ch 3, dc in next ch sp, ch 1, *(dc-cl, ch 3, tr-cl, ch 3, dc-cl) in next ch sp, ch 1, dc in next ch sp, ch 3, dc in next ch sp, ch 1; repeat from * around, join with sl st in top of beg cl, fasten off (12 ch-3 sps, 8 ch-1 sps).

Second Motif

NOTE: For **joining ch-3 sp**, ch 1, sc in corresponding ch-3 sp on other Motif, ch 1.

Rnds 1-3: Using desired scrap colors, repeat same rnds of First Motif.

Rnd 4: Join lt. green with sl st in 2nd ch sp, beg dc-cl, (ch 3, tr-cl) in same sp; joining to side of last Motif made (see Joining Diagram on page 144), work joining ch-3 sp, dc-cl in

Continued on page 143

Dear Journal,

Maggie's group is having a pot-luck luncheon tomorrow, inviting all interested parties to come and see just what a crochet guild is all about. I've been speaking to the members whenever possible hoping to educate them as to the strength a group like this can have when it comes to raising awareness. They have lots of ideas, but don't know yet how to go about making them happen. That's where I come in. I'm to be the featured speaker at the luncheon and will talk about the events we've had in Denver. I didn't volunteer, Maggie sort of railroaded me into it. I told her that regardless of the fact that I've seen more time in front of a podium than most politicians, I still get nervous. I'll be okay, I guess as long as I take along my crochet hook and some yarn. It always helps keep me calm.

I have to hand it to this group, they really do have a feel for what it's all about. Crocheters are such warm-hearted creative people, no matter where they live. That seems to be the strongest common bond between us is that we all love giving to others. Most, if not all, of the things we crochet end up going to someone else. Too bad everyone in the world can't be a willing to give of their time and effort to keep someone else warm and make them smile. As I've said before, crochet is good for the soul.

Symphony in Violet

Designed by Rosetta Harshman

SIZE: 52" x 77".

MATERIALS: Worsted-weight yarn — 24 oz. soft white, 8 oz. green, 6½ oz. purple, 4 oz. lavender and 1 oz. yellow; tapestry needle; G crochet hook or size needed to obtain gauge.

GAUGE: Rnds 1-4 of Block = 5¾" across. Each Block is 8¼" square.

SKILL LEVEL: ☆☆ Average

BLOCK (make 39, see Note)

NOTE: *Make 24 using purple for flower color; make 15 using lavender for flower color.*

Rnd 1: With yellow, ch 5, sl st in first ch to form ring, ch 3, 15 dc in ring, join with sl st in top of ch-3, fasten off (16 dc).

Rnd 2: Join flower color with sc in first st, (ch 4, 2 tr, ch 4, sc) in same st, sl st in next st, *(sc, ch 4, 2 tr, ch 4, sc) in next st, sl st in next st; repeat from * around, join with sl st in first sc (8 petals).

Rnd 3: Ch 1, sc in first st, *[ch 4, (3 dc, ch 4, sc in top of last dc made, 3 dc) in sp between next 2 tr, ch 4, sc in next sc, skip next sl st], sc in next sc; repeat from * 6 more times; repeat between [ ], join with sl st in first sc.

Rnd 4: Working behind petals, ch 5, (sc in sp between next 2 sc, ch 5) around, join with sl st in joining sl st on last rnd, fasten off (8 ch sps).

Rnd 5: Join green with sl st in any ch sp, ch 4, 5 tr in same sp, 6 tr in each ch sp around, join with sl st in top of ch-4 (48 tr).

Rnd 6: Ch 4, *[(3 tr, ch 2, 3 tr) in next st, tr in next st, dc in next st, hdc in next st, sc in next 5 sts, hdc in next st, dc in next st], tr in next st; repeat from * 2 more times; repeat between [ ], join, fasten off (17 sts across each side between corner ch sps).

Rnd 7: Join soft white with sl st in any ch sp, ch 3, (dc, ch 2, 2 dc) in same sp, ch 1, skip next 2 sts, (2 dc in next st, ch 1, skip next 2 sts) across to next ch sp, *(2 dc, ch 2, 2 dc)

Continued on page 144

Dear Ashley,

Boy, does it ever rain a lot here! I'm afraid I'm going to come home with webbed toes to go along with my callouses. It has been non-stop action ever since I arrived. We attended a performance of the London Symphony last night, then had tea today at the home of a local music professor whose wife is a part of Maggie's guild. The ladies in the guild are really getting into the swing of things and already have several charity events planned. One of which is to have a group of young musicians perform in a recital to start a scholarship fund. Where does crochet come in, well, each member of the guild would donate two afghans as door prizes for those who attend. It's small-scale for now, but they're getting the hang of it. Of course, Maggie couldn't resist telling the hostess that I held a degree in music, and then they wouldn't let up until I played something on the piano. It was truly a fine instrument though, so I didn't mind.

How's the job hunt going? I still wish you could have come out for Labor Day. We would have had a blast! We could go horseback riding, rafting, shopping, then spend our evenings in the hot tub sipping toddys. Sounds like heaven to me! London is great, but it will be good to get back home and take a long hot shower. They don't have showers here like we do, and I sure miss that every morning. I hope you'll plan on coming out at Christmas, maybe you'll be in a new position by then. You could bring your parents, too, you know. I'm sure they would enjoy seeing Colorado again. You know how lovely Morningside is at Christmas. It seems like Daddy puts up more lights each year. Last year he even put lights on the barn!

I'd better close. I sent you a package of Earl Gray tea and scones. You should get it before you get this letter. Some of the food here is great, and some is, well, different. Another reason I'll be glad to get back home. They positively do not know how to make coffee.

Take care.

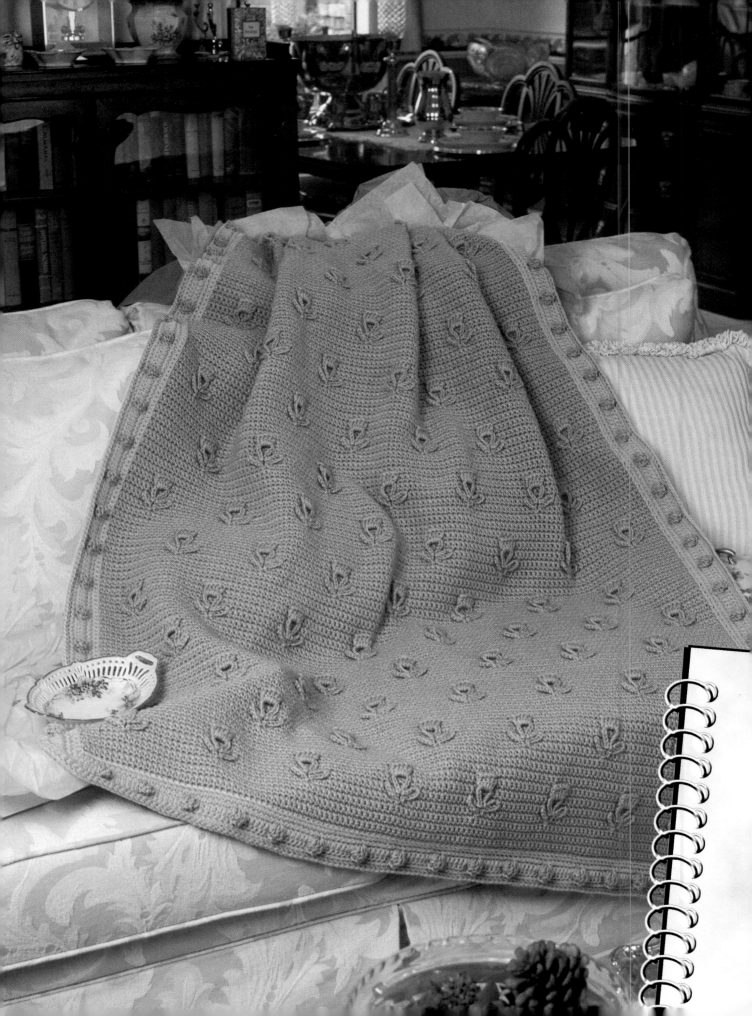

Sweet Impressions

Designed by Dot Drake

SIZE: 40" x 58".

MATERIALS: Worsted-weight yarn — 48 oz. lilac and 8 oz. mint; H crochet hook or size needed to obtain gauge.

GAUGE: 7 sc = 2"; 4 sc rows = 1".

SKILL LEVEL: ☆☆ Average

AFGHAN

Row 1: With lilac, ch 129, sc in 2nd ch from hook, sc in each ch across, turn (128 sc).

Rows 2-6: Ch 1, sc in each st across, turn.

Row 7: Ch 1, sc in first 8 sts; for **motif**, ch 10, (sl st, ch 11, sl st, ch 9, sl st) in 10th ch from hook; *sc in next 16 sts; for **motif**, ch 10, (sl st, ch 11, sl st, ch 9, sl st) in 10th ch from hook; repeat from * across to last 8 sts, sc in last 8 sts, turn (128 sc, 8 motifs).

Row 8: Skipping each motif and working in front of motifs, ch 1, sc in each st across, turn.

Rows 9-10: Ch 1, sc in each st across, turn.

Row 11: Ch 1, sc in first 4 sts, *[sc in next st and in first ch-9 lp of next motif at same time, sc in next 5 sts, skip next ch-11 lp of same motif, sc in next st and in next ch-9 lp of same motif at same time], sc in next 9 sts; repeat from * 6 more times; repeat between [ ], sc in last 5 sts, turn.

Rows 12-14: Ch 1, sc in each st across, turn.

Row 15: Ch 1, sc in first 6 sts, 5 dc in next ch-11 lp on motif below, skip next 3 sts on last row, (sc in next 13 sts, 5 dc in next ch-11 lp on motif below, skip next 3 sts on last row)

across to last 7 sts, sc in last 7 sts, turn (104 sc, 8 5-dc groups).

Row 16: Ch 1, sc in first 7 sts; (*working in front of next 5-dc group, dc in each of next 3 skipped sts on row before last*, sc in next 13 sts on last row) 7 times; repeat between **, sc in last 6 sts, turn (128 sts).

Rows 17-20: Ch 1, sc in each st across, turn.

Row 21: Ch 1, sc in first 16 sts; for **motif**, ch 10, (sl st, ch 11, sl st, ch 9, sl st) in 10th ch from hook; *sc in next 16 sts; for **motif**, ch 10, (sl st, ch 11, sl st, ch 9, sl st) in 10th ch from hook; repeat from * across to last 16 sts, sc in last 16 sts, turn (128 sc, 7 motifs).

Rows 22-24: Repeat rows 8-10.

Row 25: Ch 1, sc in first 12 sts, *[sc in next st and in first ch-9 lp of next motif at same time, sc in next 5 sts on last row, skip next ch-11 lp of same motif, sc in next st and in next ch-9 lp of same motif at same time], sc in next 9 sts on last row; repeat from * 5 more times; repeat between [ ], sc in last 13 sts, turn.

Rows 26-28: Ch 1, sc in each st across, turn.

Row 29: Ch 1, sc in first 15 sts, 5 dc in next ch-11 lp on motif below, skip next 3 sts on last row, (sc in next 13 sts, 5 dc in next ch-11 lp on motif below, skip next 3 sts on last row) 6 times, sc in last 14 sts, turn.

Row 30: Ch 1, sc in first 14 sts; (*working in front of next 5-dc group, dc in each of next 3 skipped sts on row before last*, sc in next 13 sts on last row) 6 times; repeat

Continued on page 145

Dear Journal,

Talked to Preston again today. He had received my fax and called to say he understood her feelings about having a June wedding, but that Christmas would still be better. He reminded me that neither of us is getting any younger and that it would really help him out in his professional life now to have the stability of a wife. His reasons are all very convincing, so maybe it's not such a bad idea after all. We're already planning a big get-together at Morningside for Christmas, what's a few more guests and one more event. Just one more event. Listen to me! I know better. By the time mother gets done with my wedding plans, it will be the only event. They'll have to cancel Christmas. I guess I'll call Preston tomorrow and tell him to go ahead and plan that way. We can finalize the details while he's at Morningside for Labor Day. I've pulled off bigger events in less time, so I shouldn't have any trouble doing this, either.

Right now, I have to get busy putting the finishing touches on the afghan I'm giving Maggie as a thank-you present. She's been such a sweet hostess and has really made me feel at home. I hope to come again sometime.

Daffodil Garden

Designed by Rosetta Harshman

SIZE: 52½" x 63½".

MATERIALS: Worsted-weight yarn — 30 oz. yellow, 24 oz. green, 16 oz. soft white and 1 oz. orange red; tapestry needle; F and G crochet hooks or sizes needed to obtain gauges.

GAUGES: With **G hook**, rnds 1-3 of Daffodil Block = 4" across. With **F hook**, rnds 1-3 of Plain Block = 3" across. Each Block is 5½" square.

SKILL LEVEL: ☆☆ Average

DAFFODIL BLOCK (make 50)

Rnd 1: With G hook and orange red, ch 4, sl st in first ch to form ring, ch 1, 12 sc in ring, join with sl st in first sc, fasten off (12 sc).

Rnd 2: Working this rnd in **back lps** only, join yellow with sc in first st, ch 2, skip next st, (sc in next st, ch 2, skip next st) around, join (6 ch sps).

NOTE: *For picot, ch 3, sc in top of last tr made.*

Rnd 3: Sl st in first ch sp, ch 1, (sc, ch 3, 2 tr, picot, tr, ch 3, sc) in same sp and in each ch sp around, join with sl st in first sc, fasten off (6 petals).

Rnd 4: Working behind petals, in **back lps** of rnd 1, join green with sc in any skipped st, ch 2, (sc in next skipped st, ch 2) around, join (6 ch sps).

Rnd 5: Sl st in first ch sp, ch 4, 3 tr in same sp, 4 tr in each ch sp around, join with sl st in top of ch-4 (24 tr).

Rnd 6: Ch 3, dc in same st, 2 dc in each st around, join with sl st in top of ch-3 (48 dc).

Rnd 7: Ch 3, (dc, ch 2, 2 dc) in same st, *[dc in next st, dc in next st and in picot of next petal on rnd 3 at same time, sc in next 7 sts, dc in next st and in picot of next petal on rnd 3 at same time, dc in next st], (2 dc, ch 2, 2 dc) in next st; repeat from * 2 more times; repeat between [ ], join, fasten off (15 sts across each side between corner ch sps).

Continued on page 145

Dear Ashley,

I'll be leaving London in the morning. I've had a super trip, but I need to get home. Thought I'd write and let you know that Preston has finally worn me down — were going to get married the day before Christmas. I'm still not sure how I'll get everything done that needs to be done in what little time that gives me, but I do have Mom to help. I've seen her work miracles before, too, so I guess I shouldn't worry too much.

When I called home to have the jet sent, I talked to Mom some. She's excited. She also told me that Ty has to go to Kansas City in a couple weeks to sign some papers for Daddy on a logging deal, so I decided to tell you so you could plan on getting together with him while he's in town. I'm sure he'd enjoy the company as he's not familiar with K.C. You could finally meet him face-to-face and maybe get to know each other at least a little. I'm not sure how long he's going to be there. From the sounds of it, it would probably be about two nights. I'll have to check when I get home and let you know more about it.

It's spectacular here in England today. It's been typically foggy and rainy, but today the sun is out. I'm sitting out on the veranda writing this to you. It reminds me of Mother's formal garden behind their house. You know, the one we used to play hide and seek in? Oh how I loved that garden. How I loved summer at Morningside. Mom has changed the garden some since then, but summer still holds that same old magic. Sometimes I wonder just how I'll take to life in Chicago. I've been there in summer before and didn't really like it. It will take some getting used to, I'm sure. On the other hand, it can't be any worse than some of those remote villages Steven and I camped in during summer in South America. Chicago couldn't have that many insects! Plus, I was a lot younger then and lots more resilient.

Better get this in the mail or I'll miss the post man. I'll call as soon as I can once I get back.

Love, C—

"I'm really sorry Preston didn't make it for Labor Day," said Clarice. "Me, too," said Corinne as she poured her mother another glass of tea. "This Inverness project has him so tied up that he couldn't possibly have gotten away. I had really planned on his being here so we could discuss the wedding. Guess I'll just have to do it by myself." Clarice sipped her tea thoughtfully. "Have you thought about relocating the wedding to Chicago so it would be easier for Preston." Corinne reached for her hook and yarn, frowning. "No, Mother, I haven't. I don't want to get married in Chicago. I told Preston that if he insisted on doing this at Christmas, the least he could do was let me have the wedding here."

"Okay. But I know this is getting to be a bit much for you," Clarice said, "trying to coordinate everything yourself without Preston's input, and I just thought if we moved the arrangements up there it would be easier. We should have all the arrangements finalized by Thanksgiving, so he can give his okay then. If he makes it," she added under her breath.

"Thanksgiving," said Corinne, her voice squeaking a little with agitation. "If he waits until Thanksgiving to give me the go-ahead, then there's less than a month to change anything if he doesn't agree. I don't know, Mom," Corinne put down her hook and yarn. "The way I see it is this, he is either going to have to give me free rein to do what I think is best, or he's going to have to come out and help."

"You're absolutely right, dear," Clarice smiled, patting Corinne on the shoulder. "Now, I have to get back to the house and check on Juanita. That's why I came up so early. She sprained her ankle the other day and I told her to stay off of it, but she insisted on coming up today to clean anyway. Hopefully I can run her out early by helping."

Waving goodbye to her mother, Corinne tucked her yarn back into her bag and picked up one of the fresh oatmeal cookies Clarice had brought with her earlier. Her calender lay on the edge of the desk, so she reached to pick it up, turning to the month of November. Staring wistfully at the page, she let her mind drift back to the last Thanksgiving she spent with Steven. It had been a warm and wonderful time. Filled with love, laughter and a perpetual happiness fueled by kindred spirits. She could still hear Steven calling to her from the kitchen. He loved to cook, and at Thanksgiving he was always baking something, or making his delicious homemade cocoa. It was his grandmother's recipe, and

it was the best hot chocolate on earth.

Closing her eyes, Corinne let herself drift even further into the daydream, feeling for a moment as if Steven was actually there once again. "Corinne," came a masculine voice from the back door, "are you dressed." Startled at the invasion of her thoughts by Ty's voice, Corinne blushed, embarrassed that she had allowed her mind to wander so far. "Sure, Ty, come on in." Corinne stood up, carrying her glass to the sink.

"Would you like some tea and a couple of Mom's famous oatmeal cookies." Removing his hat, Tyler shook his head, running his hand through the slightly damp strands of raven hair along his forehead. "No thanks. I know it's early, but I just came up to let you know that Mouser had her kittens last night. You'd said to let you know when she did so you could keep an eye on them." Corinne quickly opened the laundry room door and picked up her old sneakers. "Great!," Corinne shouted. "That's perfect. They'll be ready to give away just in time for Christmas. Where did she have them?"

Ty smiled mischievously. "Only Mouser and I know that little secret, but if you're really nice to us, we'll tell." Corinne smiled. "And just what do I have to do to find out?" she questioned, lowering her eyes as unsettling thoughts sprung to mind. "Well," said Ty slowly, "Mouser would like something soft to lay on and some milk. And, let's see, what else... Oh, yeah, some caviar. And I'd like one of those fresh apple cakes you bake."

Only slightly relieved, Corinne snorted with laughter, "As for the cake, okay. But you can tell Ms. Mouser that caviar is much too rich for someone who's just been through labor. I can handle the milk and bedding, but caviar is out of the question." Tyler capitulated. "Okay, then, it's a deal," he quipped, as Corinne began loading a basket with cat treats and a small bottle of milk.

Tying the laces on her shoes, Corinne jumped up grabbing a couple odd towels from above the dryer. "What are we waiting for then? Let's go!" Seeing her dash out the door, Ty couldn't help but think she looked just like a child on Christmas morning, rushing down to see what Santa had left under the tree. That was the thing he admired most about Corinne. Despite the fact that she'd never lacked for anything, she also had never let it change her loving child-like personality. She loved people, she loved animals, she loved life. A warm smile of affection lit his eyes as he followed her out the door and down the walk to the barn.

Kitten Soft

Designed by Eleanor Albano-Miles

SIZE: 51½" x 68"
MATERIALS: Worsted-weight yarn — 56 oz. white; J crochet hook or size needed to obtain gauge.
GAUGE: 3 sts = 1"; 4 rows = 1½".
SKILL LEVEL: ☆☆ Average

AFGHAN

Row 1: Ch 136, sc in 2nd ch from hook, sc in each ch across, turn (135 sc).

Row 2: Ch 3, dc in each st across, turn. Front of row 2 is right side of work.

Row 3: Ch 1, sc in each st across, turn.

NOTE: *For treble front post (fp), yo 2 times, insert hook from front to back around post of next st on row before last, yo, draw lp through, (yo, draw through 2 lps on hook) 3 times, skip next sc on last row.*

Row 4: Ch 3, fp around next 4 dc on row before last, (dc in next 5 sc, fp around each of next 2 dc on row before last, dc in next 5 sc, fp around next 4 dc on row before last) 8 times, dc in each of last 2 sc, turn.

Row 5: Ch 1, sc in each st across, turn.

Row 6: Ch 3, dc in next sc, fp around each of next 3 fp on row before last, fp around next dc on row before last, (dc in next 5 sc, fp around next fp on row before last, fp around dc on row before last, dc in next 5 sc, fp around each of next 3 fp on row before last, fp around next dc on row before last) 8 times, dc in last sc, turn.

Row 7: Repeat row 5.

Row 8: Ch 3, dc in each of next 2 sc, fp around each of next 3 fp on row before last, (fp around next dc on row before last, dc in next 5 sc, fp around next fp on row before last, fp around dc on row before last, dc in next 5 sc, fp around each of next 3 fp on row before last) 8 times, dc in last sc, turn.

Row 9: Repeat row 5.

Row 10: Ch 3, dc in each of next 3 sc, fp around each of next 3 fp on row before last, (*fp around next dc on row before last, dc in next 5 sc, fp around next fp on row before last, fp around dc on row before last, dc in next 5 sc*, fp around each of next 3 fp on row before last) 7 times; repeat between **, fp around each of next 2 fp on row before last, dc in last sc, turn.

Row 11: Repeat row 5.

Row 12: Ch 3, dc in next 4 sc, fp around each of next 3 fp on row before last, (*fp around next dc on row before last,

Continued on page 146

Dear Journal,

I don't know if I'm sad or glad. Preston called today to say we need to postpone the wedding. I guess I can't say I didn't expect it. He's been so busy that he's barely had time to talk on the rare occasions that I could even reach him. He also said he's had to put the construction of "our" house on hold, too, since he didn't have time to work with both contractors at once. Can't say that I'm all that disappointed about that either. I should be I suppose, but since I haven't been involved, it didn't seem like something I had to be concerned about anyway. I really must talk with Preston about that. I don't care about the outside as much as I do the inside. If I leave it up to him, the interior will be some ultra-modern spaceship looking place with nothing but grey and white furnishings surrounded by chrome and glass. Yuck! I'm just hoping he remembers that I prefer the warm gleam of wood and deep rich colors.

That does take one thing off my plate for now. With all the music lessons I've been giving, plus trying to make the wedding plans, I've barely had time to crochet any of the Christmas gifts I'd planned. I did finally finish the afghan I'm donating to the local Church Alliance for their annual raffle. The proceeds will be used to help a needy family from each church during the holidays. The guild has a meeting tonight to see what type of progress we're making. We hope to get at least fifty afghans.

Mouser had her kittens yesterday. She had them in the old lower barn, so Tyler and I moved them up to his back porch. They're so cute, and it's perfect timing. The kittens will be ready to give away at Christmas. I already know several people who'll get warm-fuzzies in their stockings!

Royal Treatment

Designed by Maggie Weldon

SIZE: 48½" x 71¾".

MATERIALS: Worsted-weight yarn — 24½ oz. dk. gold, 10½ oz. each dk. green and burgundy; tapestry needle; I crochet hook or size needed to obtain gauge.

GAUGE: Each Block is 7½" square.

SKILL LEVEL: ☆☆ Average

AFGHAN

BLOCK (make 48)

Rnd 1: With dk. green, ch 12, sl st in first ch to form ring, ch 1, 24 sc in ring, join with sl st in first sc (24 sc).

NOTE: *For cluster variation (cl), *yo, insert hook in next st, yo, draw lp through, yo, draw through 2 lps on hook; repeat from *, yo draw through all 3 lps on hook.*

Rnd 2: Ch 1, sc in first st, (*ch 4, cl; for **first leaf tip**, ch 4, dc in 4th ch from hook, ch 3, sl st in same ch; for **2nd leaf tip**, ch 4, tr in same ch, ch 4, sl st in same ch; for **3rd leaf tip**, ch 3, dc in same ch, ch 3, sl st in same ch; ch 4, sc in next st, ch 5, skip next 2 sts*, sc in next st) 3 times; repeat between **, join, fasten off (12 leaf tips).

Rnd 3: Join dk. gold with sc in tr of 2nd leaf tip on any 3-leaf group, ch 2, sc in same st, *[ch 5, sc in dc of next leaf tip, ch 5, sc in dc of first leaf tip on next 3-leaf group, ch 5], (sc, ch 2, sc) in tr of next leaf tip; repeat from * 2 more times; repeat between [ ], join (16 ch sps, 16 sc).

Rnd 4: Ch 1, sc in first st, *[(sc, ch 2, sc) in next corner ch sp, (sc in next st, 4 sc in next ch sp) 3 times], sc in next st; repeat from * 2 more times; repeat between [ ], join (18 sc across each side).

Rnd 5: Ch 4, skip next st, *[(dc, ch 1, dc, ch 2, dc, ch 1, dc) in next corner ch sp, ch 1, skip next 2 sts, (dc in next st, ch 1, skip next st) across to next corner ch sp]; repeat from * 2 more times; repeat between [ ], join with sl st in 3rd ch of ch-4 (12 dc across each side between corner ch-2 sps).

Rnd 6: Ch 4, (dc in next st, ch 1) around with (dc, ch 3, dc,

Continued on page 147

Dear Ashley,

Thanks for the letter. Sounds like you really had quite a time in Chicago with Preston. I so glad to here that Mr. Benedict seems in favor of hiring you for the position they have open. Preston recommended you very highly, so that should count for something. Those guys think the world of him, so it should be a cinch you'll get the job. Do you think you'll like living in Chicago? You haven't said, but I assume you'll move if they do hire you.

Mom is going nuts trying to get everything just perfect before Christmas. She and Juanita have been working frantically from dawn to dusk cleaning, rearranging and redecorating. She's so worried it won't all get done that she's about to drive everyone batty. Oh, and don't worry about trying to get plane tickets. We can just fly to Kansas City to pick you up in the jet. Maybe I can get Ty to ride along when we do so you can talk on the plane before you get lost amid the wash of people who'll be around after you arrive. I know he's anxious to meet you. He's been quite busy lately, too, though, supervising the renovation of the guest house. I must say, sometimes the man even impresses me and that's hard to do. Especially for him. He's just so "handy." He knows exactly what needs to be done and if one of the workers has a problem, he just grabs a saw or hammer and helps out. I have to laugh. Preston is a genius when it comes to designing buildings, but somehow I could never see him whielding a hammer regardless of the amount of difficulty one of the workers was having. But then again, Ty never was afraid of a little work or dirt. He also has a flair for design. Just recently he designed and oversaw the construction of a new stable.

Well, I've rambled enough. Better get going. Ty and I have to run to Denver to get paint and wallpaper for the guest house. I'll take the new afghan I just finished that will be the focal point of the living room to match colors. It's going to look great! You'll see when you're here!

See you soon!

Much love, C—

Christmas Fever

Designed by Maggie Weldon

SIZE: 46" x 55½" not including Fringe.

MATERIALS: Worsted-weight yarn — 28 oz. green, 21 oz. each white and burgundy; J crochet hook or size needed to obtain gauge.

GAUGE: 1 sc and 1 shell = 2"; 4 rows = 2".

SKILL LEVEL: ☆☆ Average

AFGHAN

NOTES: For **popcorn (pc),** *5 dc in next ch or st, drop lp from hook, insert hook in first st of 5-dc group, pick up dropped lp, draw through st, ch 1. Pop to right side of work as needed.*

*For **shell,** 5 dc in next st or ch.*

Row 1: With green, ch 142, 2 dc in 4th ch from hook, (skip next 2 chs, sc in next ch, skip next 2 chs, shell in next ch) 22 times, skip next 2 chs, sc in next ch, skip next 2 chs, 3 dc in last ch, turn (22 shells, 23 sc, 6 dc).

Row 2: Ch 1, sc in first dc, skip next dc, 2 dc in next dc, pc in next sc, (2 dc in first dc of next shell, sc in center dc of same shell, 2 dc in 5th dc of same shell, pc in next sc) across to last 3 dc, 2 dc in next dc, skip next dc, sc in last dc, turn (92 dc, 24 sc, 23 pc). Front of row 2 is right side of work.

Row 3: Ch 3, 2 dc in same st, (skip next 2 dc, sc in next pc, skip next 2 dc, shell in next sc) 22 times, skip next 2 dc, sc in next pc, skip next 2 dc, 3 dc in last sc, turn, fasten off (23 sc, 22 shells, 6 dc).

Row 4: Join white with sc in first dc, skip next dc, 2 dc in next dc, pc in next sc, (2 dc in first dc of next shell, sc in center dc of same shell, 2 dc in 5th dc of same shell, pc in next st) across to last 3 dc, 2 dc in next dc, skip next dc, sc in last dc, turn (92 dc, 24 sc, 23 pc).

Row 5: Repeat row 3.

Row 6: With burgundy, repeat row 4.

Row 7: Repeat row 3.

Row 8: With green, repeat row 4.

Rows 9-110: Repeat rows 3-8 consecutively. At end of last row, fasten off.

FRINGE

For **each Fringe,** cut 6 strands green each 15" long. With all 6 strands held together, fold in half, insert hook in st or ch, draw fold through, draw all loose ends through fold, tighten. Trim ends.

Working across last row, Fringe in first st, Fringe in center st of each shell across to last 3-dc group, Fringe in last st.

Working in starting ch on opposite side of row 1, Fringe in first ch, Fringe in ch at base of each shell across to last ch, Fringe in last ch.❧

Dear Journal,

Preston actually called me today and talked for almost forty minutes. That would be a miracle if it weren't for the fact that he apparently called to tell me that Ashley is probably going to get the job at Benedict, Darnell & Monk. He was almost effervescent! I can't remember him being so excited. I guess it does garner him quite a few brownie points with the partners, but really! I didn't see it as that big of a deal. You'd have thought he pulled off some major corporate coup. Some little part of my head says I should be jealous of the way he's bending over backward to accomodate Ashley, but I simply can't right now. I guess I'm too tired trying to carry his end of our bargain. Having Ashley in Chicago would be somewhat of a help to me though. Next time Preston gets invited to one of those boring dinner parties, I can call Ashley and ask her to stand in.

Preston also let me know he plans to be out December 15th, as he's going to take a little time off. That will give us almost two weeks together before he has to return to Chicago. I don't see how they can possibly do without him for that long! Tomorrow is Thanksgiving. I'm to go up a help Mom cook. Aside from the three of us, Ty, Ben and Juanita and one of thier sons and his family will be here and Dad's brother Theodore is coming down from Montana with his wife. It is going to be a glorius day. I can feel it already. The day after Thanksgiving, I plan to decorate. That means it wouldn't be too early to start pulling out the Christmas things now.

Chorus of Lace

Designed by Maggie Weldon

SIZE: 47½" x 62¼".

MATERIALS: Worsted-weight yarn — 21 oz. med. pink, 14 oz. white, 3½ oz. each burgundy and med. green; hairpin lace loom; tapestry needle; G and H crochet hooks or sizes needed to obtain gauges.

GAUGES: With **H hook,** 7 sts = 2"; 3 dc rows = 2". With **G hook,** Hairpin Lace Circle is 6" across. Each Block is 14½" square.

SKILL LEVEL: ☆☆ Average

AFGHAN
HAIRPIN LACE CIRCLE (make 12)

1: Position loom prongs 3" apart. Remove top bar. With G hook and white, slide slip knot lp over left prong. Replace top bar and adjust lp so slip knot is centered between the prongs and yarn held in front of loom (see Hairpin Lace illustration 1 on page 147).

2: Wrap yarn from front to back around right prong and hold in place with left hand. Insert hook in lp on left prong (see illustration 2). Draw yarn held in back of loom through lp to form a lp on hook.

3: Yo, draw through lp on hook (see illustration 3).

4: Drop lp from hook. From the back of loom, insert hook in dropped lp. Turn loom from right to left in front of you to reverse the position of the prongs.

5: Turning the loom also causes the yarn to wrap around what is now the right prong, thus forming another lp. The crochet hook is now, again, positioned in front of the loom.

6: Insert hook in front strand of lp on left prong, yo, draw yarn through lp (now there are 2 lps on hook) (see illustration 4).

7: Yo, draw through 2 lps on hook (one sc complete). Each new lp is formed by turning the loom after completing a sc between the prongs.

8: Repeat steps 4-7 83 more times for a total of 84 sc between lps, leaving 6" end for sewing, fasten off. With separate strand white, run strand through all lps on one side of loom, gather tightly; tie into knot.

9: Remove bottom bar; take off all lps. For **circle,** with

Continued on page 147

Dear Preston

Tried to reach you all day yesterday, but never did. At least if I mail you a letter I know you'll get it. We had a wonderful day! Instead of turkey this year, Mom and Juanita surprised everyone by making quail and dressing. We also had some venison and a big plump goose. The quail were what Ty had bagged during the season, and the venison and goose were some Dad got. Was it ever great! I have to hand-it to Juanita. She can sure cook wild game. I don't know what her secret is, but she must have one. I know you're not especially fond of game meat, but I do believe even you would have liked them. The rest of the fare was traditional with lots of pumpkin pie and whipped cream for dessert.

We had dinner early this year, as Uncle Theodore and Aunt Kate had another dinner to go to as well. Yuck! I can't imagine having to eat that much twice! Afterwards, Ty suggested we saddle the horses and go for a ride. I hadn't ridden in so long I thought I'd forgotten how. You should have been there. The trails were perfect. We saw quite a few deer and even a fox. By the time we got home and had taken care of the horses, it was starting to snow lightly. That really put everyone in the mood for Christmas, so we all went to the music room. Mom had already decorated there and Aunt Kate insisted I play some caroles. After a while we were all singing. It was so festive. We did-n't turn in till after midnight!

Well, enough about our day. You never said what you had planned to do. I thought maybe your parents were planning on being there, or at your Uncle Foster and Aunt Faye's. Hope you had a quite, relaxing day and didn't spend it working. You know, you shouldn't work as hard as you do. I swear you're working yourself silly. I worry about what you're doing to your health. I have lots to do, so I'd better close. I can talk to you when you get here.

Love, C—

Fireside Glow

Designed by Tammy Hildebrand

SIZE: 44¼" x 64".

MATERIALS: Worsted-weight yarn — 28 oz. off-white, 17 oz. green and 9 oz. red; P crochet hook or size needed to obtain gauge.

GAUGE: With **2 strands held together,** 2 dc = 1"; 3 dc rows = 2½". Each Strip is 4¾" across.

NOTE: Use 2 strands held together throughout.

SKILL LEVEL: ☆☆ Average

AFGHAN
FIRST STRIP

Row 1: With off-white, ch 130, dc in 4th ch from hook, dc in each ch across, **do not** turn, fasten off (128 dc).

NOTES: *Beginning ch-3 is used and counted as first st of each row.*

*For **double crochet front post (fp),** yo, insert hook from front to back around post of next st on last row, complete as dc.*

Row 2: Join green with sl st in first st, ch 3, dc in next st, (fp around next st, dc in each of next 2 sts) across, **do not** turn, fasten off.

Row 3: Join red with sl st in first st, ch 3, dc in each dc and fp around each fp across, **do not** turn, fasten off.

Row 4: With green, repeat row 3.

Row 5: With off-white, repeat row 3, **do not** turn or fasten off.

Rnd 6: Working around outer edge, ch 1, skip first row, 2 sc in end of each of next 3 rows, skip next row; working in starting ch on opposite side of row 1, (sc, ch 2, sc) in first ch, skip next ch, 2 sc in next ch, (ch 2, skip next 2 chs, 2 sc in next ch) across to last 2 chs, skip next ch, (sc, ch 2, sc) in last ch, skip end of next row, 2 sc in each of next 3 rows, skip end of next row, (sc, ch 2, sc) in first st, skip next st, 2 sc in next st, (ch 2, skip next 2 sts, 2 sc in next st) across to last 2 sts, skip next st, (sc, ch 2, sc) in last st, join with sl st in first sc, fasten off (8 sts across each short end between corner ch sps; 86 sts across each long edge between corner ch sps).

NEXT STRIP

Rows 1-5: Repeat same rows of First Strip.

Rnd 6: Working around outer edge, ch 1, skip first row, 2 sc in end of each of next 3 rows, skip next row; working in starting ch on opposite side of row 1, sc in first ch, ch 1, drop lp from hook, insert hook from front to back through corresponding corner ch-2 sp on last strip, pull dropped lp

Continued on page 148

Dear Journal,

The entire entourage arrived a few days ago, and things have been in high-speed ever since. Ashley, Preston and I spent the first couple days shopping, but today, I suggested that we get Ben to hitch up the horse-draw sleigh and go out for a run through the snow. The hunting cabin wasn't that far away, but you'd have thought it was a hundred miles by the way Preston and Ashley were complaining about the hard seat and cold wind. Once at the cabin, when Ashley started to climb out of the sleigh, she got out on the wrong side stepping right off into a ditch filled with about three feet of snow. I laughed so hard I nearly cried, but Ashley was mortified. It took both Ty and Preston to pull her out. After severals hours by the fire in the cabin, they were all dry enough for the short ride home. Since their clothes were still damp, Preston and Ashley sat in the back under all the blankets while Ty and I sat up front in the driver's seat. I get the feeling that Preston and Ashley weren't really enjoying themselves all that much. That's a shame. The weather was perfect for sledding. This evening, everyone seemed back to their old selves. We even sat around the fireplace enjoying the tree and some hot buttered rum. I had thought it would be a great chance for Ty and Ashley to talk, but unfortunately, Ashley was the only one doing the talking. Ty looked as if he was really trying to listen intently as Ashley explained what she did for a living, but I'm not sure it actually soaked in. Ty understands laws and all that, but his basic philosophy of life is just to do right by everyone. Then you wouldn't need all the other laws. Preston and I finally got some time together and he filled me in on the details of the house. It really sounds fantastic. All in all, we've had a really great beginning to this holiday. In just a few days, it will be Christmas. I'd better go to bed now, before Santa finds I stayed up past my bedtime.

Yuletide Rose

Designed by Tammy Hildebrand

SIZE: 39" x 54".

MATERIALS: Chenille yarn — 20 oz. purple and 15 oz. lt. green; Chunky yarn — 19 oz. off-white; I crochet hook or size needed to obtain gauge.

GAUGE: Rnds 1-7 = 5½" across. Each Motif is 7½" square.

SKILL LEVEL: ☆☆ Average

AFGHAN
FIRST ROW
First Motif

Rnd 1: With purple, ch 3, sl st in first ch to form ring, ch 1, (sc in ring, ch 1) 8 times, join with sl st in first sc (8 ch-1 sps).

Rnd 2: Sl st in first ch sp, ch 1; for **petal**, (sc, 3 dc, sl st) in same sp; for **petal**, (sc, 3 dc, sl st) in each ch sp around, join with sl st in first sc (8 petals).

Rnd 3: Working behind petals around sts on rnd 1, ch 1, sc around first sc, ch 2, (sc around next sc, ch 2) around, join with sl st in first sc (8 ch sps).

Rnd 4: Sl st in first ch sp, ch 1; for **petal**, (sc, 5 dc, sl st) in same sp; for **petal**, (sc, 5 dc, sl st) in each ch sp around, join with sl st in first sc (8 petals).

Rnd 5: Working behind petals around sts on rnd 3, ch 1, sc around first sc, ch 3, (sc around next sc, ch 3) around, join with sl st in first sc (8 ch sps).

Row 6: Working in rows; for **first petal**, sl st in first ch sp, ch 4, 4 tr in same sp, turn leaving remaining ch sps unworked (5 tr).

Row 7: Ch 1, sc in first st, (ch 1, sc in next st) across, turn (4 ch sps).

Row 8: (Ch 1, sc) in each ch sp across, **do not** turn (4 sc, 3 ch sps).

Row 9: For **next petal**, ch 1, 5 tr in ch-3 sp on rnd 5, turn.

Rows 10-29: Repeat rows 7-9 consecutively ending with row 8. At end of last row, join with sl st in top of ch-4 on row 6 of first petal, fasten off.

Rnd 30: Working in rnds, join lt. green with sc in any ch-1 sp between petals, (5 tr, ch 3, 5 tr) in next ch-1 sp between petals, *sc in next ch-1 sp between petals, (5 tr, ch 3, 5 tr) in next ch-1 sp between petals; repeat from *

Continued on page 148

Poinsettia Delight

Designed by Ann E. Smith

SIZE: 41½" x 51¼".

MATERIALS: Worsted-weight yarn — 15 oz. dk. green, 12½ oz. off-white, 7½ oz. red and 2½ oz. yellow; tapestry needle; G crochet hook or size needed to obtain gauge.

GAUGE: 8 sts = 2"; 8 sc rows = 2". Block is 9¾" square.

SKILL LEVEL: ☆☆ Average

AFGHAN
BLOCK (make 20)

Row 1: With off-white, ch 26, sc in 2nd ch from hook, sc in each ch across, turn (25 sc).

Row 2: Ch 1, sc in each st across, turn.

NOTES: *When changing colors (see page 159), always drop yarn to wrong side of work. Use a separate skein or ball of yarn for each color section. **Do not** carry yarn across from one section to another. Fasten off colors at end of each color section.*

Each square on graph equals 1 sc.

Work even-numbered graph rows from left to right and odd-numbered rows from right to left.

Row 3: Ch 1, sc in first 8 sts changing to green in last st made, sc in next st changing to off-white, sc in next 7 sts changing to green in last st made, sc in next st changing to off-white, sc in last 8 sts, turn.

Rows 4-25: Ch 1, sc in each st across changing colors according to graph, turn. At end of last row, **do not** turn or fasten off.

Rnd 26: Working around outer edge, in ends of rows, ch 1, *skip next row, sc in next 23 rows, skip next row*; working in starting ch on opposite side of row 1, 3 sc in first ch, sc in each ch across to last ch, 3 sc in last ch; repeat between **, 3 sc in next st, sc in each st across to last st, 3 sc in last st, join with sl st in first sc (25 sc across each side between center corner ch sps).

NOTE: *When changing colors on next rnd, work over dropped color as you carry it across to next section.*

Rnd 27: Ch 3, dc in each of next 2 sts changing to green in last st made, *dc in next st changing to off-white, (dc in each of next 3 sts changing to green in last st made, dc in next st changing to off-white) across to next center corner st, 3 dc in next st changing to green in last st made; repeat from * 3 more times, dc in next st, join with sl st in top of ch-3, fasten off (27 dc across each side between center corner sts).

NOTE: *For **front post** (fp, see page 159), yo, insert hook from front to back around post of next st, yo, draw lp through, (yo, draw through 2 lps on hook) 2 times.*

Rnd 28: Join red with sl st in any center corner st, ch 3, 2 dc in same st, dc in each off-white st and fp around each green st around with 3 dc in each center corner st, join, fasten off.

Rnd 29: Join green with sl st in any center corner st, ch 3, 2 dc in same st, dc in each dc and fp around each fp around with 3 dc in each center corner st, join, fasten off.

Continued on page 149

Dear Journal,

It's Christmas! As usual, I'm up at the crack of dawn, but I have good reason today. Preston and I are going down to help Ty feed the animals so Ben and Juanita can have the morning off. I don't think Preston was really thrilled with the idea. More than likely he was just doing it to be nice, so I'll probably be nice to him and just let him sleep. Ty and I can manage together. Ty understands how important it is to me to start this day just like every other year. He's so good about that. Only one year was different, and I can still see him standing there four years ago. I'll never forget the way the words felt when he said them. Just as I'll never forget the look in his eyes. But, then and there, I vowed to myself that I would never let that take away the joy of what Christmas really means, and I never have. This little ritual we go through every year helps us to keep our perspective. It helps us remember that Christmas is about new beginnings. It's a celebration of life itself. Steven, my love, where ever you are...I wish you a glorious Christmas and thank you so very much for having been a part of my life.

Now, I'm off to do the chores, then run on up to the house. Mom is probably up cooking by now. I can already smell the fresh cinnamon rolls she always serves. I can't wait till she sees the afghan I made for her. I know she'll love it.

Corinne poured Hemi's food into his dish and watched, smiling, as he devoured it like usual. "Not that you need the encouragement, but you'd better hurry, pretty boy. Preston will be here any minute," she said, waiting for the gray head to surface for a moment. "You're terrible, Hemi," Corinne laughed as she picked up the now-empty dish and rinsed it out in the sink. Turning to open the laundry room door, she called softly to the preening tom who sauntered casually through the opening and jumped onto the dryer. "See you later," Corinne cooed as she shut the door.

Moments later, Corinne heard tell-tale stomping on the front porch, alerting her to her fiancee's arrival. She opened the door to see him trying vainly to brush pieces of hay off his suede jacket. "Hi, darling," she called over the noise of Tyler's truck pulling away down the drive. "Did you guys have a nice morning." Now inside, Preston shed his coat and gloves then set down on the hall bench to remove his shoes. "Let's put it this way," he said, reaching up to pull a piece of straw out of his collar, "feeding cattle and chopping ice blocks off frozen water troughs will never rank at the top of my list of fun things to do." He reached into his pocket and extracted a small bottle. "What's that?" Corinne asked. "My allergy tablets," Preston replied. "All this rarified air and animal dander is just about to get the best of me." Corinne handed him a cup of steaming coffee. "I'm sorry," she said sympathetically. "I never thought it would bother you this bad, but you've never stayed this long before either."

"Where's Ashley," he asked, craning his neck to see into the living room. "Oh, she went back up to the big house. She said something about needing to check her e-mail." Preston stirred his coffee. "That must be why Tyler was headed that way," he said, reaching for the sugar bowl. "So, is everything ready for us to leave tomorrow," he asked. "Yes. Daddy has it all lined out," Corinne answered. "I don't see why you don't come with us then," Preston queried. "I'm sorry, Preston," Corinne replied. "I told you. There's just no way I can make it for New Year's. I have a press conference the second dealing with the Youth Center. With the weather being so unpredictable, I hate to take the chance on getting snowed in at Chicago."

"I understand," replied Preston, "but Ashley and I had really hoped you could make it. This is more than just a New Year's party. It's also Ashley's introduce to the rest of the firm, and to celebrate the completion of the Inverness project." Corinne sat down beside him. "I know, and again, I apologize. I hope you both have a wonderful time. I'm sure they'll love Ashley. And I'm proud of

your accomplishment, too. You're a brilliant architect. It's high time the rest of the world knew that, too." Snow was beginning to fall as Preston glanced out the window. "I'm not sure anyone else needs to know," he said with a sigh. "Heaven knows I'm busy enough already. I still haven't had a chance to get back to work on our house," he said sheepishly. "It's just been so hectic, and now with the weather and all. They're pretty well done with the exterior, but the interior is barely started. I hope you don't mind, but I took Ashley up there awhile back to show her the floor plan. She really liked it." Corinne was glad Preston couldn't see the look on her face. Was it surprise, or perhaps sudden realization? No, it was probably nothing at all. "I'm sure she did," Corinne responded after a brief silence. "Ashley appreciates good architecture as much as I do. Uh, oh! It's almost time for lunch," she said, quickly changing the subject. "Mother's expecting us up at the house." Preston drained his coffee cup and stood up. "We'd better hurry then," he replied. "This snow is getting pretty heavy, and if we're late, Juanita's disposition will be as icy as it is."

Stepping into the frigid air, Corinne turned her face up to the gently falling crystals. She stood for a moment, then turned slowly to view the towering expanse of the Rockies just to the west. Almost obscured by the snowfall, their shadowy forms loomed majestically like sentinels, faithfully guarding Morningside Ranch. Spinning around on her toes like a jubilant child, Corinne squealed. "Isn't this gorgeous! Nature's beauty at its best!" Preston snorted. "If this is its best, I'd hate to see its worst," he said. "Oh, silly! You've just lived in the city too long," Corinne called back, running ahead on the path to scope up a handful of snow. "Don't you dare," Preston yelled, ducking as a firmly packed ball sailed past his head.

Running up the front steps of her parents palatial home, Corinne stopped, laughing. "Oh, come on! Loosen up! Preston stomped up onto the shelter of the porch, brushing the snow off his sleeves. Just then Tyler opened the door. "We were just wondering where you two were," he said, glancing at the stern look on Preston's face. "Ashley's waiting in the den and Juanita's putting lunch on the table." Corinne took Preston's coat and hung it beside hers in the hall closet. "Did she make venison stew like she said," Corinne asked expectantly. "She sure did," Tyler replied, "and turkey pot pie for those with more civilized taste," he added, casting a surreptitious glance at Preston. Corinne laughed, then laced her arm through Preston's, pulling him toward the dining room. Looking back at Tyler, she winked knowingly, "What are we waiting for!"

Special Blessings

Designed by Trudy Atteberry

SIZE: 34½" square.

MATERIALS: Baby yarn — 9 oz. yellow; 2 yds. each pink, yellow and green ¼" satin ribbon; four 1½" butterfly appliqués; white sewing thread; sewing needle; H crochet hook or size needed to obtain gauge.

GAUGE: 9 dlk rows = 5".

SKILL LEVEL: ☆ Easy

BLANKET

*NOTES: For **double love knot (dlk,** see page 159), (draw up ½" long lp on hook, yo, draw lp through, sc in back strand of long lp) 2 times.*

*For **beginning love knot (beg lk),** draw up ½" long lp on hook, yo, draw lp through. Beg lk will not be used or counted as a st.*

Rnd 1: Ch 4, sl st in first ch to form ring, ch 1, (sc in ring, dlk) 4 times, join with sl st in first sc (4 sc, 4 dlks).

Rnd 2: Beg lk, (sc, dlk, sc, dlk) in center sc of each dlk around, join with sl st in first sc (8 sc, 8 dlks).

Rnds 3-23: Beg lk, (sc, dlk, sc, dlk) in center sc of first dlk, *(sc in center sc of next dlk, dlk) across to next corner dlk, (sc, dlk, sc, dlk) in center sc of next corner dlk; repeat from * 2 more times, (sc in center sc of next dlk, dlk) across, join, ending with 92 sc and 92 dlks in last rnd.

Rnd 24: For **ruffle,** beg lk, sc in center sc of first dlk, *[dlk, (sc in same sc, dlk) 3 times, (sc, dlk, sc, dlk) in center sc of next dlk across] to next corner dlk, sc in center sc of next corner dlk; repeat from * 2 more times; repeat between [ ], join (192 sc, 192 dlks).

Rnds 25-31: Repeat rnd 3, ending with 220 sc and 220 dlks in last rnd. At end of last rnd, fasten off.

FINISHING

Cut each color ribbon into 4 equal pieces. Holding one piece of each color together, tie into a bow around one corner dlk on rnd 23. Repeat with remaining pieces.

Sew one appliqué to center of each bow.❧

Dear Journal,

Got a foot of new snow last night. Good thing it waited until Preston and Ashley were on their way. I hate that I couldn't go with them, but I have to be at that Youth Center press conference. They'll just have to manage without me. Once I get through with "Bundles for Babies," I'll have a lot more time. Of all our annual events, this is the one I love most. Mom asked a funny question the other day while we were talking about this. She wanted to know if she'd ever have grandchildren. Children. That seems like such a foreign idea to me now. Steven and I talked about having children all the time, but with the fast-paced lives Preston and I lead, I can't see kids playing a part in it. I hated to say anything to her. She already seemed upset enough when I had to admit to her that Preston and I hadn't once talked about the wedding while he was here. Mom just doesn't understand that Preston and I will get married when the time is right. Once this fund-raiser is over and the Youth Center is fully functional, I can make a trip to Chicago and get everything lined out.

Had my first baby afghan done when I found that Juanita's new granddaughter had arrived, so I gave it to her. Got a second one done this morning. The third afghan is coming along very quickly, and I hope to have it done tomorrow. Talking with the guild members the other day, we were trying to think of a way to get enough afghans so the hospital didn't run out, but never decided on a solution. I've given it some thought and think I'll suggest a volunteer program of "stand-by" crocheters. These would be people who the hospital could call when they have a special need, or when the supply starts to get low. I've seen some of these children when they received their afghans. The look on their faces is enough to keep me up way past midnight crocheting.

Sweet Dreams

Designed by Roberta Maier

SIZE: 36½" x 37" not including Fringe.

MATERIALS: Baby sport yarn — 32 oz. white, 1 oz. each variegated, yellow, lt. green, peach, lt. pink and lt. blue, small amount of lavender; G crochet hook or size needed to obtain gauge.

GAUGE: 4 dc = 1"; 2 dc rows = 1", 9 sc rows = 2".

SKILL LEVEL: ☆☆ Average

AFGHAN

Row 1: With white, ch 136, dc in 4th ch from hook, dc in each ch across, turn (134 dc).

Row 2: Ch 3, dc in each st across, turn.

Row 3: Ch 3, dc in each of next 2 sts, *ch 5, skip next 2 sts, tr in next st, (skip next 2 sts, tr in next st) 2 times, ch 5, skip next 2 sts, dc in each of next 2 sts; repeat from * across to last st, dc in last st, turn, fasten off (54 sts, 20 ch-5 sps).

Row 4: Join lt. green with sl st in first st, ch 3, dc in each of next 2 sts, (ch 4, skip next 4 chs, sc in next ch, sc in each of next 3 sts, sc in next ch, ch 4, skip next 4 chs, dc in each of next 2 sts) across to last st, dc in last st, turn (74 sts, 20 ch-4 sps).

Row 5: Ch 3, dc in each of next 2 sts, (ch 5, skip next ch-4 sp and next sc, sc in each of next 3 sts, ch 5, skip next ch-4 sp, dc in each of next 2 sts) across to last st, dc in last st, turn, fasten off (54 sts, 20 ch-5 sps).

Row 6: Join white with sl st in first st, ch 3, dc in each of next 2 sts, *ch 2, (tr in next sc, ch 2) 3 times, dc in each of next 2 dc; repeat from * across to last st, dc in last st, turn (54 sts, 40 ch-2 sps).

Row 7: Ch 3, dc in each st and 2 dc in each ch-2 sp across, turn (134 dc).

Rows 8-68: Working rows 4 and 5 in color sequence of yellow, lt. pink, lt. blue, peach, lavender, peach, lt. blue, lt.

Continued on page 150

Dear Ashley,

Congratulations! Tried to call yesterday after I talked to Preston but couldn't reach you. As the newest associate of Benedict, Darnell & Monk, I guess you'll be as hard to get a hold of now as Preston. He's so excited you accepted the offer. For some reason, he seems to think you'll be the greatest thing that's happened to the company since him! I'm teasing. I know he's right. You will be a major asset to them, and they know it too, or they would never have made you the offer they did. I'd love to see the look on Doug's face when you tell him you're being spirited away by one of the most prestigious firms in Chicago.

Preston told me about the party, but I have a recital to host the night before and I'm not sure I can coordinate getting to Chicago on such short notice. But you don't need me in order to have a good time. If you'll wear that emerald green sheath dress you got in Denver before Christmas, you'll have all the attention you could possibly want. Promise me you'll keep an eye on Preston, though. Even when he's supposed to be having fun, he'll still manage to get some work done. I don't know how he does it!

The guild is working on our annual "Bundles for Babies" charity event right now. I've been crocheting baby afghans as fast as I can. I wanted to do something this year to make it a little different, so I managed to con Ty into going to Denver with me the other day and I ran all over town buying up all the stuffed animals I could find. After all, what good is a "blankie" without a teddy bear or other toy critter to share it with. I knew there was no way I could get enough toys in my Lexus, so Ty had to go so he could drive the Suburban. You should have seen the sight of this 6'2" cowboy, complete with hat and boots, carrying all those stuffed animals! He got more than his share of strange looks, but really seemed to enjoy the excursion.

Well, I'd better go. Sorry I can't make it for the big party. I'd love to see you take your first bows in the big city. Take lots of pictures!

Love, C—

Baby Stars

Designed by Ellen Anderson

SIZE: 34½" x 38½".

MATERIALS: Sport yarn — 8 oz. yellow, 6 oz. lt. blue and 3½ oz. pink; F crochet hook or size needed to obtain gauge.

GAUGE: Each Motif is 3¾" across from point to point.

SKILL LEVEL: ☆☆ Average

FIRST ROW

First Motif

Rnd 1: With pink, ch 6, sl st in first ch to form ring, ch 3, dc in ring, ch 2, (2 dc in ring, ch 2) 5 times, join with sl st in top of ch-3, fasten off (12 dc, 6 ch-2 sps).

Rnd 2: Join lt. blue with sl st in any ch sp, ch 3, (dc, ch 2, 2 dc) in same sp, ch 1, *(2 dc, ch 2, 2 dc) in next ch sp, ch 1; repeat from * around, join, fasten off (6 ch-1 sps, 6 ch-2 sps).

Rnd 3: Join yellow with sl st in any ch-2 sp, ch 3, (2 dc, ch 1, 3 dc) in same sp, sc in next ch-1 sp, *(3 dc, ch 1, 3 dc) in next ch-2 sp, sc in next ch-1 sp; repeat from * around, join, fasten off.

Next Motif

Rnds 1-2: Repeat same rnds of First Motif.

Rnd 3: Join yellow with sl st in any ch-2 sp, ch 3, 2 dc in same sp; joining to bottom of last Motif made (see Assembly Diagram on page 150), sc in first ch-2 sp on last Motif, 3 dc in same sp on this Motif, sc in next ch-1 sp, 3 dc in next ch-2 sp, sc in next ch-2 sp on last Motif, 3 dc in same sp on this Motif, sc in next ch-1 sp, *(3 dc, ch 1, 3 dc) in next ch-2 sp, sc in next ch-1 sp; repeat from * around, join, fasten off.

Repeat Next Motif 4 more times for a total of 6 Motifs on this Row.

SECOND ROW

First Motif

Rnds 1-2: Repeat same rnds of First Row First Motif.

Rnd 3: Join yellow with sl st in any ch-2 sp, ch 3, 2 dc in same sp; joining to last row made, sc in 5th ch-2 sp on First Motif of last row, 3 dc in same sp on this Motif, sc in next ch-1 sp, 3 dc in next ch-2 sp, sc in next ch-2 sp on last Motif, 3 dc in same sp on this Motif, sc in next ch-1 sp, *(3 dc, ch 1, 3 dc) in next ch-2 sp, sc in next ch-1 sp; repeat from * around, join, fasten off.

Next Motif

Rnds 1-2: Repeat same rnds of First Motif.

Rnd 3: Join yellow with sl st in any ch-2 sp, ch 3, 2 dc in same sp, sc in corresponding ch sp on last Motif, 3 dc in same sp on this Motif, sc in next ch-1 sp, 3 dc in next ch-2 sp, sc in joining sc between last Motif on this row and adjoining Motif on last row, 3 dc in same sp on this Motif, sc in next ch-1 sp, 3 dc in next ch-2 sp, sc in joining sc between last Motif and Next Motif on last row, 3 dc in same sp on this Motif, sc in next ch-1 sp, 3 dc in next ch-2 sp, sc in next ch-2 sp of same Motif on last row, 3 dc in same sp on this Motif, sc in next ch-1 sp, *(3 dc, ch 1, 3 dc) in next ch-2 sp, sc in next ch-1 sp; repeat from * around, join, fasten off.

Repeat Next Motif for the number of times indicated on Assembly Diagram on page 150.

Last Motif

Rnds 1-2: Repeat same rnds of First Motif.

Rnd 3: Join yellow with sl st in any ch-2 sp, ch 3, 2 dc in same sp, sc in corresponding ch sp on last Motif, 3 dc in same

Continued on page 150

Double Delight

Designed by Lee Mathewson

COTTON CANDY

SIZE: 33½" x 42½".

MATERIALS: Worsted-weight yarn — 20 oz. pink and 2 oz. white; J crochet hook or size needed to obtain gauge.

GAUGE: 3 sc = 1"; 3 pattern rows = 1".

SKILL LEVEL: ☆☆ Average

AFGHAN

Row 1: With pink, ch 122, sc in 2nd ch from hook, sc in each ch across, turn (121 sc).

Row 2: Ch 1, sc in each st across, turn.

Row 3: Ch 1, sc in first st, *[insert hook in same st, yo, draw lp through, (insert hook in next st, yo, draw lp through) 2 times, yo, draw through all 4 lps on hook], ch 1; repeat from * across to last 2 sts; repeat between [ ], sc in same st, turn (62 sts, 59 ch-1 sps).

Rows 4-5: Ch 1, sc in first st, *[insert hook in same st or ch sp, yo, draw lp through, (insert hook in next st or ch sp, yo, draw lp through) 2 times, yo, draw through all 4 lps on hook], ch 1; repeat from * across to last 2 sts; repeat between [ ], sc in same st, turn.

Row 6: Ch 1, sc in each st and in each ch sp across, turn (121 sc).

Row 7: Ch 1, sc in first st, (ch 1, skip next st, sc in next st) across, turn (61 sc, 60 ch-1 sps).

Rows 8-9: Ch 1, sc in first st, (ch 1, skip next ch sp, sc in next st) across, turn.

Row 10: Repeat row 6.

Rows 11-94: Repeat rows 3-10 consecutively, ending with row 6. At end of last row, **do not** fasten off.

BORDER

Rnd 1: Working around outer edge, ch 1, 3 sc in first st, sc in each st and in end of each row around with 3 sc in each corner st, join with sl st in first sc, fasten off.

Rnd 2: Working this rnd in **back lps** only, join white with sc in any center corner st, 2 sc in same st, sc in each st

Continued on page 151

My dear Preston,

Hello! Haven't heard from you for a couple days so I figured you're pretty busy. Remember my friend Denise Davis? Well, she had her twins yesterday. They are gorgeous! One boy and one girl. How lucky can you get! She'd had a sonogram and knew what they would be so I crocheted her matching pink and blue afghans to take them home in. Everyone made such a fuss when they left.

I don't know if this is the time to bring this up, but you know, you and I have never discussed the subject of children. I've thought about this a lot lately, after Mother brought it up awhile back. What do you think about starting a family shortly after we get married? Think about it and we can talk more later.

Now, I don't want you to take what I'm going to say next as correction, but I have to tell you this since I think you'd want to know. It's not too often that Chicago's grapevine tendrils reach all the way to Denver, but that's what happened. I heard the other day that Chicago is all a-buzz about you and Ashley. Don't get me wrong, I know Ashley needs someone to show her the ropes now that she's in Chicago, but you need to remember your image. Perhaps you could introduce Ashley to Patrick, that banker's son you work with occasionally. That would take the heat off you if Ashley was seen out and about more with someone else.

Okay, I know what you're thinking. You're wondering what happened to my idea to fix up Ashley and Tyler. Well, I'm beginning to think that this time my matchmaking skills may be a little off. Ty and Ashley don't really seem to have a thing in common. Ashley certainly didn't seem to enjoy the country lifestyle while at Morningside for Christmas. And, I can't see Ty moving to the city anytime soon, so where does that leave me? I'd probably better chalk this one up as a loss and go on.

Again, I've missed talking to you these past few days, so please call as soon as you can!

Love, C—

Pastel Puzzle

Designed by Diane Poellot

SIZE: 45½" square.

MATERIALS: Sport-weight yarn — 17 oz. white, 11 oz. pink and 7 oz. lt. green; G crochet hook or size needed to obtain gauge.

GAUGE: Each Motif is 1½" square.

SKILL LEVEL: ☆☆ Average

FIRST ROW

First Motif

With white, ch 4, sl st in first ch to form ring, ch 3, 2 dc in ring, ch 3, (3 dc in ring, ch 3) 3 times, join with sl st in top of ch-3, fasten off (12 dc, 4 ch-3 sps).

Second Motif

With color indicated on Color Diagram (see page 151), ch 4, sl st in first ch to form ring, ch 3, 2 dc in ring, ch 1; joining to side of last Motif (see Joining Diagram on page 151), sl st in corresponding conrer ch sp on other Motif, ch 1, 3 dc in ring on this Motif, ch 1, sl st in next corner ch sp on other Motif, ch 1, (3 dc in ring on this Motif, ch 3) 2 times, join with sl st in top of ch-3, fasten off.

With color indicated on Color Diagram, repeat Second Motif 28 more times for a total of 30 Motifs.

SECOND ROW

First Motif

Joining to bottom of First Motif on last row, with color indicated on Color Diagram, work same as First Row Second Motif.

Second Motif

With color indicated on Color Diagram, ch 4, sl st in first ch to form ring, ch 3, 2 dc in ring, ch 1; joining to bottom of next Motif on last row, sl st in corresponding corner ch sp (see Joining Diagram) on other Motif, ch 1, 3 dc in ring on

Continued on page 151

Dear Journal,

Tyler and I flew to Wichita today — for several reasons. I was slated to speak about "Bundles for Babies" at a charity luncheon hosted by the Wichita Crochet Guild and Ty had to check out some cattle at a local ranch for Daddy. He's really getting into this registered here-ford craze that's going around now, and heard that some ranch near Augusta had the best herefords you could buy. Phillip was scheduled to take the jet for an appraisal by the people at Beech, as Daddy's thinking about getting a new one.

The weather was slightly choppy, so we didn't get to Wichita until about ten. The limo was already waiting, and Phillip had to hurry to get to the Beech office for his appointment. It was a hectic start to a hectic day. Ty had farther to go than I did, so they dropped me off at the River Center early. Little did I know there wasn't a thing to do there, so I just walked around by the river for almost an hour waiting on someone to show up. By the time the limo returned after the luncheon, it was raining, and I didn't have an umbrella. But here's the good part. When I ran across the little tiled area just outside the door, I slipped, fell unceremoniously on my rear and twisted my ankle. Tyler, bless his heart, came over and scooped me up just like a child. I'm so glad there wasn't anyone else around at the time! I would have been so embarrassed.

The only problem was that while I laid there against Ty's chest, I felt this strange sense of dejavú. Steven used to carry me like that sometimes, maybe that's why. Tyler had his hat on though, so I don't think it was that. Steven never wore a cowbow hat. Perhaps it's because I haven't really been that close to Tyler for ages, and I'd forgotten just how handsome he really is.

We did finally make it home, despite the rain and minor mishaps. But now, sitting here on my bed, I can't understand why that incident made me feel so odd. While I was hiding the ends on my latest afghan awhile ago, I couldn't get that feeling out of my head. I draped that afghan over the rocker when I was done and for some strange reason, I can't seen to shake the thought of Ty seated in that rocker lovingly cradling a child in his arms. Everytime I close my eyes, that's all I see. Come on, Corinne! You're really losing it now!

Butterfly Kisses

Designed by Erma Fielder

SIZE: 38" square.

MATERIALS: Size-10 bedspread cotton — 2200 yds. white; size-20 crochet cotton — small amount each yellow, variegated pink, variegated lavender, green and brown; tapestry needle; No. 1 and No. 10 steel crochet hooks or sizes needed to obtain gauges.

GAUGES: With **No. 1 steel hook and size-10 bedspread cotton,** 6 sc and 6 ch-5 sps = 5"; 6 pattern rows = 2½". With **No. 10 steel hook and size-20 crochet cotton,** Butterfly is 1¼" x 1½"; Flower is ⅜" across.

SKILL LEVEL: ☆☆ Average

AFGHAN

NOTES: *For beginning picot (beg picot), sl st in 3rd ch from hook.*

*For **picot,** ch 3, sl st in top of last st made.*

Use No. 1 steel hook and size-10 bedspread cotton unless otherwise stated.

Row 1: With white, ch 242, sc in 2nd ch from hook, *ch 6, beg picot, (dc in same ch, picot) 4 times, skip next 5 chs, sc in next ch; repeat from * across, turn (200 picots, 41 sc).

Row 2: Ch 8, skip next 4 picots, sc in next picot, (ch 5, skip next 4 picots, sc in next picot) across, turn (40 ch-5 sps).

Row 3: Ch 1, sc in first st, *[ch 6, beg picot, (dc in same sc, picot) 4 times], skip next ch–5 sp, sc in next sc; repeat from * 38 more times; repeat between [ ], sc in 3rd ch of last ch-8, turn.

Rows 4-78: Repeat rows 2 and 3 alternately, ending with row 2. At end of last row, **do not** fasten off.

BORDER

Rnd 1: Working around outer edge, ch 3, 2 dc in same st, 4 dc in next ch-5 sp, (dc in next st, 4 dc in next ch-5 sp) 39 times, 3 dc in 3rd ch of last ch-8; working in ends of rows, 4 dc in this row, (dc in next row, 4 dc in next row) 38 times, 3 dc in last row; working in starting ch on opposite side of row 1, 4 dc in next ch-5 sp, (dc in next ch, 4 dc in next ch-5 sp) 39 times, 3 dc in last ch; working in ends of rows, 2 dc around next ch-3, 2 dc around next picot, (dc in next sc row,

Continued on page 152

My dear friend Ashley,

Hello! Thank you so much for the heartfelt letter. First let me say, there's no need to apologize. I had already alerted Preston to the rumors, so it wasn't news to me. And no, don't feel that you've somehow hurt me. I know Preston's help is very important to you right now, and it doesn't bother me that he's turned into your "personal business guru" as you call it. This is a different situation entirely, even if some of the functions can't exactly be called business. Preston doesn't do anything anymore unless it relates to his business. I'm thrilled he took you to the faculty dinner at the University. And, if you managed to get Preston on a dance floor, power to you.

Trust me. I'm not worried. I know this talk will all blow over and I'm thrilled that you're becoming such an overnight success. If Preston can help with the right connections, then I say go for it. However, I am a little miffed with Preston. I haven't heard from him in two weeks. I've called a couple times, but he was always out and hasn't yet returned my calls. I know he's been extremely busy trying to iron out the difficulties they are having with the Hill Creek project, but I'd think he could at least call for a minute. Please relay a message to him to call soon. I had planned to fly to Chicago in a week or so and wanted Preston to know so he could coordinate his schedule.

I had lots of fun the other night. Remember I said Juanita had a new granddaughter. Well, she was baby-sitting the other evening when Ben cut his arm and had to be taken to the emergency room for stitches, so I got to baby-sit. It was great. Melissa is such a sweet baby. It really made me start thinking. Here I am already 29. I probably need to think about motherhood if I'm going to.

Well, enough for now! Again, don't you worry about this thing with Preston. It will blow over.

Love, C—

Zigzag Adventures

Designed by Rusti

SIZE: 34" square.

MATERIALS: Baby sport pompadour yarn — 24 oz. variegated and 18 oz. white; F crochet hook or size needed to obtain gauge.

GAUGE: 9 dc and 3 ldc worked in pattern = 2¼"; 5 dc rows worked in pattern = 2¾".

SKILL LEVEL: ☆☆ Average

AFGHAN

Row 1: With variegated, ch 114, sc in 2nd ch from hook, sc in each ch across, turn (113 sc).

Row 2: Ch 3, *dc in each of next 3 sts; for **back long double crochet (back ldc) on this row only,** working behind last 3 sts, yo, insert hook in same st as 3rd st to the right, yo, draw up long lp, (yo, draw through 2 lps on hook) 2 times; repeat from * across to last st, dc in last st, turn (113 dc, 37 back ldc).

NOTES: *For back long double crochet (back ldc) on remaining rows; working behind last 3 dc, yo, insert hook in skipped ldc, yo, draw up long lp, (yo, draw through 2 lps on hook) 2 times.*

*For **front long double crochet (front ldc) on remaining rows,** working in front of last 3 dc, yo, insert hook in skipped ldc, yo, draw up long lp, (yo, draw through 2 lps on hook) 2 times.*

Row 3: Ch 3, (skip next ldc, dc in each of next 3 sts, front ldc) across to last st, dc in last st, turn (113 dc, 37 front ldc).

Row 4: Ch 3, (skip next ldc, dc in each of next 3 sts, back ldc) across to last st, dc in last st, turn (113 dc, 37 back ldc).

Rows 5-53: Repeat rows 3 and 4 alternately, ending with row 3.

Row 54: Skipping each ldc, ch 1, sc in each dc across, turn, fasten off (113 sc).

BORDER

Rnd 1: Working around outer edge, join white with sc in first st, sc in next 14 sts, skip next st, (sc in next 15 sts, skip next st) across to last st, sc in last st, ch 2; *working in ends of rows, sc in first sc row, 2 sc in each dc row across to last sc row, sc in last sc row, ch 2*; working in starting ch on opposite side of row 1, (sc in next 15 chs, skip next ch) across to last ch, sc in last ch, ch 2; repeat between **, join with sl st in first sc (106 sc across each edge between corner ch-2 sps).

Rnd 2: Ch 3, dc in each st across with (2 dc, ch 2, 2 dc) in each corner ch sp, join with sl st in top of ch-3 (110 dc

Continued on page 152

Dear Journal,

Spoke to Preston today. He was in a huge hurry, so we didn't talk long, but he'd gotten the message from Ashley to call. She'd told him I was going to come up but he said that wouldn't work. Apparently he and Ashley are slated to fly to California to consult with some world-renowned firm there about designing and overseeing the construction of a new convention center in San Diego. This could be the biggest job of his career, but if they accept, it will take at least a year to do the project. That's when he said we'd probably have to postpone the wedding again. He did suggest I come along, but he knows I hate California. I guess I really must begin to face the fact that Preston's job will always take precedence over me unless I'm willing to tag along every time he gets swept up in a new adventure. I should probably be upset, but I'm not. That's probably because we just finished the "Bundles for Babies" program today with a presentation at the hospital and being around all those children gives your spirits a lift that even Preston's news can't dampen. We had such a great time. Ty helped out by driving the Suburban to deliver the boxes of toys and blankets. When we walked into the childrens' ward, the kids were fascinated by Ty's "cowboy" outfit. They pummeled him with questions about his horse, his guns, etc., all of which Ty answered with great dignity, treating the youngsters with such kindness and respect that it was all I could do to keep from crying. At one point, he even got down on all fours, pretending to be a rocking horse so one little boy could pretend he was a real cowboy like Ty. After a day like that it's hard to be upset by such trivial stuff as having to postpone our wedding date, again. I've done it several times, and by now it seems to be getting pretty easy.

"What's bothering you, dear," Clarice asked her daughter. Corinne was sitting on the sofa in her parents' den crocheting madly. "Oh, nothing, Mom. I just want to get this afghan done." Clarice frowned at Corinne's blatant cover-up. "Corinne, I know when you're keeping something from me, so don't say it's nothing." Corinne stopped for a moment, looking up to smile at the beautiful woman sitting beside her. Clarice had always been the perfect mother. Never too controlling, always willing to let Corinne find her own way, but always there to help and support whenever necessary. "Okay. If you really want to know. I've been having some serious doubts lately about my relationship with Preston." Clarice tried hard not to display the shock she felt. "When did this come about?" Corinne's hands stilled again and she laid her work aside, reaching for the mug of chocolate sitting next to her on the table. "It didn't just come to me. It's something that I've thought about quite a bit over the past few months. I mean..." she paused thoughtfully, sipping her cocoa. "Look at the circumstances now. Preston and I have been engaged for almost two years, and we're no closer to finalizing our wedding than we were the day he proposed. He's off in Chicago doing his thing and loving it. I'm out here, doing the same. Does that sound like two people who are madly in love and itching to spend the rest of their lives together?" Clarice's eyes softened. "I don't know, Mother. When Preston and I first got together it seemed like the perfect match. No, it didn't have all the fireworks of my relationship with Steven, but Preston and I are really good friends. We respect and trust each other, and what a better basis for a marriage than that?"

"It sounds like a perfect foundation to me, if you have everything else, too," answered Clarice. "If you can't blend the other pursuits in your life, you only end up respecting and trusting each other from afar." Corinne sighed audibly, sitting the mug down. "What am I going to do? I don't think it would be fair to either me or Preston to continue thinking we can really pull this off. I don't think I'll be happy if I move to Chicago, and I know Preston could never be happy here." Clarice stood up. "Have you thought about settling in Denver? That would be close enough to Morningside for you to come out often, and Preston wouldn't have to give up the big city life he's accustomed to."

Corinne sat, staring off in space a moment, then purposely grabbed her hook and yarn and began stitching. "I'm really confused, Mom, and I don't like it. I need to have a serious talk with Preston so we can reevaluate our priorities and goals. If we can line it all out and come to a mutually acceptable plan, then we could still marry. He's

really a wonderful man with steadfast character. He has a fabulous career and respects me immensely. I couldn't ask for more than that, could I?" Clarice lovingly laid her hand on Corinne's arm. "Yes, you could dear." Corinne fingers ceased momentarily, then flew into action again as Clarice continued. "You could ask for a wonderful man with steadfast character who understood that the person the public sees when you're wearing your society smile is only a part of you. You could ask for a man who can put you at the top of the list, at least occasionally, and still tend to his responsibilities. You could ask for a man who not only respects you but who can sweep you off your feet, make your knees weak and your heart flutter, just by touching your shoulder."

Corinne stopped crocheting and dropped her chin. Clarice reached over, cupping Corinne's chin and gently raised her head. A shimmery tear glided down Corinne's cheek as she took a shaky breath. "I had that once, Mother. I don't know if I dare to dream of having it again. I know Steven wanted me to go on with my life, and when Preston and I got engaged, I felt mutual respect and friendship was a comfortable combination, even if a pounding pulse wasn't part of the deal." She pulled a tissue from a nearby box and wiped her eyes. "Preston and I do have many things in common," she continued, sniffing, "but there are just as many areas where we clash."

Clarice leaned over and hugged her daughter. Sitting up, she smiled lovingly. "Baby, you know I've never told you what to do, and I'm not going to start now. This is a decision you have to make on your own. You need to think long and hard about all the ramifications of being Mrs. Preston Richards. Then, and only then, can you make a choice that's fair to you both." Corinne began gathering up her things and stuffing them in her ever-present yarn bag. Smiling, she leaned over and kissed her mother's cheek. "I guess you're right. It is time to make a choice," she stated strongly. Standing up, bag in hand, she turned for the door. "I'm going to take a walk down to the stables, then go home and have a hot bath and do some thinking. Getting outdoors always helps clear my head."

Opening the door, Corinne was surprised to see her father coming up the path. "Hi, Daddy!" She said. "You're back early." Milt gave his daughter a quick hug, then turned to Clarice. "Would you please ask Juanita to fix some coffee, I'm going to go to the den to rest. I think I overdid it moving the hay." Corinne's questioning eyes darted to her mother. "Certainly, sweetheart," Clarice replied and quickly headed for the kitchen, concern clouding her face. "Corinne," she called back, "go with your father and see if he needs anything else."

Solid Comfort

Designed by Eleanor Albano-Miles

SIZE: 48½" x 72".

MATERIALS: Worsted-weight yarn — 60 oz. buff fleck; J crochet hook or size needed to obtain gauge.

GAUGE: 13 sc = 4"; 2 sc rows and 2 cluster/dc rows worked in pattern = 1¾".

SKILL LEVEL: ☆☆ Average

AFGHAN

Row 1: Ch 154, sc in 2nd ch from hook, sc in each ch across, turn (153 sc).

NOTES: *For cluster, yo, insert hook in next st, yo, draw lp through, yo, draw through 2 lps on hook, (yo, insert hook in same st, yo, draw lp through, yo, draw through 2 lps on hook) 3 times, yo, draw through all 5 lps on hook.*

Ch-4 at beginning of next row counts as first dc and ch sp.

Row 2: Ch 4, skip next st, cluster in next st, ch 1, skip next st, dc in next st, (ch 1, skip next st, cluster in next st, ch 1, skip next st, dc in next st) across, turn (76 ch sps, 39 dc, 38 clusters).

Row 3: Ch 1, sc in each st and in each ch sp across, turn.

Rows 4-5: Repeat rows 2 and 3.

Row 6: Ch 1, sc in first st, (tr in next st, sc in next st) across, turn.

Row 7: Ch 1, sc in each st across, turn.

Rows 8-173: Repeat rows 2-7 consecutively, ending with row 5. At end of last row, **do not** turn.

Rnd 174: Working around outer edge in ends of rows and in sts, ch 1, (skip first row; skipping cluster rows, 2 sc in each dc row and sc in each sc row across to last row, skip last row); working in starting ch on opposite side of row 1, 3 sc in first ch, sc in each ch across with 3 sc in last ch; repeat between ( ); working in sts across last row, 3 sc in first st, sc in each st across with 3 sc in last st, join with sl st in first sc, **turn** (153 sc across each short end between center corner sts, 221 sc across each long edge between center corner sts).

Rnd 175: Ch 4, (sc in next st, tr in next st) across to next center corner st, (sc, tr, sc) in next st, *tr in next st, (sc in next st, tr in next st) across to next center corner st, (sc, tr, sc) in next st; repeat from * around, join with sl st in top of ch-4, **turn.**

Rnd 176: Ch 1, sc in each st around with 3 sc in each center corner st, join with sl st in first sc, fasten off. ❦

Dear Journal,

We had to take Daddy to the emergency room last night. He was having chest pains. After some initial tests, they say it may be a blocked artery. They will do more tests tomorrow, then schedule him for angio-plasty in a day or so to determine if surgery is necessary. I was so scared. I've never thought about what would happen to Morningside if something happened to Daddy. I know a lot about the day-to-day business of running the ranch, but I'd be hard-pressed to deal with it myself. Mom would be of no use. Even though she's lived here for almost 40 years, she wouldn't last a week. She simply doesn't understand any of it. Daddy has always taken care of the ranching and Mom took care of domestic and social affairs. While sitting in the waiting room it suddenly hit me. I don't ever want to live anywhere else. But then, that brought to mind Preston. If he and I do get married, he'll expect me to move to Chicago. I've never minded visiting, but I wouldn't want to live there. This is just too much to think about right now.

It's after eleven and I'm at Daddy's office. I've been going over his daily planner for the next week and there are several checks that must be written. There's a note from Ty saying he left a feed order with the Co-Op which is due to arrive tomorrow, so I'll need to find out if we pay them right away or if they will send a bill. Jim Martin is coming, as well, to pick up the 50 steers he bought, but I'm not sure which herd it is. The new herd of cows is due to be pregnancy tested, so we have to contact the vet. There's also a notation about calling the logging firm again to set up a time for them to come survey the west slope. Thank heavens Ty will be home tomorrow. He'll know what to do about this stuff.

Interlaced Images

Designed by Jennifer Christiansen McClain

SIZE: 49" x 61" not including Fringe.

MATERIALS: Fuzzy worsted-weight yarn — 22 oz. each tan, lt. gray, and dk. gray; J crochet hook or size needed to obtain gauge.

GAUGE: 11 dc = 3½"; rows 1-4 worked in pattern = 2".

SKILL LEVEL: ☆☆ Average

AFGHAN

NOTE: Entire Afghan is worked with right side facing you. **Do not** *turn at end of each row. Leave 7"-long strand at beginning and end of each row.*

Row 1: With dk. gray, ch 192, dc in 4th ch from hook, dc in each ch across, **do not** turn, fasten off (190 dc).

Row 2: Join dk. gray with sc in first st, (ch 2, skip next 2 sts, sc in next st) across, fasten off (64 sc, 63 ch sps).

Row 3: Join lt. gray with sc in first st; (working behind next ch sp, dc in each of next 2 skipped sts on row before last, sc in next st on last row) across, fasten off.

Row 4: Join lt. gray with sl st in first st, ch 6, skip next st, dc next 3 sts tog, (ch 3, dc next 3 sts tog) across to last 2 sts, ch 3, skip next st, dc in last st, fasten off.

Row 5: Join med. gray with sc in 3rd ch of ch-6; working behind next ch sp, 2 dc in next skipped st on row before last, sc in next st; (working behind next ch sp, 2 dc in same st as last part of next decrease, sc in next st) across to last ch sp;

Continued on page 153

My dearest Preston,

I started to call, but just couldn't. I think you need time to read what I have to say and think about it. This is very hard for me because you are such a wonderful man and such a good friend, but with everything that's happened lately, I've done quite a bit of thinking. I know now that I just can't marry you. Our relationship is good, but not good enough. Don't get me wrong, that has nothing to do with you.

Actually, I've seen this coming for some time now. You and I both have our dreams, and they just don't mesh. More and more I've come to realize that your dreams hinge around your career. Mine are wrapped up in Morningside and my charity work. But I also think there isn't anyone who would be better suited to help you to realize all your dreams than Ashley. I believe Ashley is the one you really need.

Thinking back over the past two years, I'm convinced you and I could never have a normal life together. Your life is in Chicago, and my heart is here at Morningside. Sitting here in Daddy's studio gazing out over the valley I can feel my love of the land and all its creatures well up inside me. That sounds silly doesn't it. But I see now, my future is here, not in Chicago, or San Diego, or New York. I hope you understand, darling. I wish you all the best in your career and in your life. You deserve someone who will always be at your side, wherever you go, and I simply can't make that promise.

I know my decision to stay at Morningside is right. I spent the day helping Ty work cattle before taking them to the sale. They had to be tagged and dipped. It's very dirty work that left me looking like something the dog drug in. Despite the dirt and sweat, I loved the sense of well-being and accomplishment that came from being a part of this operation. I must hurry and close now. Thankfully, I brought my things so I can run next door to Ty's and change there. I'm going with him to the senator's reception in Denver this evening to take Daddy's place. They have been working hard to get the state to back a grant that would create a fund for low-income families to buy land to be reclaimed, and Daddy insists we can't miss this opportunity. Even from his hospital bed he's a force to be reckoned with.

You've been a true friend, Preston dear, and I truly hope you understand that my reasons have nothing to do with you. I think you need to look in another direction. Ashley is a very special person and would be perfect for you, career wise and personally. Maybe this is going to work out for the best after all. Let me hear from you soon, and I'll send you a picture of me in my ranch-hand outfit.

Love, C—

Morning's Glow

Designed by Vicki M. Watkins

SIZE: 51½" x 70".

MATERIALS: Worsted-weight yarn — 36 oz. brown, 25 oz. brown/tan/green variegated and 14 oz. green; H crochet hook or size needed to obtain gauge.

GAUGE: Rnds 1-3 of Block = 2½" square. Each Block is 5¾" square.

SKILL LEVEL: ☆☆ Average

BLOCK (make 88)

Rnd 1: With green, ch 4, sl st in first ch to form ring, ch 1, sc in ring, ch 2, (3 sc in ring, ch 2) 3 times, 2 sc in ring, join with sl st in first sc (12 sc, 4 ch sps).

Rnd 2: Sl st in first ch sp, ch 1, (sc, ch 2, sc, tr, sc) in same sp, ch 1, skip next 3 sts, *(sc, tr, sc, ch 2, sc, tr, sc) in next ch sp, ch 1, skip next 3 sts; repeat from * around, (sc, tr) in same ch sp as first st, join with sl st in first sc (4 ch-2 sps, 4 ch-1 sps).

Rnd 3: Sl st in first ch-2 sp, ch 1, (sc, ch 2, sc, tr, sc) in same sp, ch 1, (sc, tr, sc) in next ch-1 sp, ch 1, *(sc, tr, sc, ch 2, sc, tr, sc) in next ch-2 sp, ch 1, (sc, tr, sc) in next ch-1 sp, ch 1; repeat from * around, (sc, tr) in same ch sp as first st, join, fasten off (8 ch-1 sps, 4 ch-2 sps).

Rnd 4: Join brown with sc in any corner ch-2 sp, ch 2, sc in same sp, ch 1, (2 sc in next ch-1 sp, ch 1) 2 times, *(sc, ch 2, sc) in next ch-2 sp, ch 1, (2 sc in next ch-1 sp, ch 1) 2 times; repeat from * around, join, fasten off (24 sc, 12 ch-1 sps, 4 ch-2 sps).

Rnd 5: Join variegated with sl st in any corner ch-2 sp, ch 5, dc in same sp, dc in each st and in each ch-1 sp across to next corner ch-2 sp, *(dc, ch 2, dc) in next ch-2 sp, dc in each st and in each ch-1 sp across to next corner ch-2 sp; repeat from * around, join with sl st in 3rd ch of ch-5 (11 dc across each side between ch-2 sps).

NOTE: *For* **double crochet back post (dc bp,** *see page 159), yo, insert hook from back to front around post of next st, yo, draw lp through, (yo, draw through 2 lps on hook) 2 times.*

Rnd 6: Sl st in first ch sp, ch 5, dc in same sp, dc bp around next 11 sts, *(dc, ch 2, dc) in next ch-2 sp, dc bp around next 11 sts; repeat from * around, join, fasten off (13 sts across each side between ch-2 sps).

Rnd 7: Join brown with sl st in any ch-2 sp, ch 5, dc in same sp, dc bp around next 13 sts, *(dc, ch 2, dc) in next ch-2 sp, dc bp around next 13 sts; repeat from * around, join, fasten off.

JOINING

Place two Blocks side-by-side, join brown with sc in first

Continued on page 153

Dear Journal,

It's four in the morning and I'm wide awake. Actually, I've been wide awake since about two, but I finally gave in and got up to make coffee. No need to fight it. I don't know why I can't sleep. Ty and I had a wonderful time at the reception. The senator seems more in favor of the land grant than ever. I'm going to the hospital today to see Daddy. He's recovering well from his triple by-pass surgery and I can't wait to give him the newest afghan I stitched for him along with the good news about the grant. Later today, Ty and I must go over some paperwork for the sale of the jet.

This is stupid, but for some reason these images from the reception last night keep running around in my head, but they don't make sense. I keep seeing Tyler on the dance floor last night, feeling his strong arms holding me as we waltzed together. I haven't felt that free since Steven was still here. I thought I'd forgotten what it felt like. I'm a grown woman, so I shouldn't be thinking this way. Tyler is like a brother to me and we have a wonderful set-up. He'd think I was crazy for sure if I began to think of anything more intimate than that. These crazy notions are probably just because I've been under so much stress lately. Right now I need to get dressed, I have to go to Ty's bungalow and sign some papers. He also wanted me to see where he put the afghan I gave him for Christmas. If there's really nothing to this, why does that make my palms sweat.

Peaceful Surroundings

Designed by Carol Smith

SIZE: 60" x 80½".

MATERIALS: Worsted-weight yarn — 25 oz. each green fleck, navy fleck and burgundy fleck; tapestry needle; K crochet hook or size needed to obtain gauge.

GAUGE: Rnds 1-2 of Square = 3½" square. Each Square is 6¼" square; each Strip is 10" wide.

SKILL LEVEL: ☆☆ Average

STRIP (make 6)
Square (make 12)

Rnd 1: With green fleck, ch 5, sl st in first ch to form ring, ch 3, 4 dc in ring, ch 2, (5 dc in ring, ch 2) 3 times, join with sl st in top of ch-3, fasten off (20 dc, 4 ch sps).

NOTE: For **treble crochet front post (tr fp,** see page 159), yo 2 times, insert hook from front to back around post of next st, yo, draw lp through, (yo, draw through 2 lps on hook) 3 times.

For **double treble crochet front post (dtr fp),** yo 3 times, insert hook from front to back around post of next st on rnd before last, yo, draw lp through, (yo, draw through 2 lps on hook) 4 times. Skip next st on last rnd.

Rnd 2: Join burgundy fleck with sl st in any ch sp, ch 3, (dc, ch 2, 2 dc) in same sp, dc in next st, (tr fp around next st, dc in next st) 2 times, *(2 dc, ch 2, 2 dc) in next ch sp, dc in next st, (tr fp around next st, dc in next st) 2 times; repeat from * around, join, fasten off (9 sts across each side between ch sps).

Rnd 3: Join navy fleck with sl st in any ch sp, ch 3, (dc, ch 2, 2 dc) in same sp, *[dc in each of next 2 sts, tr fp around next st, dc in next st, dtr fp around next st on rnd before last, dc in next st on last rnd, tr fp around next st, dc in each of next 2 sts], (2 dc, ch 2, 2 dc) in next ch sp; repeat from * 2 more times; repeat between [ ], join, fasten off (13 sts

Continued on page 153

Dear Ashley,

Just read your letter. You and I have been friends for years now, so there's not much we haven't been through, but let me start by saying that I don't hold any ill feelings toward you. If you have fallen in love with Preston, then that is what was meant to be. I guess I hadn't really told you that awhile back I had written Preston and told him I couldn't marry him. It's not that he's not a wonderful man, it's just that our lifestyles are too different. My advice to you is to go ahead and tell Preston. I think you two would make a great couple. Remember now, he's not the romantic sort, so you need to be up front with him. And don't worry if he doesn't respond right away. He can't stay blind or busy forever. He's bound to see that you would make a splendid partner for him, both in his businesses and at home. With your business sense, you and Preston could become a world-ranked team in the field of architecture and design, and you'd be able to handle all the legal things, too.

Now it's time for a confession of my own. I have fallen in love, too. I mean mad-about-you, crazy-school-girl love. Who, you ask? Would you believe Tyler? Probably not. I couldn't believe it either. The only problem though is that I can't bring myself to say a thing to him. We have the perfect set-up here with him running the ranch and it's very important for Daddy to keep him here. If he and I started anything and it didn't work out, I don't know what we'd do. Neither of us would ever want to leave Morningside. Yesterday, after riding out all day with him to check the fences, he offered to cook dinner for me and I couldn't say no. It was all I could do to keep from just blurting out the words. To make matters worse, it had been a long, tiring day, and with a great meal under my belt, I ended up falling asleep on his couch. I woke up this morning on his bed, where he had apparently carried me and covered me with an afghan. When I woke up, I snuck into the living room and found him asleep on the sofa. How did we end up in this predicament, Ashley? We're grown women. We're supposed to know how to handle ourselves. Maybe our hearts don't count.

Please write again soon, and remember, I love you. You're a very special friend, and I know this will all work out for both of us.

Love, C.—

Warm & Welcome

Designed by Katherine Eng

SIZE: 40½" x 54½" not including Fringe.

MATERIALS: Worsted-weight yarn — 26 oz. multicolor, 15 oz. black and 15 oz. tan; K crochet hook or size needed to obtain gauge.

GAUGE: With **2 strands yarn held together,** 3 sc = 1"; 6 rows worked in pattern = 2¼".

NOTE: Work entire pattern with 2 strands yarn held together throughout.

SKILL LEVEL: ☆ Easy

AFGHAN

Row 1: For **first side,** with one strand each black and multicolor, ch 165, sc in 2nd ch from hook, sc in each of next 2 chs, ch 2, skip next 2 chs, (sc in each of next 2 chs, ch 2, skip next 2 chs) across to last 3 chs, sc in each of last 3 chs, turn (84 sc, 40 ch sps).

Rows 2-3: Ch 1, sc in each of first 3 sts, ch 2, skip next ch sp, (sc in each of next 2 sts, ch 2, skip next ch sp) across to last 3 sts, sc in each of last 3 sts, turn. At end of last row, **do not** turn, fasten off.

Row 4: With right side facing you, using one strand each tan and multicolor, join with sc in first st, ch 2, skip next 2 sts, (2 sc in next ch sp, ch 2, skip next 2 sts) across to last st, sc in last st, turn.

Rows 5-7: Ch 1, sc in first st, ch 2, skip next ch sp, (sc in each of next 2 sts, ch 2, skip next ch sp) across to last st, sc in last st, turn. At end of last row, fasten off.

Row 8: With one strand each black and multicolor, join with sc in first st, 2 sc in next ch sp, (ch 2, skip next 2 sts, 2 sc in next ch sp) across to last st, sc in last st, turn.

Rows 9-13: Ch 1, sc in each of first 3 sts, ch 2, skip next ch sp, (sc in each of next 2 sts, ch 2, skip next ch sp) across to last 3 sts, sc in each of last 3 sts, turn. At end of last row, fasten off.

Rows 14-53: Repeat rows 4-13 consecutively. At end of last row, **do not** fasten off.

Row 54: Ch 1, sc in first st, ch 1, skip next st, sc in next st, 3 dc in next ch sp, (skip next st, sc in next st, 3 dc in next ch sp) across to last 3 sts, sc in next st, ch 1, skip next st, sc in last st, fasten off.

Row 55: For **2nd side,** working in starting ch on opposite side of row 1, with right side facing you, using one strand each black and multicolor, join with sc in first ch, sc in each of next 2 chs, ch 2, skip next 2 chs, (sc in each of next 2 chs, ch 2, skip next 2 chs) across to last 3 chs, sc in each of last 3 chs, turn.

Rows 56-108: Repeat rows 2-54 of first side.

FRINGE

For **each Fringe,** cut two strands yarn each 12" long. Holding both strands together, fold in half, insert hook in end of row, draw fold through, draw all loose ends through fold, tighten. Trim ends.

Matching row colors, Fringe in end of each row across each short end of Afghan. ❧

Dear Preston

I don't have a lot of time now, so I'm going to get to the point. I know I shouldn't meddle, but I can't let you throw away a good thing just because you didn't know about it. I don't think she's said anything to you, but Ashley is in love with you and if you have any brains, you'll marry her. You two are perfect for each other. You both love the city highlife, both love the business. What more could you want? Ashley is the perfect foil for you, Preston, personally and professionally. With her having already made her mark in Chicago, you can only benefit.

I never told you this, but I never felt for you what I felt for Steven, and it wouldn't have been fair to you for us to marry. You deserve to have someone who loves you totally and completely, like Ashley. I know you're going to think this is strange, but lately, I've had some very strong feelings for Ty. Please don't say anything, as I don't want Ty to know.

Please give some thought to what I said. I wouldn't let Ashley get away. When Steven died, I learned that we never know how long we have to enjoy our life, so live it to the fullest. Daddy is coming home this afternoon and we're planning a surprise party to welcome him so I'd better close now. Take care.

Love always, C—

Revelations

Designed by Frances Hughes

SIZE: 53" x 61".

MATERIALS: Worsted-weight yarn — 18 oz. each brown/rust/tan variegated and rust, 14 oz. tan; tapestry needle; G crochet hook or size needed to obtain gauge.

GAUGE: Each motif is 2¼" across. Each Block is 8" square.

SKILL LEVEL: ☆☆ Average

BLOCK (make 42)
Center

Rnd 1: For **first motif,** with variegated, ch 4, sl st in first ch to form ring, ch 3, 13 dc in ring, join with sl st in top of ch-3, turn (14 dc).

Rnd 2: Ch 1, sc in first 6 sts, 2 sc in next st, sc in next 6 sts, 2 sc in last st, join with sl st in first sc, fasten off (16 sc).

Rnd 1: For **second motif,** repeat same rnd of first motif.

Rnd 2: Ch 1, sc in first 6 sts, 2 sc in next st, sc in next 6 sts, 2 sc in last st; to **join,** drop lp from hook, insert hook in any st on first motif, draw dropped lp through, join with sl st in first sc, fasten off.

Rnds 1-2: For **third motif,** work same as second motif, joining to second motif according to Joining Diagram on page 154.

Rnd 1: For **fourth motif,** repeat same rnd of first motif.

Rnd 2: Ch 1, sc in first 3 sts; to **join,** drop lp from hook, insert hook in corresponding st (see Joining Diagram) on first motif, draw dropped lp through; sc in each of next 2 sts on this motif, 2 sc in next st, sc in next 6 sts, 2 sc in last st; to **join,** drop lp from hook, insert hook in corresponding st on third motif, draw dropped lp through, join with sl st in first sc, fasten off.

Border

NOTES: For **beginning shell (beg shell),** ch 3, (2 dc, ch 1, 3 dc) in same st or ch sp.

For **shell,** (3 dc, ch 1, 3 dc) in next st or ch sp.

For **popcorn (pc),** 4 dc in next st, drop lp from hook, insert hook in first st of 4-dc group, draw dropped lp through, pushing sts toward wrong side of work, ch 1.

Rnd 1: Working around outer edge of Center, join tan with sl st in 6th st after any joining, beg shell, (*ch 1, skip next st, sc in next st, ch 1, skip next st, 3 dc in next st, ch 1, skip next st, skip next joining, skip next st on next motif, 3 dc in next st, ch 1, skip next st, sc in next st, ch 1, skip next st*, shell in next st) 3 times; repeat between **, join with sl st in top of ch-3 (20 ch-1 sps, 8 3-dc groups, 8 sc, 4 shells).

Rnd 2: Sl st in each of next 2 sts, sl st in next ch sp, beg shell, *[pc in next ch-1 sp, (3 dc in next ch-1 sp, pc in next

Continued on page 154

The early morning sun was streaming through the trees as Corinne ran up the path to her father's office situated at the end of the new stable building. As she opened the door the smell of fresh coffee assailed her senses. Milt looked up from his desk as Corinne walked in. A handsome man in his mid fifties, Milt was a perpetual gentleman. Tall and slender, his impeccable taste showed in every aspect of his life. Always amiable and polite, he treated everyone with equal fairness, regardless of social or economic status, a trait that drew high regards and respect from the community.

"You just couldn't wait, could you," she chided, walking around behind the desk to give him a hug. "You know me, kitten. Work, work, work." Milt said, depositing some papers in one of the pigeon holes on his desk. Corinne perched herself on the edge of the massive oak desk, pushing still more papers out of the way. "I know that's how you used to be, Daddy, but you know what the doctor said." Milt snorted, closing his planner with a slight slap. "What does he know. I'm in better shape than he is," he said with a defiant tone. "Now, Daddy," Corinne cooed, "don't get your dander up. He's just trying to see to it that you behave. We'd all like to keep you around for awhile longer, you know."

Milt leaned back in his chair and sighed. "I know. You don't have to remind me! I'm not getting any younger, that's for sure. But, I have to say, I'm really impressed with the job you and Tyler did of keeping the place going smoothly while I was in the hospital." At the thought of the many hours spent in Ty's company, day and night, coordinating the daily ranching affairs, Corinne blushed slightly. Turning her head quickly so her father wouldn't notice, she struggled for an air of composure. "It was truly a labor of love and you know it. We just did what we had to do. I couldn't possibly have done it without Tyler, though. He really understands the workings of the ranch and takes care of everything like it was his own."

Nodding in agreement, Milt stood up and walked across to the window. Surveying the peaceful scene outside, he spoke quietly. "I've never told you this, Corinne, but I think you're old enough to listen to some fanciful ramblings from your old dad. Before you married Steven, I had always secretly hoped some day you would grow up and marry Tyler." Corinne's hand jerked, spilling a few drops of coffee onto the desk. Scrambling to get a tissue, she tried desperately to appear unflustered. "No, I never knew that, Daddy. I can't imagine why you'd ever think that. Tyler has always been like a brother to me. We grew up together."

Striding purposefully toward the kitchenette for more coffee, Milt turned to look at the daughter he loved so much. "Well, Corinne, I guess I've always known that you and Tyler shared a love for this place, and without a son to leave it to, I had hoped that things would work where I could leave it to both of you." Corinne's heart beat erratically in her chest and she looked away, inwardly cringing at the thought of Morningside Ranch without Tyler.

"You do have provisions in your will for Tyler, Daddy, I know you do. Mother told me once," she said somewhat tightly. "Yes, I do," Milt stated a little too emphatically. "He's like a son to me, and if anything ever happens to me, he'll be well taken care of, just as if he were my own flesh and blood. But, if he ever had to leave Morningside, it would break his heart."

Corinne swallowed hard. "If I ever had to leave Morningside, it would break my heart," she admitted. "That's one of the biggest reasons I broke my engagement to Preston." Her father nodded in agreement and his features softened. "I know that, baby," he said softly, "and I want you to know how sorry I am, but I think you made the smart choice. For all your brilliance, shining in the bright lights of the big cities like you do, you're still a country girl at heart. You've just learned how to play both sides of the court, so to speak." Corinne laughed, easing the tension. "I guess you're right," she replied, smiling. "I really do enjoy all the glitz and glamour of the social scene, but nothing makes me happier than coming home to Morningside. Living out here amidst all Nature's beauty is what keeps my spirit going. It makes me appreciate everything I have."

Milt walked over and placed his arms lovingly around his daughter and gave her a squeeze. "I love you, Corinne, and my hope is that you're happy, whatever path you choose," he said. "Don't worry, I'm not losing any sleep over your not being married. I know how much you loved Steven, and I realized years ago that you and Ty were probably too much like brother and sister to ever get married. But, then again, you couldn't ask for a better man." Corinne grinned mischievously. "Not unless they figure out how to clone you," she added flippantly.

Milt chuckled and shook his head, resuming his seat behind the desk. "Never mind, kitten. I think all that medication they gave me in the hospital made my brain go soft or something. I'd better get busy. I've got too much to do today to be sitting around her chatting with a female. Even if she is my favorite daughter." Corinne laughed and stood up, planting a kiss on Milt's cheek just as Ty walked in the door. "I love you, Daddy! Don't you work too hard, now, hear?" she said, waving as she slipped out the door. "See you at dinner!"

Wedding Lace

Designed by Lucia Biunno

SIZE: 65½" x 74".

MATERIALS: Worsted-weight yarn — 56 oz. white; tapestry needle; H and I crochet hooks or sizes needed to obtain gauges.

GAUGES: With **H hook,** 7 dc = 2"; 2 dc rows = 1". With **I hook,** 3 sts = 1"; 3 dc rows = 2".

SKILL LEVEL: ☆☆ Average

AFGHAN

Row 1: With H hook, ch 231, dc in 4th ch from hook, dc in each of next 3 chs, *ch 1, skip next ch, (dc in next ch, ch 1, skip next ch) 4 times, dc in next 5 chs; repeat from * across, turn (149 dc, 80 ch sps).

Row 2: Ch 3, dc in next 4 sts, *ch 1, skip next ch sp, (dc in next st, ch 1, skip next ch sp) 4 times, dc in next 5 sts; repeat from * across, turn.

NOTE: *For **puff st,** yo, insert hook in next st, yo, draw up long lp, (yo, insert hook in same st, yo, draw up long lp) 3 times, yo, draw through all 9 lps on hook.*

Row 3: Ch 3, dc in next 4 sts, *(ch 1, skip next ch sp, dc in next st) 2 times, puff st in next ch sp, (dc in next st, ch 1, skip next ch sp) 2 times, dc in next 5 sts; repeat from * across, turn.

Row 4: Ch 3, dc in next 4 sts, (ch 1, skip next ch sp, dc in next st, puff st in next ch sp, dc in next st, ch 1, skip next puff st, dc in next st, puff st in next ch sp, dc in next st, ch 1, skip next ch sp, dc in next 5 sts) across, turn.

Row 5: Ch 3, dc in next 4 sts, (ch 1, skip next ch sp, dc in next st, ch 1, skip next puff st, dc in next st, puff st in next ch sp, dc in next st, ch 1, skip next puff st, dc in next st, ch 1, skip next ch sp, dc in next 5 sts) across, turn.

Row 6: Ch 3, dc in next 4 sts, *(ch 1, skip next ch sp, dc in next st) 2 times, ch 1, skip next puff st, (dc in next st, ch 1, skip next ch sp) 2 times, dc in next 5 sts; repeat from * across, turn.

Rows 7-117: Repeat rows 2-6 consecutively, ending with row 2.

Row 118: Ch 3, dc in each st and in each ch sp across, fasten off.

Row 119: Working in starting ch on opposite side of row 1, join with sl st in first ch, ch 3, dc in each ch across, fasten off.

BORDER (make 2)

Row 1: With I hook, ch 25, dc in 4th ch from hook, dc in next 4 chs, *ch 3, skip next 2 chs, sc in next ch, ch 3, skip next 2 chs*, dc in next 6 chs; repeat between **, (dc, ch 5, sl st) in last ch, turn (13 dc, 4 ch-3 sps, 2 sc, 1 ch-5 sp).

Row 2: Ch 1, (sc, 2 hdc, 5 dc) in first ch-5 sp, dc in next dc, (ch 5, skip next 2 ch-3 sps and one sc, dc in next dc, ch 5, skip next 4 dc, dc in next dc) across, turn.

Row 3: Ch 3, (4 dc in next ch-5 sp, dc in next dc, ch 3, sc in next ch-5 sp, ch 3, dc in next dc) 2 times, ch 5, sl st in same st as last dc made leaving remaining sts unworked, turn.

Rows 4-98: Repeat rows 2 and 3 alternately, ending with row 2. At end of last row, **do not** turn.

Row 99: Working across long edge, ch 3, 2 dc in end of each row across, fasten off.

Easing to fit, working in **back lps,** sew last row of one Border to each short end of Afghan.❦

Dear Preston & Ashley,

I just got your letter, Ashley, and had to write as soon as possible to say Congratulations! I knew you'd see it my way eventually. And, yes, I'd love to coordinate your wedding, if for no other reason than to prove there are no hard feelings. June is perfect, although that doesn't give us much time. I truly wish for you the same wonderful kind of marriage that I had with Steven. Everyone should experience that. Maybe some day I'll get another chance, but I'm not going to push it. I'm content living at Morningside. Daddy is well again, my guild is preparing for their next big auction to benefit the children's music center and I'm planning the party for Mom and Dad's 40th wedding anniversary so I have a very full life. No time to sit around wondering what to do next. I'd love for you to attend if you can find time, if not, I'll see you when I get to Chicago to hunt for the perfect place to have your reception. Oh, and you can expect your engagement present in the mail shortly. I've been working on it for awhile now in anticipation of this moment, but you will be surprised — it's not just the usual.

Love to you both, C—

Timeless Treasure

Designed by Erma Fielder

SIZE: 47½" x 56½".

MATERIALS: Size-10 bedspread cotton — 3650 yds. white, 150 yds. pink and 100 yds. green; tapestry needle; No. 1 steel and No. 12 steel crochet hooks or sizes needed to obtain gauges.

GAUGES: With **No. 1 steel hook,** 6 dc = 1"; 7 dc rows = 2". With **No. 12 steel hook,** each Rose is ⅞" across.

SKILL LEVEL: ☆☆ Average

AFGHAN

NOTES: *For **treble crochet front post (tr-fp,** see page 159), yo 2 times, insert hook from front to back around post of next st, yo, draw lp through, (yo, draw through 2 lps on hook) 3 times.*

*For **popcorn (pc),** 5 dc in next st, drop lp from hook, insert hook in first st of 5-dc group, draw dropped lp through.*

*For **double crochet front post (dc-fp),** yo, insert hook from front to back around post of next st, yo, draw lp through, (yo, draw through 2 lps on hook) 2 times.*

*For **double crochet back post (dc-bp),** yo, insert hook from back to front around post of next st, yo, draw lp through, (yo, draw through 2 lps on hook) 2 times.*

*For **back twist,** skip next 2 sts, tr-fp around each of next 2 sts; working behind tr just made, dc in each of 2 skipped sts.*

*For **front twist,** skip next 2 sts, dc in each of next 2 sts; working in front of dc just made, tr in each of 2 skipped sts.*

Row 1: With No. 1 steel hook and white, ch 282, dc in 4th ch from hook, dc in each ch across, turn (280 dc).

Row 2: Ch 3, dc in next 8 sts, *[skip next 2 sts, tr-fp around each of next 2 sts; working in front of tr just made, tr-fp around each of 2 skipped sts, dc in next 9 sts], pc in next st, (dc in each of next 3 sts, pc in next st) 5 times, dc in next 9 sts; repeat from * 5 more times; repeat between [ ], turn (216 dc, 36 pc, 28 tr-fp). Front of row 2 is right side of work.

Row 3: Ch 3, dc in next 8 sts, dc-bp around next 4 sts, (dc in next 8 sts, hdc in next 23 sts, dc in next 8 sts, dc-bp around next 4 sts) 6 times, dc in last 9 sts, turn.

Row 4: Ch 3, dc in next 6 sts, back twist, front twist, *dc in next 9 sts, pc in next st, (dc in each of next 3 sts, pc in next st) 4 times, dc in next 9 sts, back twist, front twist; repeat from * 5 more times, dc in last 7 sts, turn.

Row 5: Ch 3, dc in next 6 sts, dc-bp around each of next 2 sts, dc in next 4 sts, dc-bp around each of next 2 sts, (dc in next 6 sts, hdc in next 23 sts, dc in next 6 sts, dc–bp around each of next 2 sts, dc in next 4 sts, dc-bp around each of next 2 sts) 6 times, dc in last 7 sts, turn.

Row 6: Ch 3, dc in next 4 sts, back twist, dc in next 4 sts, front twist, *dc in next 5 sts, pc in next st, (dc in each of next 3 sts, pc in next st) 5 times, dc in next 5 sts, back twist, dc in next 4 sts, front twist; repeat from * 5 more times, dc in last 5 sts, turn.

Row 7: Ch 3, dc in next 4 sts, dc-bp around each of next

Continued on page 154

Dear Journal,

Went to Denver with Tyler today to make the final arrangements for Mom and Dad's anniversary dinner. The menu is prepared and the wine is purchased. The band is booked and the flowers ordered. All is ready. On the way home, I stopped by to pick up part of their gift, a matching set of custom made gold and diamond watches. On the back of each are the words "Happy 40th Anniversary, Love Corinne" inscribed in a circle. Inside the circle it says "Milt & Clarice June 14." On our way out of the jeweler's, Ty suddenly stopped at a counter filled with diamonds. I asked him what he was looking for and he reminded me that I have a birthday coming up soon. Then he asked me what I'd buy if I was choosing a ring for myself. I was caught totally off-guard, but after thinking about it for a while, I can't help but wonder just what he has up his sleeve. Plus, Daddy made a strange comment earlier in the day when they were getting ready to leave for Denver. What was that he said, something about checking on the wedding? But then he corrected himself and said he meant anniversary. Then he laughed, winked at Ty and said "you know I only like chocolate!" I can't imagine what he meant by that. It probably was just some inside "guy" joke and nothing more, but still their strange exchange left me quite puzzled.

I have to close for now. I have to finish the afghan I'm sending to Maggie in London. Her youngest daughter, Marissa, is going to be confirmed in a couple weeks and I've crocheted a special commemorative afghan for her.

Enduring Love

Designed by Maggie Weldon

SIZE: 51½" x 70½".

MATERIALS: Worsted-weight yarn — 35 oz. winter white, 11 oz. each med. rose and green, 8 oz. lt. rose; tapestry needle; I crochet hook or size needed to obtain gauge.

GAUGE: Rnds 1-6 of Block = 5" across. Each Block is 9½" square.

SKILL LEVEL: ☆☆ Average

BLOCK (make 35)

NOTES: *For beginning popcorn (beg pc), ch 3, 3 dc in same sp, drop lp from hook, insert hook in top of ch-3, draw dropped lp through.*

For popcorn (pc), 4 dc in ring, drop lp from hook, insert hook in first st of 4-dc group, draw dropped lp through.

Rnd 1: With winter white, ch 4, sl st in first ch to form ring, beg pc, ch 2, (pc in ring, ch 2) 7 times, join with sl st in top of beg pc, fasten off (8 pc, 8 ch sps).

Rnd 2: Join lt. rose with sc in any ch sp, (2 dc, 2 tr, 2 dc, sc, sl st) in same sp, (sc, 2 dc, 2 tr, 2 dc, sc, sl st) in each ch sp around, join with sl st in first sc (8 petals).

Rnd 3: Working behind petals, ch 4, (sl st in next sp between petals, ch 4) around, join with sl st in joining sl st of last rnd, fasten off (8 ch sps).

Rnd 4: With med. rose, repeat rnd 2.

Rnd 5: Working behind petals, ch 5, (sl st in next sp between petals, ch 5) around, join with sl st in joining sl st of last rnd, fasten off.

Rnd 6: Join green with sc in any ch sp, ch 3, (2 dc, 3 tr, ch 2, 3 tr, 2 dc) in next ch sp, ch 3, *sc in next ch sp, ch 3, (2 dc, 3 tr, ch 2, 3 tr, 2 dc) in next ch sp, ch 3; repeat from * around, join with sl st in first sc, fasten off (44 sts, 8 ch-3 sps, 4 ch-2 sps).

Rnd 7: Join winter white with sc in any corner ch-2 sp, ch 3, sc in same sp, *[ch 3, skip next 2 sts, sc in next st, ch 3, skip next st, sc in next st, ch 3, skip next ch-3 sp, sc in next st, ch 3, skip next ch-3 sp, sc in next st, ch 3, skip next st, sc in next st, ch 3, skip next 2 sts], (sc, ch 3, sc) in next ch-2 sp; repeat from * 2 more times; repeat between [ ], join with sl st in first sc (6 ch sps across each side between corner ch sps).

Rnds 8-10: Sl st in first ch sp, ch 1, (sc, ch 3, sc) in same sp, ch 3, (sc in next ch sp, ch 3) across to next corner ch sp, *(sc, ch 3, sc) in next corner ch sp, ch 3, (sc in next ch sp, ch 3) across to next corner ch sp; repeat from * around, join, ending with 9 ch sps across each side between corner ch sps.

Rnd 11: Sl st in first ch sp, ch 3, (2 dc, ch 2, 3 dc) in same sp, 2 dc in next ch sp, (3 dc in next ch sp, 2 dc in next ch sp)

Continued on page 155

Dear Maggie,

Hello! Got your letter and the thank-you note from Marissa. She was so sweet to write what she did. You've got a great girl there, Maggie, but I'm sure you know that. I'm so pleased to hear that the guild has really come along. I knew your members would have what it takes to make a big contribution to the community. When you work as a team, you can do so much more than you can alone.

This will probably come as a shock, since I haven't written you in a long time, but Preston and I are no longer engaged. We broke it off awhile back, and you won't believe what's happened since. Preston and Ashley are engaged to be married in June and I'm coordinating the wedding. Now does that sound like the plot from a soap-opera or what? No, really. I had finally realized that the lives that Preston and I lead are just so different that we didn't stand a chance of actually making it together. As long as we had our separate lives we were okay, but every-time we tried to mix the two for very long it didn't work. Anyway, Ashley and Preston make a great pair, and I wish them all the happiness in the world.

Speaking of happiness, Mom and Dad will celebrate their 40th anniversary on June 14th. I have a huge party planned with a catered dinner and dancing and lots of champagne. I've enclosed a picture of the afghan I made them so you can see it, too.

Need to go now. Give Marissa a hug for me and write again soon.

Love, C—

Sunshine & Roses

Designed by Maggie Weldon

SIZE: 45½" x 67½".

MATERIALS: Worsted-weight yarn — 39 oz. maize, 18 oz. coral rose, 7 oz. each green and white; tapestry needle; G crochet hook or size needed to obtain gauge.

GAUGE: 4 sc = 1"; 4 sc rows = 1". Each Block is 11" square.

SKILL LEVEL: ☆☆ Average

BLOCK (make 24)

Row 1: With maize, ch 38, sc in 2nd ch from hook, sc in each ch across, turn (37 sc).

Row 2: Ch 1, sc in each st across, turn.

*NOTES: When changing colors (see page 159), always drop yarn to wrong side of work. Use a separate skein of yarn for each color section. **Do not** carry yarn across from one section to another. Fasten off colors at end of each color section.*

Work odd-numbered graph rows from right to left; work even-numbered rows from left to right.

Each square on graph equals one sc.

Row 3: For **row 3 of graph** (see page 156), ch 1, sc in first 30 sts changing to green in last st made, sc in each of next 3 sts changing to maize in last st made, sc in last 4 sts, turn.

Rows 4-37: Ch 1, sc in each st across changing colors according to graph, turn. At end of last row, **do not** turn.

Rnd 38: Working around outer edge in sts and in ends of rows, ch 1, skip first row, sc in next 35 rows, skip last row; working in starting ch on opposite side of row 1, 3 sc in first ch, sc in each ch across with 3 sc in last ch, skip first row, sc in next 35 rows, skip last row, 3 sc in first st, sc in each st across with 3 sc in last st, join with sl st in first sc, fasten off (37 sc across each side between center corner sts).

Rnd 39: Join white with sl st in any center corner st, ch 6, dc in same st, ch 1, skip next st, (dc in next st, ch 1, skip next st) across to next center corner st, *(dc, ch 3, dc) in next st, ch 1, skip next st, (dc in next st, ch 1, skip next st) across to next center corner st; repeat from * around, join with sl st in 3rd ch of ch-6, fasten off (20 dc and 19 ch-1 sps across each side between corner ch-3 sps).

Rnd 40: Join coral rose with sc in any corner ch-3 sp, 4 sc in same sp, 2 sc in each ch-1 sp around with 5 sc in each corner ch-3 sp, join with sl st in first sc, fasten off (42 sc across each side between center corner sts).

Holding Blocks wrong sides together, matching sts, with coral rose, sew together through **back lps** in 4 rows of 6 Blocks each according to Assembly Diagram on page 156.

EDGING

Working around entire outer edge, join coral rose with sl st in any center corner st, ch 3, (dc, ch 2, 2 dc) in same st, dc in each st around with (2 dc, ch 2, 2 dc) in each center corner st, join with sl st in top of ch-3, fasten off.❦

Dear Journal,

Didn't have time to write this morning, so thought I'd take advantage of the peace and quiet of the flight. We're to land in Chicago by three and tomorrow I begin working on the preparations for Preston and Ashley's wedding. I already have some ideas, but now just need to solidify them.

Tyler drove me to the airport this morning. Said he had to pick something up. Whatever it is, it must be important. Ty usually has everything delivered. While we were driving, he talked about some of his future plans for Morningside. He has some great ideas and I encouraged him to talk to Daddy about them. According to him, he's already discussed this all with him. He just wanted to get my input. That seems strange. Since when does my imput come into play. Oh, well. Maybe he's still in that mode from when Daddy was sick. I did manage to finish the afghan for Carol before we arrived in Denver. She's retiring soon to Florida and I plan to give it to her at the party we'll throw at the Youth Center next week.

Endless Romance

Designed by Maggie Weldon

SIZE: 63" x 84" not including Tassels.

MATERIALS: Worsted-weight yarn — 49 oz. black, 21 oz. red and 7 oz. green; tapestry needle; G crochet hook or size needed to obtain gauge.

GAUGE: Rnds 1-6 of Large Square = 3½" across. Each Large Square measures 10½" from point to point; each Small Square measures 4" from point to point.

SKILL LEVEL: ☆☆ Average

LARGE SQUARE (make 83)

Rnd 1: With red, ch 4, sl st in first ch to form ring, ch 1, (sc in ring, ch 3) 4 times, join with sl st in first sc (4 sc, 4 ch sps).

Rnd 2: (Sc, 4 dc, sc, sl st) in each ch sp around, **do not** join (4 petals).

Rnd 3: Working behind petals, ch 3, sl st in next sl st between petals, (ch 3, sl st in next sl st between petals) around, **do not** join (4 ch sps).

Rnd 4: (Sc, 5 dc, sl st, 5 dc, sc, sl st) in each ch sp around, **do not** join (8 petals).

Rnd 5: Repeat rnd 3, fasten off (8 ch sps).

NOTES: For **cluster (cl),** yo, insert hook in next ch sp, yo, draw lp through, yo, draw through 2 lps on hook, (yo, insert hook in same ch sp, yo, draw lp through, yo, draw through 2 lps on hook) 2 times, yo, draw through all 4 lps on hook.

For **beginning V-stitch (beg V-st),** ch 4, dc in same sp.

For **V-stitch (V-st),** (dc, ch 1, dc) in next ch sp.

Rnd 6: Join green with sc in any ch sp, ch 3, (cl, ch 3, cl) in next ch sp, ch 3, *sc in next ch sp, ch 3, (cl, ch 3, cl) in next ch sp, ch 3; repeat from * around, join with sl st in first sc, fasten off (12 ch sps, 8 cls, 4 sc).

Rnd 7: Join black with sl st in first ch sp, beg V-st, ch 1, (V-st, ch 3, V-st) in next ch sp, ch 1, *(V-st in next ch sp, ch 1) 2 times, (V-st, ch 3, V-st) in next ch sp, ch 1; repeat from * 2 more times, V-st in last ch sp, ch 1, join with sl st in 3rd ch of ch-4 (16 V-sts, 12 ch-1 sps, 4 ch-3 sps).

Rnds 8-9: Sl st in next ch-1 sp, sl st in next st, sl st in next ch-1 sp, beg V-st, ch 1, skip next V-st, (V-st, ch 3, V-st) in next ch-3 sp, ch 1, skip next V-st, *(V-st in next ch-1 sp, ch 1, skip next V-st) across to next corner ch-3 sp, (V-st, ch 3, V-st) in next ch-3 sp, ch 1, skip next V-st; repeat from * 2 more times, (V-st in next ch-1 sp, ch 1, skip next V-st)

Continued on page 156

Dear Ashley,

You'll never guess what happened. It came as a complete surprise to me — Tyler proposed. I tried to call, but you were gone, so I decided to write instead. I can't believe I never saw it coming. Mom and Dad are so happy they are practically beside themselves. They can't wait! We haven't set a date yet, but it will probably be in June. We may even get married on the 14th, the same day as their anniversary, just kill two birds with one stone.

After I got back from Chicago, Ty asked me over one evening saying he wanted some ideas on redecorating his bungalow. Well, you know me. I didn't think a thing of it and went right along never suspecting a thing! He'd cooked this fabulous chicken pasta dish and had wine and strawberries for dessert. After dinner we went to the living room supposedly to go over paint and fabric swatches. When I was showing him the new afghan I'd made for Juanita and Ben's anniversary, next thing I know he's down on his knees in front of me asking if I'll marry him. I was so stunned I couldn't say a word. He said he's been in love with me for years, but never said or did anything because he didn't want to ruin a good thing. At least living here he got to be around me, even if he couldn't have me. It was so touching I cried. He even had a bottle of my favorite chablis handy because he was so sure I'd say yes!

Oh, Ashley! I'm so happy. Life does give you second chances! I thought when I lost Steven that I'd never love like that again, but now I know better.

I have to go now. There's so much to do!

Love, C—

Dear Journal,

Through the journey of life, it seems some people are blessed beyond measure. But I believe those people are also given a responsiblity to share those blessing with others. I know I am one of those people. I have wonderful, loving parents who were fortunate enough to be able to give me everything that was good for me, but who were also wise enough to teach me the value of those things. I've been blessed with health, and with true friends like Ashley and Preston. I know their happiness is a source of strength to them, just as their continued friendship is to me. I was lucky enough to marry the love of my life, and thanks to my faith, didn't turn bitter when that life was taken from this world. This year, though, a new life has begun for me, along with Tyler. This loving, gentle man has stood by me through thick and thin, and has now pledged to stand by me for the rest of his life. Sometimes you don't appreciate home until you've traveled the world over, and sometimes you don't see what's right under your nose until your perspective changes. Each new day is a new opportunity to help make the world a better place. I pray I never lose my ability to do everything I can to make a difference — no matter how big or how small.

Mountain Sunrise

Continued from page 9

Rnd 6: Ch 3, *[(2 dc, ch 2, 2 dc) in next corner ch-2 sp, dc in each of next 2 sts; twist next ch lp of rnd 4 to right, dc in ch lp and in next st on last row at same time; dc in each of next 3 sts; twist next ch lp of rnd 2 to right, pull corresponding ch lp of rnd 4 through first lp, twist to right, dc in ch lp and in next st on last row at same time, dc in each of next 3 sts; twist next ch lp of rnd 4 to left, dc in ch lp and in next st of last row at same time], dc in each of next 2 sts; repeat from * 2 more times; repeat between [ ], dc in last st, join with sl st in top of ch-3, fasten off (17 sts across each side between corner ch sps).

Rnd 7: Join variegated with sc in any corner ch sp, 2 sc in same sp, sc in each st around with 3 sc in each corner ch sp, join with sl st in first sc, fasten off (19 sts across each side between center corner sts).

Holding Blocks wrong sides together, matching sts, with variegated, sew together through **back lps** in 6 rows of 9 Blocks each.

BORDER

Rnd 1: Join variegated with sc in center corner st before one short end, 2 sc in same st; working in corner sts on each side of seams, (skip next st, sc in each st across to next center corner st, 3 sc in next st, sc in each st across to next center corner st), 3 sc in next st; repeat between ( ), join with sl st in first sc (127 sc across each short end between center corner sts, 191 sc across each long edge between center corner sts).

Rnd 2: Sl st in next st, ch 1, (sc, ch 3, sc) in same st, *[ch 3, skip next st, (sc in next st, ch 3, skip next st) across] to next center corner st, (sc, ch 3, sc) in next st; repeat from * 2 more times; repeat between [ ], join, fasten off.❧

Faithful Friends

Continued from page 13

Holding Blocks wrong sides together, matching sts, with pink, sew together through **back lps** in 5 rows of 6 Blocks each.

BORDER

Working around entire outer edge, join pink with sl st in any corner ch sp, ch 3, (dc, ch 2, 2 dc) in same sp, dc in each st, in each ch sp on each side of seams and in each seam around with (2 dc, ch 2, 2 dc) in each corner ch sp, join with sl st in top of ch-3, fasten off.

FINISHING

For **eyes**, glue or sew 2 buttons to face of each cat according to Graph.

For **each Block**, cut piece black yarn 3" long; tie knot in center. Unravel yarn ends. For **whisker**, sew or glue centered below eyes of each cat according to Graph.❧

GRAPH

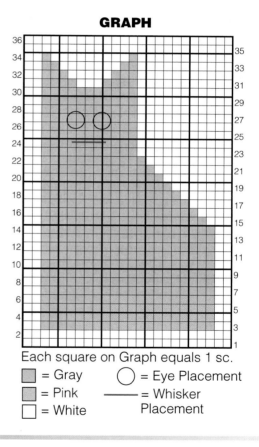

Each square on Graph equals 1 sc.

◼ = Gray ◯ = Eye Placement
◼ = Pink —— = Whisker
◻ = White Placement

Tropical Evening

Continued from page 15

next lg shell; repeat between **, join, **do not** turn, fasten off.

To **join Strips,** beginning and ending with sm shells on long edges, holding Strips wrong sides together, matching sts, working through both thicknesses in **back lps,** with green, sc in each st across leaving 22 sts on each end unworked, fasten off.

BORDER

Rnd 1: Working around entire outer edge, in **back lps** only, skipping seams, with G hook and green, join with sc in any st, sc in each st and in each ch around, join with sl st in first sc, fasten off.

Rnd 2: Working this rnd in **back lps** only, join blue with sl st in first st, ch 3, dc in each st around with 2 dc in st at each point and in each corner on each end of Strips, join with sl st in top of ch-3, fasten off. ❧

Grandma's Favorite

Continued from page 19

To **lace rows together,** lay 2 rows side by side on flat surface, beginning in corner ch lp on bottom left Motif, insert hook from bottom to top in first corner ch lp on this Motif and from top to bottom in corner ch lp on other Motif at same time, draw 2nd lp through; *insert hook from bottom to top in next lp on left Motif, draw lp through, insert hook from top to bottom in next lp on right Motif, draw lp through; repeat from * across joining secured lps as you work; secure last lp with safety pin to use when working Border.
Repeat with remaining 8 strips.

BORDER

Working from right to left, in ch lps around entire outer edge, beginning in any corner ch lp, insert hook from bottom to top in first 2 lps, draw 2nd lp through, *insert hook from bottom to top in next lp, draw lp through; repeat from * around to last ch lp joining secured lps as you work, twist last ch-12 lp left over right, draw last ch-12 lp through; to **join last ch lp to first ch lp,** tack top of last ch lp to base of first ch lp.❦

Roses & Lace

Continued from page 23

same as First Row Second Large Motif.

Second Large Motif

Rnds 1-7: Repeat same rnds of First Row First Large Motif.

Rnd 8: Ch 1, sc in first st; joining to bottom of next Motif on last row,*(ch 2, sl st in 3rd ch of corresponding ch sp on other Motif—see diagram, ch 2, skip next 2 sts on this Motif, sc in next st) 4 times*, (ch 5, skip next 2 sts, sc in next st) 4 times; joining to side of last Moitf on this row; repeat between **, ch 5, skip next 2 sts, (sc in next st, ch 5, skip next 2 sts) around, join with sl st in first sc, fasten off.

Repeat Second Large Motif 3 more times for a total of 5 Large Motifs.

Repeat Second Row 5 more times for a total of 7 Rows.

FILLER MOTIF

Rnds 1-2: Repeat same rnds of First Row First Large Motif.

Rnd 3: Joining to unworked ch-5 sps between Large Motifs, sl st in next ch sp, beg pc, ch 2, sl st in 3rd ch of any ch-5 sp on Large Motifs, (*ch 2, dc in next st on this Motif, ch 2, sl st in 3rd ch of next ch-5 sp on Large Motifs, ch 2*, pc in next ch sp on this Motif, ch 2, sl st in 3rd ch of next ch-5 sp on Large Motifs) 7 times; repeat between **, join with sl st in top of beg pc, fasten off.

Repeat in each sp between joined Large Motifs.

LEAVES (make 35)

With green, ch 20, sl st in 3rd ch from hook, *sc in next ch, hdc in each of next 3 chs, sc in next ch, sl st in next 6 chs, sc in next ch, hdc in each of next 3 chs, sc in next ch*, (sl st, ch 1, sl st) in last ch; working on opposite side of ch, repeat between **, join with sl st in next ch, fasten off.

Sew each pair of Leaves horizontally to center of each Large Motif.

ROSE (make 35)

Row 1: With burgundy, ch 8, 4 hdc in 3rd ch from hook, 4 hdc in each ch across, turn (25 hdc).

Row 2: Ch 3, skip first 2 sts, sl st in next st, (ch 3, skip next st, sl st in next st) across. Leaving 8" end for sewing, fasten off.

Roll into Rose shape; secure at bottom. Sew one Rose in center of each Motif over Leaves.❦

JOINING DIAGRAM

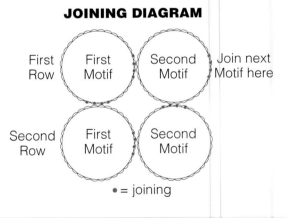

First Row — First Motif — Second Motif — Join next Motif here

Second Row — First Motif — Second Motif

• = joining

Wildflowers

Continued from page 25

*from *, yo, draw through all 4 lps on hook.*

Rnd 5: Join flower color as indicated in Flower Color Diagram on page 137 with sl st in any pc, beg tr-cl, *[(ch 5, tr-cl) 2 times in same st, ch 5, skip next ch sp, (sc in next ch sp, ch 5) 2 times, skip next ch sp], tr-cl in next pc; repeat from * 2 more times; repeat between [ ], join with sl st in top of beg tr-cl, fasten off (20 ch-5 sps, 12 tr-cls, 8 sc).

Rnd 6: Join variegated with sl st in 2nd tr-cl, beg dc-cl, ch 5, dc-cl in same st, *[ch 5, sc in next tr-cl, ch 5, skip next ch sp, (tr-cl, ch 5, tr-cl) in next ch sp, ch 5, skip next ch sp, sc in next tr-cl, ch 5], (dc-cl, ch 5, dc-cl) in next tr-cl; repeat from * 2 more times; repeat between [ ], join with sl st in top of beg dc-cl, fasten off.

Rnd 7: Join white with sl st in first ch-5 sp, beg dc-cl, ch 5, dc-cl in same sp, *[ch 4, skip next ch sp, (dc-cl, ch 5, dc-cl) in next sc, ch 4, skip next ch sp, (dc-cl, ch 5, dc-cl) in next ch sp, ch 4, skip next ch sp, (dc-cl, ch 5, dc-cl) in next sc, ch 4, skip next ch sp], (dc-cl, ch 5, dc-cl) in next ch sp; repeat from * 2 more times; repeat between [ ], join.

Rnd 8: Sl st in first ch sp, beg dc-cl, ch 5, dc-cl in same sp, ch 5, (sc in next ch sp, ch 5) 7 times, *(dc-cl, ch 5, dc-cl) in next ch sp, ch 5, (sc in next ch sp, ch 5) 7 times; repeat from * around, join, fasten off (36 ch-5 sps).

Rnd 9: Join dk. green with sl st in first corner ch sp, beg dc-cl, ch 5, dc-cl in same sp, ch 5, (sc in next ch sp, ch 5) 8 times, *(dc-cl, ch 5, dc-cl) in next corner ch sp, ch 5, (sc in next ch sp, ch 5) 8 times; repeat from * around, join, fasten off (40 ch-5 sps).

Second Motif
Rnds 1-8: Repeat same rnds of First Motif.

Rnd 9: Join dk. green with sl st in first corner ch sp, beg dc-cl; joining to side of last Motif, ch 2, sl st in corresponding corner ch sp on other Motif, ch 2, dc-cl in same sp on this Motif, ch 2, sl st in next ch sp on other Motif, ch 2, (sc in next ch sp on this Motif, ch 2, sl st in next ch sp on other Motif, ch 2) 8 times, dc-cl in next corner ch sp on this Motif, ch 2, sl st in next corner ch sp on other Motif, ch 2, dc-cl in same sp on this Motif, ch 5, (sc in next ch sp, ch 5) 8 times, *(dc-cl, ch 5, dc-cl) in next corner ch sp, ch 5, (sc in next ch sp, ch 5) 8 times; repeat from * around, join, fasten off.

Repeat Second Motif 2 more times for a total of 4 Motifs.

SECOND ROW
First Motif
Joining to bottom of First Motif on last row, work same as First Row Second Motif.

Second Motif
Rnds 1-8: Repeat same rnds of First Row First Motif.

Rnd 9: Join dk. green with sl st in first corner ch sp; joining to bottom of next Motif on last row, beg dc-cl, ch 2, sl st in corresponding corner ch sp on other Motif, ch 2, dc-cl in same sp on this Motif, *ch 2, sl st in next ch sp on other Motif, ch 2, (sc in next ch sp on this Motif, ch 2, sl st in next ch sp on other Motif, ch 2) 8 times, dc-cl in next corner ch sp on this Motif, ch 2, sl st in next corner ch sp on other Motif, ch 2, dc-cl in same sp on this Motif*; joining to side of last Motif on this row, repeat between **, ch 5, (sc in next ch sp, ch 5) 8 times, (dc-cl, ch 5, dc-cl) in next corner ch sp, ch 5, (sc in next ch sp, ch 5) 8 times, join, fasten off.

Repeat Second Motif 2 more times for a total of 4 Motifs.
Repeat Second Row 3 more times for a total of 5 Rows.

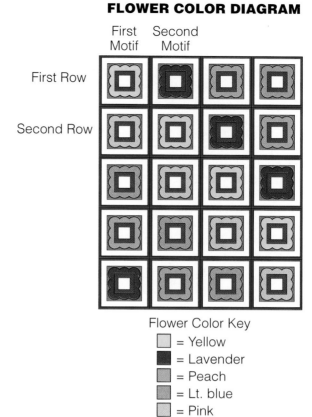

FLOWER COLOR DIAGRAM

First Motif · Second Motif

First Row

Second Row

Flower Color Key
☐ = Yellow
■ = Lavender
▨ = Peach
▨ = Lt. blue
☐ = Pink

EDGING
Working around outer edge, join white with sl st in any corner ch sp, beg tr-cl, (ch 5, tr-cl) 2 times in same sp, ◊•ch 4, sc in next ch sp, *(dc-cl, ch 4, tr-cl, ch 4, dc-cl) in next ch sp, sc in next ch sp*; repeat between ** 3 more times, [ch 4, skip next ch sp, (tr-cl, ch 4, tr-cl, ch 4, tr-cl) in next joining sl st, ch 4, skip next ch sp, sc in next ch sp; repeat between ** 4 more times]; repeat between [ ] across to next corner ch sp•, (tr-cl, ch 5, tr-cl, ch 5, tr-cl) in next corner ch sp; repeat from ◊ 2 more times; repeat between ••, join with sl st in top of beg tr-cl, fasten off.❦

Midnight Mosaic

Continued from page 27

repeat between [ ], join, fasten off.

NEXT STRIP (make 9)
Flowers
Work same as First Strip's Flowers on page 27.

Border
Rnd 1: Repeat same rnd of First Strip's Border.

Rnd 2: Sl st in each of next 2 sts, sl st in next ch-3 sp, ch 3, (2 dc, ch 2, 3 dc) in same sp, (2 dc, ch 1, 2 dc) in next ch-1 sp; joining to last Strip made, 3 dc in next ch-1 sp, ch 1, drop lp from hook, insert hook in 2nd ch of corresponding ch-3 sp on last Strip, draw dropped lp through, ch 1, 3 dc in same sp on this Strip, (skip next ch-1 sp, dc in next tr, skip next ch-1 sp, 3 dc in next ch-1 sp, ch 1, drop lp from hook, insert hook in 2nd ch of next ch-3 sp on last Strip, ch 1, draw dropped lp through, 3 dc in same sp on this Strip) 29 times, (2 dc, ch 1, 2 dc) in next ch-1 sp, (3 dc, ch 2, 3 dc) in next ch-3 sp, (2 dc, ch 1, 2 dc) in next ch-1 sp, (3 dc, ch 3, 3 dc) in next ch-1 sp, *skip next ch-1 sp, dc in next tr, skip next ch-1 sp, (3 dc, ch 3, 3 dc) in next ch-1 sp; repeat from * 28 more times, (2 dc, ch 1, 2 dc) in last ch-1 sp, join, fasten off.

TASSEL (make 20)
Cut 30 strands desired color scrap yarn each 12" long. Tie separate strand same color tightly around middle of all strands; fold strands in half. Wrap another strand of same color around all strands 1½" from top of fold; secure and hide ends inside Tassel. Trim all ends evenly.

Tie one Tassel to ch sp at tip of each Strip on each short end of Afghan.❦

Eternal Blooms

Continued from page 29

sp on next rnd after same (sl st, ch 5, sl st) group, ch 1, sc in next ch-1 sp on last rnd, ch 3, sc in next ch-1 sp, ch 1, sl st in 2nd ch of corresponding ch-3 sp on other Motif, ch 1 (see diagram), sc in next ch-1 sp on this Motif, ch 3, sc in next ch-1 sp, ch 1*, sl st in next ch-2 sp on rnd 3 before next (sl st, ch 5, sl st) group on last rnd; repeat between **; [sl st in next ch-2 sp of rnd 3 before next (sl st, ch 5, sl st) group on last rnd, ch 3, (sl st in next ch-2 sp on next rnd, ch 3) 2 times, sl st in ring between next 2 dc on rnd 1, ch 3, (sl st in same ch-2 sp on next rnd, ch 3) 2 times, sl st in same ch-2 sp on next rnd after same (sl st, ch 5, sl st) group, ch 1, sc in next ch-1 sp on last rnd, (ch 3, sc in next ch-1 sp) 3 times, ch 1]; repeat between [ ] around, join with sl st in first sl st, fasten off.

Repeat Second Motif 10 more times for a total of 12 Motifs.

SECOND ROW
First Motif

Rnds 1-3: Repeat same rnds of First Row First Motif.

Rnd 4: Sl st in next st, sl st in next ch-1 sp, ch 4, dc in same sp, (ch 1, dc in same sp) 3 times, sl st in next ch-2 sp; joining to First Motif on last row, ch 2, sl st in 3rd ch of ch-5 sp on other Motif (see point A on diagram), ch 2, sl st in same sp on this Motif, dc in next ch-1 sp, (ch 1, dc in same sp) 4 times, sl st in next ch-2 sp; joining to next Motif on last row, ch 2, sl st in 3rd ch of next ch-5 sp on other Motif (see point B), ch 2, sl st in same sp on this Motif, *dc in next ch-1 sp, (ch 1, dc in same sp) 4 times, (sl st, ch 5, sl st) in next ch-2 sp; repeat from * around, join with sl st in 3rd ch of ch-4, fasten off.

Rnd 5: Working over top of rnds 1-4, join dk. peach with sl st in ch-2 sp of rnd 3 before last (sl st, ch 5, sl st) group on last rnd, *ch 3, (sl st in next ch-2 sp on next rnd, ch 3) 2 times, sl st in ring between next 2 dc on rnd 1, ch 3, (sl st in same ch-2 sp on next rnd, ch 3) 2 times, sl st in same ch-2 sp on next rnd after same (sl st, ch 5, sl st) group, ch 1, sc in next ch-1 sp on last rnd, ch 3, sc in next ch-1 sp*, ch 1, sl st in 2nd ch of corresponding ch-3 sp on other (see point 1), ch 1, sc in next ch-1 sp on this Motif, ch 3, sc in next ch-1 sp, ch 1, sl st in ch-2 sp on rnd 3 before next (sl st, ch 5, sl st) group on last rnd; repeat between **, ch 1, sl st in joining sl st between last Motif and next Motif on last row (see point 2), ch 1, sc in next ch-1 sp on this Motif, ch 3, sc in next ch-1 sp, ch 1, sl st in ch-2 sp on rnd 3 before next (sl st, ch 5, sl st) group on last rnd; repeat between **, ch 1, sl st in 2nd ch of corresponding ch-3 sp on other Motif (see point 3), ch 1, sc in next ch-1 sp on this Motif, ch 3, sc in next ch-1 sp, ch 1, [sl st in ch-2 sp on rnd 3 before next (sl st, ch 5, sl st) group on last rnd, ch 3, (sl st in next ch-2 sp on next rnd, ch 3) 2 times, sl st in ring between next 2 dc on rnd 1, ch 3, (sl st in same ch-2 sp on next rnd, ch 3) 2 times, sl st in same ch-2 sp on next rnd after same (sl st, ch 5, sl st) group, ch 1, sc in next ch-1 sp on last rnd, (ch 3, sc in next ch-1 sp) 3 times, ch 1]; repeat between [ ] around, join with sl st in first sl st, fasten off.

Second Motif

Rnds 1-3: Repeat same rnds of First Row First Motif.

Rnd 4: Sl st in next st, sl st in next ch-1 sp, ch 4, dc in same sp, (ch 1, dc in same sp) 3 times, sl st in next ch-2 sp; joining to last Motif on this row, ch 2, sl st in 3rd ch of center bottom ch-5 sp on other Motif (see point C), ch 2, sl st in same sp on this Motif, dc in next ch-1 sp, (ch 1, dc in same sp) 4 times, sl st in next ch-2 sp; joining to next Motif on last row, ch 2, sl st in 3rd ch of next unworked ch-5 sp on other Motif (see point D), ch 2, sl st in same sp on this Motif, dc in next ch-1 sp, (ch 1, dc in same sp) 4 times, sl st in next ch-2 sp; joining to next Motif on last row, ch 2, sl st in 3rd ch of next unworked ch-5 sp on other Motif (see point E), ch 2, sl st in same sp on this Motif, *dc in next ch-1 sp, (ch 1, dc in same sp) 4 times, (sl st, ch 5, sl st) in next ch-2 sp; repeat from * around, join with sl st in 3rd ch of ch-4, fasten off.

Rnd 5: Working over top of rnds 1-4, join dk. peach with sl st in ch-2 sp of rnd 3 before last (sl st, ch 5, sl st) group on last rnd, *ch 3, (sl st in next ch-2 sp on next rnd, ch 3) 2 times, sl st in ring between next 2 dc on rnd 1, ch 3, (sl st in same ch-2 sp on next rnd, ch 3) 2 times, sl st in same ch-2 sp on next rnd after same (sl st, ch 5, sl st) group, ch 1, sc in next ch-1 sp on rnd 4, ch 3, sc in next ch-1 sp*, ch 1, sl st in 2nd ch of corresponding ch-3 sp on other Motif (see point 4), ch 1, sc in next ch-1 sp on this Motif, ch 3, sc in next ch-1 sp, ch 1, sl st in next ch-2 sp on rnd 3 before next (sl st, ch 5, sl st) group; repeat between **, ch 1, sl st in joining sl st between last Motif on this row and next Motif on last row (see point 5), ch 1, sc in next ch-1 sp on this Motif, ch 3, sc in next ch-1 sp, ch 1, sl st in next ch-2 sp on rnd 3 before next (sl st, ch 5, sl st) group; repeat between **, ch 1, sl st in joining sl st between last Motif and next Motif on last row (see point 6), ch 1, sc in next ch-1 sp on this Motif, ch 3, sc in next ch-1 sp, ch 1, sl st in next ch-2 sp on rnd 3 before next (sl st, ch 5, sl st) group; repeat between **, ch 1, sl st in 2nd ch of next ch-3 sp on other Motif (see point 7), ch 1, sc in next ch-1 sp on this Motif, ch 3, sc in next ch-1 sp, ch 1, [sl st in next ch-2 sp on rnd 3 before next (sl st, ch 5, sl st) group, ch 3, (sl st in next ch-2 sp on next rnd, ch 3) 2 times, sl st in ring between next 2 dc on rnd 1, ch 3, (sl st in same ch-2 sp on next rnd, ch 3) 2 times, sl st in same ch-2 sp on next rnd after same (sl st, ch 5, sl st) group, ch 1, sc in next ch-1 sp on rnd 4, (ch 3, sc in next ch-1 sp) 3 times, ch 1]; repeat between [ ] around, join with sl st in first sl st, fasten off.

Repeat Second Motif 9 more times for a total of 11 Motifs.

THIRD ROW
First Motif

Rnds 1-3: Repeat same rnds of First Row First Motif.

Rnd 4: Sl st in next st, sl st in next ch-1 sp, ch 4, dc in same sp, (ch 1, dc in same sp) 3 times, sl st in next ch-2 sp; joining to First Motif on last row, ch 2, sl st in 3rd ch of corresponding ch-5 sp on other Motif (see point F), ch 2, sl st in same sp on this Motif, *dc in next ch-1 sp, (ch 1, dc in same sp) 4 times, (sl st, ch 5, sl st) in next ch-2 sp; repeat from * around, join with sl st in 3rd ch of ch-4, fasten off.

Rnd 5: Working over top of rnds 1-4, join dk. peach with sl st in ch-2 sp of rnd 3 before last (sl st, ch 5, sl st) group on last rnd, *ch 3, (sl st in next ch-2 sp on next rnd, ch 3) 2 times, sl st in ring between next 2 dc on rnd 1, ch 3, (sl st in same ch-2 sp on next rnd, ch 3) 2 times, sl st in same ch-2 sp on next rnd after same (sl st, ch 5, sl st) group, ch 1, sc in next ch-1 sp on rnd 4, ch 3, sc in next ch-1 sp*, ch 1, sl st in 2nd ch of corresponding ch-3 sp on other Motif (see point 8), ch 1, sc in next ch-1 sp on this Motif, ch 3, sc in next ch-1 sp, ch 1, sl st in next ch-2 sp on rnd 3 before next (sl st, ch 5, sl st) group; repeat between **, ch 1, sl st in 2nd ch of next ch-3 sp on other Motif (see point 9), ch 1, sc in next ch-1 sp on this Motif, ch 3, sc in next ch-1 sp, ch 1, [sl st in ch-2 sp of rnd 3 before next (sl st, ch 5, sl st) group on last rnd, ch 3, (sl st in next ch-2 sp on next rnd, ch 3) 2 times, sl st in ring between next 2 dc on rnd 1, ch 3, (sl st in same ch-2 sp on next rnd, ch 3) 2 times, sl st in same ch-2 sp on next rnd after same (sl st, ch 5, sl st) group, ch 1, sc in next ch-1 sp on rnd 4, (ch 3, sc in next ch-1 sp) 3 times, ch 1]; repeat between [ ] around, join with sl st in first sl st, fasten off.

Second Motif

Rnds 1-3: Repeat same rnds of First Row First Motif.

Rnd 4: Sl st in next st, sl st in next ch-1 sp, ch 4, dc in same sp, (ch 1, dc in same sp) 3 times, sl st in next ch-2 sp; joining to last Motif on this row, ch 2, sl st in 3rd ch of center bottom ch-5 sp on last Motif (see point G), ch 2, sl st in same sp on this Motif, dc in next ch-1 sp, (ch 1, dc in same sp) 4 times, sl st in next ch-2 sp; joining to next Motif on last row, ch 2, sl st in 3rd ch of next unworked ch-5 sp on other Motif (see point H), ch 2, sl st in same sp on this Motif, dc in next ch-1 sp, (ch 1, dc in same sp) 4 times, sl st in next ch-2 sp; joining to next Motif on last row, ch 2, sl st in 3rd ch of next unworked ch-5 sp on other Motif (see point I), ch 2, sl st in same sp on this Motif, *dc in next ch-1 sp, (ch 1, dc in same sp) 4 times, (sl st, ch 5, sl st) in next ch-2 sp; repeat from * around, join with sl st in 3rd ch of ch-4, fasten off.

Rnd 5: Working over top of rnds 1-4, join dk. peach with sl st in ch-2 sp of rnd 3 before last (sl st, ch 5, sl st) group on last rnd, *ch 3, (sl st in next ch-2 sp on next rnd, ch 3) 2 times, sl st in ring between next 2 dc on rnd 1, ch 3, (sl st in same ch-2 sp on next rnd, ch 3) 2 times, sl st in same ch-2 sp on next rnd after same (sl st, ch 5, sl st) group, ch 1, sc in next ch-1 sp on rnd 4, ch 3, sc in next ch-1 sp*, ch 1, sl st in 2nd ch of corresponding ch-3 sp on other Motif (see point 10), ch 1, sc in next ch-1 sp on this Motif, ch 3, sc in next ch-1 sp, ch 1, sl st in next ch-2 sp on rnd 3 before next (sl st, ch 5, sl st) group; repeat between **, ch 1, sl st in joining sl st between last Motif on this row and next Motif on last row (see point 11), ch 1, sc in next ch-1 sp on this Motif, ch 3, sc in next ch-1 sp, ch 1, sl st in next ch-2 sp on rnd 3 before next (sl st, ch 5, sl st) group; repeat between **, ch 1, sl st in joining sl st between last Motif and next Motif on last row (see point 12), ch 1, sc in next ch-1 sp on this Motif, ch 3, sc in next ch-1 sp, ch 1, sl st in next ch-2 sp on rnd 3 before next (sl st, ch 5, sl st) group; repeat between **, ch 1, sl st in 2nd ch of next ch-3 sp on other Motif (see point 13), ch 1, sc in next ch-1 sp on this Motif, ch 3, sc in next ch-1 sp, ch 1, [sl st in next ch-2 sp on rnd 3 before next (sl st, ch 5, sl st) group, ch 3, (sl st in next ch-2 sp on next rnd, ch 3) 2 times, sl st in ring between next 2 dc on rnd 1, ch 3, (sl st in same ch-2 sp on next rnd, ch 3) 2 times, sl st in same ch-2 sp on next rnd after same (sl st, ch 5, sl st) group, ch 1, sc in next ch-1 sp on rnd 4, (ch 3, sc in next ch-1 sp) 3 times, ch 1]; repeat between [ ] around, join with sl st in first sl st, fasten off.

Repeat Second Motif 8 more times for a total of 11 Motifs.

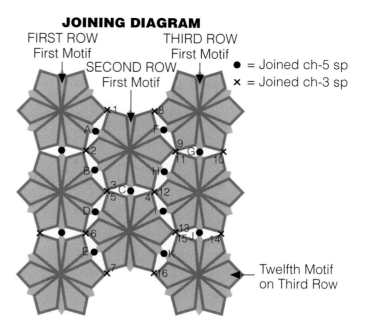

JOINING DIAGRAM

FIRST ROW
First Motif

THIRD ROW
First Motif

SECOND ROW
First Motif

● = Joined ch-5 sp
✕ = Joined ch-3 sp

Twelfth Motif
on Third Row

Twelfth Motif

Rnds 1-3: Repeat same rnds of First Row First Motif.

Rnd 4: Sl st in next st, sl st in next ch-1 sp, ch 4, dc in same sp, (ch 1, dc in same sp) 3 times, sl st in next ch-2 sp; joining to last Motif on this row, ch 2, sl st in 3rd ch of center bottom ch-5 sp on last Motif (see point J), ch 2, sl st in same sp on this Motif, dc in next ch-1 sp, (ch 1, dc in same sp) 4 times, sl st in next ch-2 sp; joining to next Motif on last row, ch 2, sl st in 3rd ch of next unworked ch-5 sp on other Motif (see point K), ch 2, sl st in same sp on this Motif, *dc in next ch-1 sp, (ch 1, dc in same sp) 4 times, (sl st, ch 5, sl st) in next ch-2 sp; repeat from * around, join with sl st in 3rd ch of ch-4, fasten off.

Rnd 5: Working over top of rnds 1-4, join dk. peach with sl st in ch-2 sp of rnd 3 before last (sl st, ch 5, sl st) group on last rnd, *ch 3, (sl st in next ch-2 sp on next rnd, ch 3) 2 times, sl st in ring between next 2 dc on rnd 1, ch 3, (sl st in same ch-2 sp on next rnd, ch 3) 2 times, sl st in same ch-2 sp on next rnd after same (sl st, ch 5, sl st) group, ch 1, sc in next ch-1 sp on rnd 4, ch 3, sc in next ch-1 sp*, ch 1, sl st in 2nd ch of corresponding ch-3 sp on other Motif (see point 14), ch 1, sc in next ch-1 sp on this Motif, ch 3, sc in next ch-1 sp, ch 1, sl st in next ch-2 sp on rnd 3 before next (sl st, ch 5, sl st) group; repeat between **, ch 1, sl st in joining sl st between last Motif on this row and next Motif on last row (see point 15), ch 1, sc in next ch-1 sp on this Motif, ch 3, sc in next ch-1 sp, ch 1, sl st in next ch-2 sp on rnd 3 before next (sl st, ch 5, sl st) group; repeat between **, ch 1, sl st in 2nd ch of corresponding ch-3 sp on other Motif (see point 16), ch 1, sc in next ch-1 sp on this Motif, ch 3, sc in next ch-1 sp, ch 1, [sl st in next ch-2 sp on rnd 3 before next (sl st, ch 5, sl st) group, ch 3, (sl st in next ch-2 sp on next rnd, ch 3) 2 times, sl st in ring between next 2 dc on rnd 1, ch 3, (sl st in same ch-2 sp on next rnd, ch 3) 2 times, sl st in same ch-2 sp on next rnd after same (sl st, ch 5, sl st) group, ch 1, sc in next ch-1 sp on last row, (ch 3, sc in next ch-1 sp) 3 times, ch 1]; repeat between [ ] around, join with sl st in first sl st, fasten off.

Repeat Second and Third Rows alternately 3 times for a total of 9 rows.❦

Anticipation

Instructions on page 33

ASSEMBLY DIAGRAM

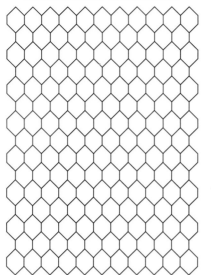

Sculpted Sapphires

Continued from page 37

Row 22: Repeat row 2.
Row 23: Ch 1, sc in each st across skipping ch sps, turn.
Row 24: Ch 1, sc in each st across, turn, fasten off.
Rows 25-164: Repeat rows 11-24 consecutively.

FRINGE

For **each Fringe,** cut 12 strands yarn each 16" long. Holding all strands together, fold in half, insert hook in end of row, draw fold through, draw all loose ends through fold, tighten. Trim ends.

Make one lt. blue Fringe in end of center row on each lt. blue section; make 2 dk. blue Fringe evenly spaced across ends of each dk. blue section.❦

Grandiloquence

Continued from page 41

1, (sc, ch 2, sc) in first ch, sc in each ch across to last ch, (sc, ch 2, sc) in last ch; repeat between **, join with sl st in first sc, **turn** (135 sc across each short end between corner ch sps, 161 sc across each long edge between corner ch sps).

Rnd 2: Ch 1, sc in first st, *[(puff st, sc in next st) across to next corner ch sp, (sc, ch 2, sc) in next ch sp], sc in next st; repeat from * 2 more times; repeat between [ ], join, **turn.**

Rnd 3: Ch 1, sc in each st around with (sc, ch 2, sc) in each corner ch sp, join, **turn.**

Rnd 4: Ch 1, sc in first st, *(puff st, sc in next st) across to next corner ch sp, (sc, ch 2, sc) in next ch sp, sc in next st; repeat from * 3 more times, puff st in last st, join, **turn.**

Rnd 5: Repeat rnd 3.

Rnd 6: Ch 1, sc in first st, *[(puff st in next st, sc in next st) across to next corner ch sp, (sc, ch 2, sc) in next ch sp], sc in next st; repeat from * 2 more times; repeat between [ ], (sc in next st, puff st) 2 times, join, **turn.**

Rnd 7: Repeat rnd 3.❦

Carved Ivory

Continued from page 43

next st, cr st across to last st, dc in last st, fasten off.

Rows 13-15: Working these rows in **back lps** only, join soft white with sc in first st, sc in each st across, fasten off. At end of last row, **turn.**

Rows 16-96: Repeat rows 8-15 consecutively, ending with row 8.

Rows 97-103: Working these rows in **back lps** only, join soft white with sc in first st, sc in each st across, fasten off.

For **each fringe,** tie 6" ends at ends of rows in Overhand Knot (see illustration) in groups of 3, ending with last fringe in a group of 4. Trim to desired length.❦

OVERHAND KNOT

City Lights

Continued from page 47

on this Motif, skip next 2 sts, sc in sp between last skipped st and next st, 5 dc in next shell, ch 1, drop lp from hook, insert hook in center ch of next ch-3 sp on other Motif, draw dropped lp through, ch 1, 5 dc in same sp on this Motif, *[skip next 3 sts, sc in sp between last skipped st and next

st, (3 sc, ch 1, 3 sc) in next ch-2 sp, skip next 2 sts, sc in sp between last skipped st and next st], (5 dc, ch 3, 5 dc) in next shell; repeat from *; repeat between [ ], join, fasten off.
Repeat Second Motif 7 more times for a total of 9 Motifs.

SECOND ROW
First Motif
Joining to bottom of First Motif on last row, work same as First Row Second Motif.

Second Motif

Rnds 1-3: Repeat same rnds of First Row First Motif.

Rnd 4: Join black with sl st in first shell, ch 3, 4 dc in same sp; joining to bottom of next Motif on last row (see diagram), ch 1, drop lp from hook, insert hook in center ch of corresponding ch-3 sp on other Motif, draw dropped lp through, ch 1, 5 dc in same sp on this Motif, *skip next 3 sts, sc in sp between last skipped st and next st, 3 sc in next ch-2 sp, drop lp from hook, insert hook in next ch-1 sp on other Motif, draw dropped lp through, 3 sc in same sp on this Motif, skip next 2 sts, sc in sp between last skipped st and next st, 5 dc in next shell, ch 1, drop lp from hook, insert hook in center ch of next ch-3 sp on other Motif, draw dropped lp through, ch 1, 5 dc in same sp on this Motif*; joining to side of last Motif on this row; repeat between **, [skip next 3 sts, sc in sp between last skipped st and next st, (3 sc, ch 1, 3 sc) in next ch-2 sp, skip next 2 sts, sc in sp between last skipped st and next st], (5 dc, ch 3, 5 dc) in next shell; repeat between [ ], join, fasten off.

Repeat Second Motif 7 more times for a total of 9 Motifs.

Repeat Second Row 10 more times for a total of 12 rows.

BORDER

Working around entire outer edge, join black with sl st in any corner ch-3 sp, ch 3, (4 dc, ch 3, 5 dc) in same sp, ◊●*[skip next 2 dc, sc in next dc, skip next 2 dc, sc in next sc, (2 sc, ch 1, 2 sc) in next ch-1 sp, skip next 3 sc, sc in next sc, skip next 2 dc, sc in next dc], (5 dc, ch 1, 5 dc) in next joining between Motifs; repeat from * across to last Motif before next corner; repeat between [ ]●, (5 dc, ch 3, 5 dc) in next corner ch-3 sp; repeat from ◊ 2 more times; repeat between ●●, join with sl st in top of ch-3, fasten off.🐦

JOINING DIAGRAM

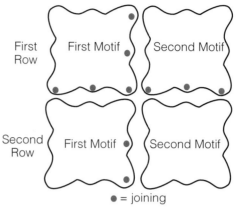

● = joining

Circles of Love

Continued from page 51

around with (2 dc, ch 2, 2 dc) in each corner ch sp, join with sl st in top of ch-3, fasten off (169 dc on each short end between corner ch sps, 217 dc across each long edge between corner ch sps).

EDGING

Row 1: Working across one short end of Afghan, join navy with sc in first corner ch sp, ch 5, skip next st, (sc in next st, ch 5, skip next 2 sts) across to next corner ch sp, sc in next corner ch sp leaving remaining sts unworked, turn (57 ch sps).

Row 2: Ch 7, sc in next ch sp, (ch 5, sc in next ch sp) across, ch 3, tr in last st, turn.

Row 3: Ch 1, sc in first st, ch 5, (sc in next ch sp, ch 5) across to last ch sp, sc in 4th ch of ch-7, fasten off.

Repeat on other short end of Afghan.

FRINGE

For **each Fringe,** cut 6 strands green each 14" long. Holding all strands together, fold in half, insert hook in ch sp, draw fold through, draw all loose ends through fold, tighten. Trim ends.

Fringe in each ch sp across each short end of Afghan.🐦

Musical Days

Continued from page 55

med. purple, repeat Next Strip 20 more times, ending with dk. purple and 22 strips.

BORDER

Rnd 1: Working around entire outer edge of Strips, join green with sl st in center top of right-hand end Strip, ch 7, (sl st around side of next joining sc between Strips, ch 7, sl st in center top of next Strip, ch 7) 21 times; working across side of Strip, (sl st in next ch-2 sp, ch 7) across; working in ends of Strips, sl st in center bottom of next Strip, ch 7, (sl st around side of next joining sc between Strips, ch 7, sl st in center bottom of next Strip, ch 7) 21 times; working across side of opposite end Strip, (sl st in next ch-2 sp, ch 7) across, join with sl st in first sl st.

NOTE: *For leaf cluster (leaf cl), *yo 2 times, insert hook in ch sp, yo, draw lp through, (yo, draw through 2 lps on hook) 2 times; repeat from * 2 more times in same sp, yo, draw through all 4 lps on hook.*

Rnd 2: Sl st in first ch-7 sp, (ch 4, leaf cl, ch 3, sl st) 2 times in same sp, *sl st in next ch sp, (ch 4, leaf cl, ch 3, sl st) 2 times in same sp; repeat from * around, join with sl st in first sl st, fasten off.🐦

Love's Devotion

Continued from page 59

ch across with 3 sc in last ch, skip first row, sc in next 23 rows, skip last row, 3 sc in first st, sc in next 23 sts, 3 sc in last st, join with sl st in first sc, fasten off (25 sc across each side between center corner sts).

Rnd 27: Join purple with sl st in any center corner st, ch 3, (dc, ch 2, 2 dc) in same st, dc in each st around with (2 dc, ch 2, 2 dc) in each corner st, join with sl st in top of ch-3, fasten off.

Holding Blocks wrong sides together, matching sts, with

Continued on next page

Love's Devotion

Continued from page 141

purple, sew together through **back lps** in 5 rows of 7 Blocks each.

BORDER

Rnd 1: Working around outer edge, join white with sc in any corner ch sp, 2 sc in same sp, sc in each st and in each ch sp on each side of seams around with 3 sc in each corner ch sp, join with sl st in first sc, fasten off.

Rnd 2: Join green with sl st in any center corner st, ch 3, (dc, ch 2, 2 dc) in same st, dc in each st around with (2 dc, ch 2, 2 dc) in each center corner st, join with sl st in top of ch-3, fasten off.❦

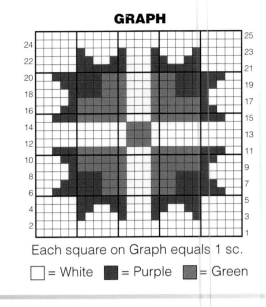

GRAPH

Each square on Graph equals 1 sc.

☐ = White   ■ = Purple   ▨ = Green

Country Communion

Instructions on page 57

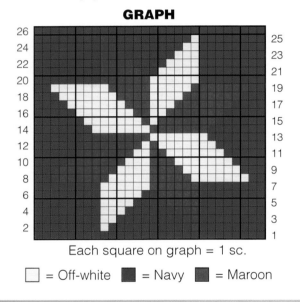

GRAPH

Each square on graph = 1 sc.

☐ = Off-white   ■ = Navy   ▨ = Maroon

Rave Reviews

Continued from page 61

same sp, *ch 3, skip next st, (sc in next st, ch 3, skip next st) across to next corner ch sp, (sc, ch 3, sc) in next ch sp, (ch 3, skip next st, sc in next st) across to next corner ch sp, ch 3*, (sc, ch 3, sc) in next ch sp; repeat between **, join with sl st in first sc, fasten off.

Rnd 97: Join navy with sl st in first corner ch sp, ch 3, (dc, ch 2, 2 dc) in same sp, 2 dc in each ch sp around with (2 dc, ch 2, 2 dc) in each corner ch sp, join with sl st in top of ch-3, fasten off.

Holding Strips wrong sides together, matching sts, with navy, sew long edges together through **back lps.**

EDGING

Working around entire outer edge, join navy with sl st in any corner ch sp, ch 3, (dc, ch 2, 2 dc) in same sp, dc in each st, in each ch sp on each side of seams and in each seam around with (2 dc, ch 2, 2 dc) in each corner ch sp, join with sl st in top of ch-3, fasten off.❦

Royal Bows

Continued from page 65

around with (2 dc, ch 2, 2 dc) in each corner ch sp, join with sl st in top of ch-3, fasten off (153 dc across each short end between corner ch sps, 213 dc across each long edge between corner ch sps).

Rnd 2: Join lt. blue with sc in any corner ch sp, (ch 3, sc) in same sp, ch 3, skip next st, (sc in next st, ch 3, skip next st) across to next corner ch sp, *(sc, ch 3, sc) in next ch sp, ch 3, skip next st, (sc in next st, ch 3, skip next st) across to next corner ch sp; repeat from * around, join with sl st in first sc, fasten off.❦

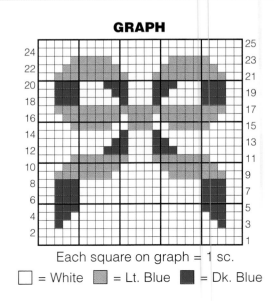

GRAPH

Each square on graph = 1 sc.

☐ = White   ▨ = Lt. Blue   ■ = Dk. Blue

Picot Paradox

Continued from page 67

in 3rd ch of ch-6, fasten off (36 picots, 4 ch-3 sps).

Second Large Motif
Rnds 1-6: Repeat same rnds of First Large Motif.
NOTES: *For **joining picot**, ch 1, sl st in corresponding picot on other Large Motif, ch 1, sl st in top of last st made on this Large Motif.*
Join Large Motifs according to Joining Diagram.
Rnd 7: Ch 6, sl st in 3rd ch from hook, ch 2, (dc in next dc, picot, ch 2) 5 times, dc in next dc; joining to side of last Large Motif made, work joining picot, (ch 2, dc in next dc on this Large Motif, work joining picot) 2 times, ch 3, skip next 2 ch-3 sps on this Large Motif, dc in next dc, work joining picot, (ch 2, dc in next dc on this Large Motif, work joining picot) 2 times, (ch 2, dc in next dc, picot) 6 times, ch 3, skip next 2 ch-3 sps, *dc in next dc, picot, (ch 2, dc in next dc, picot) 8 times, ch 3, skip next 2 ch-3 sps; repeat from *, join with sl st in 3rd ch of ch-6, fasten off.
Repeat Second Large Motif 5 more times for a total of 7 Large Motifs.

SECOND ROW
First Large Motif
Joining to bottom of First Large Motif on last row, work same as First Row Second Large Motif.

Second Large Motif
Rnds 1-6: Repeat same rnds of First Row First Large Motif.
Rnd 7: Ch 6, sl st in 3rd ch from hook, ch 2, (dc in next dc, picot, ch 2) 5 times, dc in next dc; joining to bottom of next Large Motif on last row made, *work joining picot, (ch 2, dc in next dc on this Large Motif, work joining picot) 2 times, ch 3, skip next 2 ch-3 sps on this Large Motif, dc in next dc, work joining picot, (ch 2, dc in next dc on this

JOINING DIAGRAM

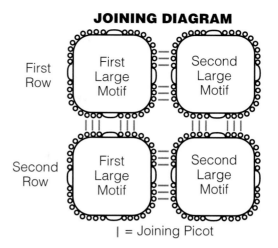

| = Joining Picot

Large Motif, work joining picot) 2 times*, ch 2, (dc in next dc, picot, ch 2) 3 times, dc in next dc; joining to side of last Large Motif on this row; repeat between **, (ch 2, dc, picot) 6 times, ch 3, skip next 2 ch-3 sps, dc in next dc, picot, (ch 2, dc in next dc, picot) 8 times, ch 3, skip next 2 ch-3 sps, join with sl st in 3rd ch of ch-6, fasten off.
Repeat Second Large Motif 5 more times for a total of 7 Motifs.
Repeat Second Row 7 more times for a total of 9 rows.

FILLER MOTIF
Rnd 1: With variegated, ch 7, sl st in first ch to form ring, ch 1, 12 sc in ring, join with sl st in first sc (12 sc).
Rnd 2: Joining to sps between Large Motifs, ch 7, sl st in first unworked picot on any Large Motif, ch 1, sl st in 5th ch of ch-7, ch 2, (dc in next st on this Motif, work joining picot in next picot on Large Motif, ch 2) 2 times, *dc in next st on this Motif, work joining picot in first unworked picot on next Large Motif, ch 2, (dc in next st on this Motif, work joining picot in next picot on Large Motif, ch 2) 2 times; repeat from * around, join with sl st in 3rd ch of ch-7, fasten off.
Repeat Filler Motif in each sp between Large Motifs.

Petunia Potluck

Continued from page 69

same sp on this Motif, ch 1, dc in next ch sp, work joining ch-3 sp, dc in next ch sp on this Motif, ch 1, dc-cl in next ch sp, work joining ch-3 sp, (tr-cl, ch 3, dc-cl) in same sp on this Motif, ch 1, dc in next ch sp, ch 3, dc in next ch sp, ch 1, *(dc-cl, ch 3, tr-cl, ch 3, dc-cl) in next ch sp, ch 1, dc in next ch sp, ch 3, dc in next ch sp, ch 1; repeat from *, join with sl st in top of beg dc-cl, fasten off.
Repeat Second Motif 9 more times for a total of 11 Motifs.

SECOND ROW
First Motif
Joining to bottom of First Motif on last row, work same as First Row Second Motif.

Second Motif
Rnds 1-3: Using desired scrap colors, repeat same rnds of First Row First Motif.
Rnd 4: Join lt. green with sl st in 2nd ch sp, beg dc-cl, (ch 3, tr-cl) in same sp; joining to bottom of next Motif on last row, *work joining ch-3 sp, dc-cl in same sp on this Motif, ch 1, dc in next ch sp, work joining ch-3 sp, dc in next ch sp on this Motif, ch 1, dc-cl in next ch sp, work joining ch-3 sp*, tr-cl in same sp on this Motif; joining to side of last Motif on this row; repeat between **, (tr-cl, ch 3, dc-cl) in same sp on this Motif, ch 1, dc in next ch sp, ch 3, dc in next ch sp, ch 1, (dc-cl, ch 3, tr-cl, ch 3, dc-cl) in next ch sp, ch 1, dc in next ch sp, ch 3, dc in next ch sp, ch 1, join with sl st in top of beg dc-cl, fasten off.
Repeat Second Motif 9 more times for a total of 11 Motifs.
Repeat Second Row 13 more times for a total of 15 rows.

BORDER
Rnd 1: Working around entire outer edge, join lt. green with sc in any corner tr-cl, (ch 7, sc) in same st; skipping ch-1 sps and joined ch-3 sps between Motifs, ch 5, (sc in next
Continued on next page

Petunia Potluck

Continued from page 143

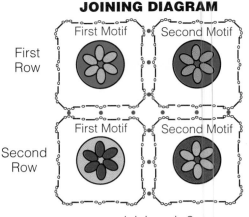

ch-3 sp, ch 5) across to next corner tr-cl *(sc, ch 7, sc) in next tr-cl; skipping ch-1 sps and joined ch-3 sps between Motifs, ch 5, (sc in next ch-3 sp, ch 5) across to next corner tr-cl; repeat from * around, join with sl st in first sc (34 ch-5 sps across each short end between corner ch-7 lps, 46 ch-5 sps across each long edge between corner ch-7 lps).

Rnd 2: Sl st in each of next 2 chs, ch 1, sc in same ch, *[(ch 3, skip next ch, sc in next ch) 2 times, (ch 3, sc in 2nd ch of next ch-5 sp, ch 3, skip next ch, sc in next ch) across to next corner ch-7 lp], ch 3, sc in 2nd ch of next ch-7 lp; repeat from * 2 more times; repeat between [ ]; to **join,** ch 1, hdc in first sc (71 ch sps across each short end, 95 ch sps across each long edge).

Rnd 3: Ch 1, sc around joining hdc, [◊(dc-cl, ch 3, dc-cl) in next ch sp, ch 3, (dc-cl, ch 3, dc-cl) in next ch sp, *sc in next ch sp, (dc-cl, ch 3, dc-cl, ch 3, dc-cl) in next ch sp; repeat from * across◊ to last ch sp before next 2 corner ch sps, sc in next ch sp]; repeat between [ ] 2 more times;

• = Joining ch-3 sp

repeat between ◊◊, join with sl st in first sc, fasten off.

Rnd 4: Join med. green with sc in any corner ch sp, (sc, ch 3, 2 sc) in same sp, [◊(sc, ch 3, sc) in next dc-cl, *3 sc in each of next 2 ch sps, (sc, ch 3, sc) in next dc-cl; repeat from * across to next corner ch sp◊, (2 sc, ch 3, 2 sc) in next ch sp]; repeat between [ ] 2 more times; repeat between ◊◊, join, fasten off.❦

Symphony in Violet

Continued from page 71

in next ch sp, ch 1, skip next 2 sts, (2 dc in next st, ch 1, skip next 2 sts) across to next ch sp; repeat from * around, join with sl st in top of ch-3.

Rnd 8: Sl st in next st, sl st in next ch sp, ch 3, (dc, ch 2, 2 dc) in same sp, ch 1, (2 dc in next ch-1 sp, ch 1) across to next corner ch-2 sp, *(2 dc, ch 2, 2 dc) in next ch-2 sp, ch 1, (2 dc in next ch-1 sp, ch 1) across to next corner ch-2 sp; repeat from * around, join, fasten off.

Rnd 9: Join green with sc in any corner ch-2 sp, (ch 3, sc) in same sp, ch 2, (sc in next ch-1 sp, ch 2) across to next corner ch-2 sp, *(sc, ch 3, sc) in next ch-2 sp, ch 2, (sc in next ch-1 sp, ch 2) across to next corner ch-2 sp; repeat from * around, join with sl st in first sc, fasten off.

Rnd 10: Join soft white with sl st in any corner ch-3 sp, ch 6, dc in same sp, (dc, ch 2, dc) in each ch-2 sp across to next corner ch-3 sp, *(dc, ch 3, dc) in next ch-3 sp, (dc, ch 2, dc) in each ch-2 sp across to next corner ch-3 sp; repeat from * around, join with sl st in 3rd ch of ch-6, fasten off.

Holding Blocks wrong sides together, matching sts and ch sps, with soft white, sew together through **back lps** according to Assembly Diagram.

BORDER

Rnd 1: Working around entire outer edge, join soft white with sl st in ch-3 sp of first outer point on top of Afghan according to diagram, ch 5, (dc, ch 2, dc, ch 2, dc) in same sp, [(dc, ch 2, dc) in each of next 8 ch-2 sps, *dc in next ch-3 sp, (ch 2, dc in same sp) 3 times, (dc, ch 2, dc) in each of next 8 ch-2 sps, dc next 2 ch-3 sps tog, (dc, ch 2, dc) in each of next 8 ch-2 sps*; repeat between ** 2 more times, dc in next ch-3 sp, (ch 2, dc in same sp) 3 times, (dc, ch 2, dc) in each of next 8 ch-2 sps; repeat between ** 5 more times], dc in next ch-3 sp, (ch 2, dc in same sp) 3 times; repeat between [ ], join with sl st in 3rd ch of ch-5, fasten off.

Rnd 2: Join purple with sl st in 2nd ch sp, ch 5, (dc, ch 2, dc, ch 2, dc) in same sp, [(dc, ch 2, dc) in each of next 10 ch sps, *dc in next ch sp, (ch 2, dc in same sp) 3 times, (dc, ch 2, dc) in each of next 8 ch sps, dc next 2 ch sps tog, (dc, ch 2, dc) in each of next 8 ch sps*; repeat between ** 2 more times, dc in next ch sp, (ch 2, dc in same sp) 3 times, (dc, ch 2, dc) in each of next 10 ch sps; repeat between ** 5 more times], dc in next ch sp, (ch 2, dc in same sp) 3 times; repeat between [ ], join, fasten off.

NOTE: *For picot, ch 4, sl st in 4th ch from hook.*

Rnd 3: Join soft white with sl st in 2nd ch sp, ch 7, sl st in 4th ch from hook (first picot made), (dc, picot, dc) in same sp, [(dc, picot, dc) in each of next 12 ch sps, *(dc, picot, dc, picot, dc) in next ch sp, (dc, picot, dc) in each of next 8 ch sps, dc next 2 ch sps tog, (dc, picot, dc) in each of next 8 ch sps*; repeat between ** 2 more times, (dc, picot, dc, picot, dc) in next ch sp, (dc, picot, dc) in each of next 12 ch sps; repeat between ** 5 more times], (dc, picot, dc, picot, dc) in next ch sp; repeat between [ ], join with sl st in 3rd ch of ch-7, fasten off.❦

ASSEMBLY DIAGRAM

Join Rnd 1 of Border here.

Sweet Impressions

Continued from page 73

between **, sc in last 15 sts, turn.

Rows 31-34: Ch 1, sc in each st across, turn.

Rows 35-212: Repeat rows 7-34 consecutively, ending with row 16.

Rows 213-218: Ch 1, sc in each st across, turn. At end of last row, fasten off.

BORDER

Rnd 1: Working around outer edge, with right side facing you, join mint with sl st in first st of last row, sl st in each st and in end of each row around, join with sl st in first sl st (128 sl sts across each short end, 218 sl sts across each long edge).

Rnd 2: Working this rnd in **back lps** only, ch 1, 3 sc in first st, *sc in next 126 sts, 3 sc in next st, sc in next 218 sts*, 3 sc in next st; repeat between **, join with sl st in first sc (128 sc across each short end between corner sc, 220 sc across each long edge between corner sc).

Rnd 3: Ch 1, sc in each st around with 3 sc in each center corner st, join, fasten off (130 sc across each short end between corner sc, 222 sc across each long edge between corner sc).

NOTE: *For popcorn (pc), 5 dc in next st, drop lp from hook, insert hook in first st of 5-dc group, draw dropped lp through.*

Rnd 4: Join lilac with sl st in center corner st before either short end, *ch 5, skip next 5 sts, pc in next st, (ch 8, skip next 7 sts, pc in next st) 15 times, ch 5, skip next 4 sts, sl st in next center corner st, ch 7, skip next 7 sts, pc in next st, (ch 8, skip next 7 sts, pc in next st) 26 times, ch 7, skip next 6 sts*, sl st in next center corner st; repeat between **, join with sl st in first sl st, fasten off.

Rnd 5: Working over ch sps and sl sts of last rnd, in skipped sts on rnd before last, join mint with sl st in any center corner st on rnd before last, ch 3, 3 dc in same st, dc in each skipped st and in each pc on last rnd around with 4 dc in each center corner st on rnd before last, join with sl st in top of ch-3.

Rnd 6: Ch 1, sc in each st around with 2 sc in each of 2 center corner sts on each corner, join with sl st in first sc.

Rnd 7: Sl st in each st around, join with sl st in first sl st, fasten off.

Rnd 8: Join lilac with sl st in first sl st, sl st in each sl st around, join, fasten off.❧

Daffodil Garden

Continued from page 75

Rnd 8: With F hook and soft white, join with sl st in any corner ch sp, ch 3, (2 dc, ch 3, 3 dc) in same sp, *[skip next 3 sts, (3 dc in next st, skip next 2 sts) across to next corner ch sp], (3 dc, ch 3, 3 dc) in next ch sp; repeat from * 2 more times; repeat between [ ], join, fasten off (6 3-dc groups across each side between corner ch sps).

Daffodil Top

Rnd 1: Working in **front lps** of rnd 1, with G hook and yellow, join with sc in any st, sc in each st around, join with sl st in first sc (12 sc).

Rnd 2: Ch 2, (sl st in next st, ch 2) around, join with sl st in joining sl st of last rnd, fasten off.

PLAIN BLOCK (make 49)

Rnd 1: With F hook and yellow, ch 4, sl st in first ch to form ring, ch 3, 2 dc in ring, ch 3, (3 dc in ring, ch 3) 3 times, join with sl st in top of ch-3 (12 dc, 4 ch sps).

Rnd 2: Sl st in each of next 2 sts, sl st in next ch sp, ch 3, (2 dc, ch 3, 3 dc) in same sp, (3 dc, ch 3, 3 dc) in each ch sp around, join (8 3-dc groups, 4 ch sps).

Rnd 3: Sl st in each of next 2 sts, sl st in next ch sp, ch 3, (2 dc, ch 3, 3 dc) in same sp, 3 dc in sp between next 2 3-dc groups, *(3 dc, ch 3, 3 dc) in next ch sp, 3 dc in sp between next 2 3-dc groups; repeat from * around, join, fasten off (12 3-dc groups, 4 ch sps).

Rnd 4: Join green with sl st any corner ch sp, ch 3, (2 dc, ch 3, 3 dc) in same sp, (3 dc in sp between next 2 3-dc groups) 2 times, *(3 dc, ch 3, 3 dc) in next ch sp, (3 dc in sp between next 2 3-dc groups) 2 times; repeat from * around, join (16 3-dc groups, 4 ch sps).

ASSEMBLY DIAGRAM

Rnd 5: Sl st in each of next 2 sts, sl st in next ch sp, ch 3, (2 dc, ch 3, 3 dc) in same sp, (3 dc in sp between next 2 3-dc groups) 3 times, *(3 dc, ch 3, 3 dc) in next ch sp, (3 dc in sp between next 2 3-dc groups) 3 times; repeat from * around, join, fasten off (20 3-dc groups, 4 ch sps).

Rnd 6: Join soft white with sl st in any corner ch sp, ch 3, (2 dc, ch 3, 3 dc) in same sp, (3 dc in sp between next 2 3-dc groups) 4 times, *(3 dc, ch 3, 3 dc) in next ch sp, (3 dc in sp between next 2 3-dc groups) 4 times; repeat from *

Continued on next page

145

Daffodil Garden

Continued from page 145

around, join, fasten off (24 3-dc groups, 4 ch sps).

Holding Blocks wrong sides together, matching sts, with soft white, sew together through **back lps** according to Assembly Diagram on page 145.

BORDER

Rnd 1: Working around entire outer edge, with F hook and soft white, join with sl st in any corner ch sp, ch 3, (2 dc, ch 3, 3 dc) in same sp, [◊(3 dc in sp between next 2 3-dc groups) 5 times, *3 dc in each of next 2 ch sps skipping seam in between, (3 dc in sp between next 2 3-dc groups) 5 times; repeat from * across to next corner ch sp◊, (3 dc, ch 3, 3 dc) in next ch sp]; repeat between [ ] 2 more times; repeat between ◊◊, join with sl st in top of ch-3.

Rnd 2: Sl st in each of next 2 sts, sl st in next ch sp, ch 3, (2 dc, ch 3, 3 dc) in same sp, 3 dc in each sp between 3-dc groups around with (3 dc, ch 3, 3 dc) in each corner ch sp, join.

Rnd 3: Sl st in each of next 2 sts, sl st in next ch sp, ch 3, (dc, picot, 4 dc, picot, 2 dc) in same sp, (2 dc, picot, 2 dc) in each sp between 3-dc groups around with (2 dc, picot, 4 dc, picot, 2 dc) in each corner ch sp, join, fasten off.❦

Kitten Soft

Continued from page 79

dc in next 5 sc, fp around next fp on row before last, fp around dc on row before last, dc in next 5 sc*, fp around each of next 3 fp on row before last) 7 times; repeat between **, fp around next fp on row before last, dc in last sc, turn.

Row 13: Repeat row 5.

Row 14: Ch 3, dc in next 5 sc, (fp around each of next 3 fp on row before last, fp around next dc on row before last, dc in next 5 sc, fp around next fp on row before last, fp around dc on row before last, dc in next 5 sc) 8 times, dc in last sc, turn.

Row 15: Repeat row 5.

Row 16: Ch 3, fp around next dc on row before last, dc in next 5 sc, (fp around each of next 3 fp on row before last, fp around next dc on row before last, dc in next 5 sc, fp around next fp on row before last, fp around next dc on row before last, dc in next 5 sc) 8 times, turn.

Row 17: Repeat row 5.

Row 18: Ch 3, fp around next fp on row before last, (fp around next dc on row before last, dc in next 5 sc, fp around each of next 3 fp on row before last, fp around next dc on row before last, dc in next 5 sc, fp around next fp on row before last) 8 times, fp around next dc on row before last, dc in last 4 sc, turn.

Row 19: Repeat row 5.

Row 20: Ch 3, dc in next sc, (*fp around next fp on row before last, fp around next dc on row before last*, dc in next 5 sc, fp around each of next 3 fp on row before last, fp around next dc on row before last, dc in next 5 sc) 8 times; repeat between **, dc in each of last 3 sc, turn.

Row 21: Repeat row 5.

Row 22: Ch 3, dc in each of next 2 sc, (*fp around next fp on row before last, fp around next dc on row before last*, dc in next 5 sc, fp around each of next 3 fp on row before last, fp around next dc on row before last, dc in next 5 sc) 8 times; repeat between **, dc in each of last 2 sc, turn.

Row 23: Repeat row 5.

Row 24: Ch 3, dc in each of next 3 sc, (*fp around next fp on row before last, fp around next dc on row before last*, dc in next 5 sc, fp around each of next 3 fp on row before last, fp around next dc on row before last, dc in next 5 sc) 8 times; repeat between **, dc in last sc, turn.

Row 25: Repeat row 5.

Row 26: Ch 3, dc in next 4 sc, (fp around next fp on row before last, fp around next dc on row before last, dc in next 5 sc, fp around each of next 3 fp on row before last, fp around next dc on row before last, dc in next 5 sc) 8 times, fp around next fp on row before last, dc in last sc, turn.

Row 27: Repeat row 5.

Row 28: Ch 3, (dc in next 5 sc, fp around next fp on row before last, fp around next dc on row before last, dc in next 5 sc, fp around each of next 3 fp on row before last, fp around next dc on row before last) 8 times, dc in last 6 sc, turn.

Row 29: Repeat row 5.

Row 30: Ch 3, (fp around next dc on row before last, dc in next 5 sc, fp around next fp on row before last, fp around next dc on row before last, dc in next 5 sc, fp around each of next 3 fp on row before last) 8 times, fp around next dc on row before last, dc in last 5 sc, turn.

Row 31: Repeat row 5.

Row 32: Ch 3, fp around next fp on row before last, fp around next dc on row before last, (dc in next 5 sc, fp around next fp on row before last, fp around next dc on row before last, dc in next 5 sc, fp around each of next 3 fp on row before last, fp around next dc on row before last) 8 times, dc in last 4 sc, turn.

Row 33: Repeat row 5.

Row 34: Ch 3, fp around each of next 2 fp on row before last, (fp around next dc on row before last, dc in next 5 sc, fp around next fp on row before last, fp around next dc on row before last, dc in next 5 sc, fp around each of next 3 fp on row before last) 8 times, fp around next dc on row before last, dc in each of last 3 sc, turn.

Row 35: Repeat row 5.

Row 36: Ch 3, (fp around each of next 3 fp on row before last, fp around next dc on row before last, dc in next 5 sc, fp around next fp on row before last, fp around next dc on row before last, dc in next 5 sc) 8 times, fp around each of next 3 fp on row before last, fp around each of next 3 fp on row before last, fp around next dc on row before last, dc in each of last 2 sc, turn.

Rows 37-165: Repeat rows 5-36 consecutively, ending with row 5. At end of last row turn, **do not** fasten off.

BORDER

Rnd 1: Ch 1, (sc, ch 2, sc) in first st,*sc in each st across to next corner st, (sc, ch 2, sc) in next st; working in ends of rows, sc in each row across* to next corner st, (sc, ch 2, sc) in next corner st; repeat between **, join with sl st in first sc (135 sts across each short end between corner ch sps; 167 sts across each long edge between corner ch sps).

Rnd 2: Ch 3, dc in each st around with (dc, ch 2, dc) in each corner ch sp, join with sl st in top of ch-3, **turn** (137 sts across each short end between corner ch sps; 169 sts across each long edge between corner ch sps).

Rnd 3: Ch 1, sc in each st around with (sc, ch 2, sc) in each corner ch sp, join with sl st in first sc, **turn**.

Rnd 4: Ch 3, fp around next dc on rnd before last, skip next st, *[(dc, ch 2, dc) in next corner ch sp, skip next st, fp around next dc on rnd before last, (dc in next st, fp around next dc on rnd before last) across] to st before next corner ch sp, skip next st; repeat from * 2 more times; repeat between [ ], join with sl st in top of ch-3, **turn**.

Rnd 5: Repeat rnd 3.

Rnd 6: Ch 3, fp around next fp on rnd before last, dc in each of next 2 sc, *[(dc, ch 2, dc) in next corner ch sp, dc in each of next 2 sc, fp around next fp on rnd before last, (dc in next sc, fp around next fp on rnd before last) across] to 2 sc before next corner ch sp, dc in each of next 2 sc; repeat from * 2 more times; repeat between [ ], join with sl st in top of ch-3, **turn**.

Rnd 7: Repeat rnd 3.

Rnd 8: Ch 3, fp around next fp on rnd before last, dc in next sc, fp around next dc on rnd before last, dc in each of next 2 sc, *[(dc, ch 2, dc) in next corner ch sp, dc in each of next 2 sc, fp around next dc on rnd before last, (dc in next sc, fp around next fp on rnd before last) across] to 4 sc before next corner ch sp, dc in next sc, fp around next dc on rnd before last, dc in each of next 2 sc; repeat from * 2 more times; repeat between [ ], join with sl st in top of ch-3, **turn**.

Rnd 9: Repeat rnd 3, fasten off.❦

Royal Treatment

Continued from page 81

ch 1) in each corner ch-2 sp, join, fasten off (14 sts across each side between corner ch sps).

Holding Blocks wrong sides together, matching sts, with dk. gold, sew together through **back lps** in 6 rows of 8 Blocks each.

ROSE (make 48)

With burgundy, ch 17, (4 sc, sl st) in 2nd ch from hook and in each of next 2 chs, (4 hdc, sl st) in each of next 3 chs, (4 dc, sl st) in each of next 3 chs, (4 tr, sl st) in each of next 7 chs, leaving long end for sewing, fasten off.

Roll into a Rose shape; tack to secure. Sew Rose to ring of rnd 1 on each Block.

EDGING

NOTE: *For picot, ch 4, sl st in 4th ch from hook.*

Join dk. gold with sl st in any corner ch sp, ch 7, sl st in 4th ch from hook, (dc, picot) in same sp, (dc, picot) in each st and in each seam around with (dc, picot, dc, picot) in each corner ch sp, join with sl st in top of ch-3, fasten off.❦

Chorus of Lace

Continued from page 85

6" end, tack first sc and last sc together.

BLOCK (make 12)

Rnd 1: Working in remaining lps on opposite side of hairpin lace, with white, insert hook from left to right in first 3-lps (see 3-lp group illustration A on page 148), yo, draw lp through all 3 lps, ch 1, 3 sc in same 3-lp group (see illustration B), (insert hook in next 3 lps, yo, draw lp through all 3 lps, ch 1, 3 sc in same 3-lp group) around, join with sl st in first sc (84 sc).

Rnd 2: Working this rnd in **front lps** only, ch 1, sc in first st, ch 3, skip next st, (sc in next st, ch 3, skip next st) around, join, fasten off.

Rnd 3: Working this rnd in **back lps** of rnd 1, join med. pink with sl st in any st, ch 4, (tr, ch 2, 2 tr) in same st, *[skip next st, 2 dc in next st, skip next st, (2 hdc in next st, skip next st) 2 times, 2 sc in next st, skip next st, sc in each of next 2 sts, skip next st, 2 sc in next st, skip next st, (2 hdc in next st, skip next st) 2 times, 2 dc in next st, skip next st], (2 tr, ch 2, 2 tr) in next st; repeat from * 2 more times; repeat between [ ], join with sl st in top of ch-4 (22 sts across each side between corner ch sps).

Rnds 4-5: Ch 3, dc in each st around with (2 dc, ch 2, 2 dc) in each corner ch sp, join with sl st in top of ch-3 ending with 30 dc across each side between corner ch sps.

HAIRPIN LACE ILLUSTRATION

3-LP GROUP ILLUSTRATION

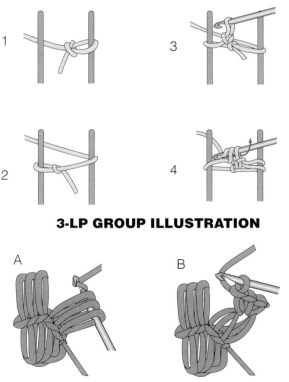

Rnd 6: Ch 3, dc in each st around with (dc, ch 2, dc) in each corner ch sp, join, fasten off (32 sts across each side

Continued on next page

Chorus of Lace

Continued from page 147

between corner ch sps).

Rnd 7: Join white with sc in any corner ch sp, ch 5, sc in same sp, *[ch 5, skip next 2 sts, (sc in next st, ch 5, skip next 2 sts) across to next corner ch sp], (sc, ch 5, sc) in next sp; repeat from * 2 more times; repeat between [ ], join with sl st in first sc, fasten off (11 ch-5 sps across each side between corner ch sps).

Rnd 8: Join med. pink with sl st in any corner ch sp, ch 3, (dc, ch 2, 2 dc) in same sp, 3 dc in each ch sp around with (2 dc, ch 2, 2 dc) in each corner ch sp, join with sl st in top of ch-3 (37 dc across each side between corner ch sps).

Rnd 9: Ch 3, dc in each st around with (2 dc, ch 2, 2 dc) in each corner ch sp, join, fasten off (41 dc across each side between corner ch sps).

Holding Blocks wrong sides together, matching sts, with med. pink, sew together through **back lps** in 3 rows of 4 Blocks each.

ROSE (make 12)

With H hook and burgundy, ch 7, (hdc, ch 2) 5 times in 3rd ch from hook, (hdc, ch 2) 5 times in each ch across to last ch, (hdc, ch 2) 5 times in last ch, sl st in same ch, fasten off.

LEAVES (make 12)

With H hook and med. green, ch 18, sl st in 3rd ch from hook, *sc in next ch, hdc in next ch, dc in next ch, hdc in next ch, sc in next ch, sl st in next 4 chs, sc in next ch, hdc in next ch, dc in next ch, hdc in next ch, sc in next ch*, (sl st, ch 2, sl st) in end ch; working on opposite side of starting ch, repeat between **, sl st in last ch, fasten off.

Roll Rose into a Rose shape, tack to secure; sew Rose centered on Leaves. With Leaves pointed toward long edges of Afghan, tack to center of Hairpin Lace Circle as shown in photo on page 84.

Repeat with remaining Roses and Leaves.

BORDER

Rnd 1: Working around entire outer edge, with H hook and white, join with sc in any corner ch sp, ch 5, sc in same sp, [◊ch 5, skip next 2 sts, (sc in next st, ch 5, skip next 2 sts) 13 times, *sc in ch sp before next seam, ch 5, sc in ch sp after same seam, ch 5, skip next 2 sts, (sc in next st, ch 5, skip next 2 sts) 13 times; repeat from * across to next corner ch sp◊, (sc, ch 5, sc) in next ch sp]; repeat between [ ] 2 more times; repeat between ◊◊, join with sl st in first sc.

Rnds 2-3: Sl st in each of next 3 chs on corner ch-5 sp, (sc, ch 5, sc) in same sp, *ch 5, (sc in next ch sp, ch 5) across to next corner ch sp, (sc, ch 5, sc) in corner ch sp; repeat from * 2 more times, ch 5, (sc in next ch sp, ch 5) across, join. At end of last rnd, fasten off.❦

Fireside Glow

Continued from page 87

through, ch 1, sc in same ch on this Strip, skip next ch, 2 sc in next ch, (ch 1, drop lp from hook, insert hook from front to back through corresponding ch-2 sp on last Strip, pull dropped lp through, ch 1, skip next 2 chs on this Strip, 2 sc in next ch) across to last 2 chs, skip next ch, sc in last ch, ch 1, drop lp from hook, insert hook from front to back through corresponding corner ch-2 sp on last Strip, pull dropped lp through, ch 1, sc in same ch on this Strip, ch 1, skip end of next row, 2 sc in each of next 3 rows, skip end of next row, (sc, ch 2, sc) in first st, skip next st, 2 sc in next st, (ch 2, skip next 2 sts, 2 sc in next st) across to last 2 sts, skip next st, (sc, ch 2, sc) in last st, join with sl st in first sc, fasten off.

Repeat Next Strip 7 more times for a total of 9 Strips.

BORDER

Working around entire outer edge, join green with sl st in corner ch-2 sp before one short end, ch 3, (dc, ch 2, 2 dc) in same sp, [*(sc in next st, dc in each of next 2 sts, sc in each of next 2 sts, dc in each of next 2 sts, sc in next st*, 2 tr around joining ch-2 sp between Strips) 8 times; repeat between **; (2 dc, ch 2, 2 dc) in next corner ch-2 sp, sc in each of next 2 sts, (2 dc in next ch sp, sc in each of next 2 sts) across], (2 dc, ch 2, 2 dc) in next corner ch sp; repeat between [ ], join with sl st in top of ch-3, fasten off.❦

Yuletide Rose

Continued from page 89

around, join with sl st in first sc, fasten off.

NOTES: *For **small V-st** (sm V-st), (dc, ch 1, dc) in next st.*

*For **large V-st** (lg V-st), (dc, ch 3, dc) in next st.*

Rnd 31: Join off-white with sl st in any corner ch-3 sp, ch 3, (2 dc, ch 3, 3 dc) in same sp, *[skip next 2 tr, sm V-st in next tr, (2 tr, ch 1, 2 tr) in next sc, skip next 2 tr, sm V-st in next tr], (3 dc, ch 3, 3 dc) in next corner ch-3 sp; repeat from * 2 more times; repeat between [ ], join with sl st in top of ch-3.

Rnd 32: Sl st in each of next 2 sts, sl st in next ch sp, ch 3, (dc, ch 5, 2 dc) in same sp, *[lg V-st in sp between next 3-dc group and next sm V-st, lg V-st between last sm V-st and next 2-tr group, (sc, ch 1, sc) in next ch-1 sp, lg V-st in sp between next 2-tr group and next sm V-st, lg V-st between last sm V-st and next 3-dc group], (2 dc, ch 5, 2 dc) in next corner ch sp; repeat from * 2 more times; repeat between [ ], join with sl st in top of ch-3, fasten off (5 ch sps across each side between corner sts).

Second Motif

Rnds 1-31: Repeat same Rnds of First Motif.

NOTE: *For **joining lg V-st**, dc in next sp, ch 1, drop lp from hook, insert hook from front to back through center ch of corresponding V-st on last Motif, pull dropped lp through, ch 1, dc in same sp on this Motif.*

Rnd 32: Sl st in each of next 2 sts, sl st in next ch sp, ch 3, (dc, ch 5, 2 dc) in same sp, lg V-st in sp between next 3-dc group and next sm V-st, lg V-st between last sm V-st and next

2-tr group, (sc, ch 1, sc) in next ch-1 sp, lg V-st in sp between next 2-tr group and next sm V-st, lg V-st between last sm V-st and next 3-dc group; joining to side of last Motif made (see Joining Diagram), 2 dc in next corner ch-5 sp, ch 2, drop lp from hook, insert hook from front to back through corresponding corner ch-5 sp on other Motif, pull dropped lp through, ch 2, 2 dc in same corner ch-5 sp on this Motif, joining lg V-st in sp between next 3-dc group and next sm V-st, joining lg V-st between last sm V-st and next 2-tr group, sc in next ch-1 sp, drop lp from hook, insert hook from front to back through corresponding ch-1 sp on other Motif, pull dropped lp through, sc in same ch-1 sp on this Motif, joining lg V-st in sp between next 2-tr group and next sm V-st, joining lg V-st between last sm V-st and next 3-dc group, 2 dc in next corner ch-5 sp, ch 2, drop lp from hook, insert hook from front to back through corresponding corner ch-5 sp on other Motif, pull dropped lp through, ch 2, 2 dc in same ch sp on this Motif, *lg V-st in sp between next 3-dc group and next sm V-st, lg V-st between last sm V-st and next 2-tr group, (sc, ch 1, sc) in next ch-1 sp, lg V-st in sp between next 2-tr group and next sm V-st, lg V-st between last sm V-st and next 3 dc group*, (2 dc, ch 5, 2 dc) in next corner ch sp; repeat between **, join with sl st in top of ch-3, fasten off.

Repeat Second Motif 3 more times for a total of 5 Motifs.

SECOND ROW
First Motif
Joining to bottom of First Row First Motif on last row, work same as First Row Second Motif on page 89.

Second Motif
Rnds 1-31: Repeat same rnds of First Row First Motif on page 89.

Rnd 32: Sl st in each of next 2 sts, sl st in next ch sp, ch 3, (dc, ch 5, 2 dc) in same sp, *lg V-st in sp between next 3-dc group and next sm V-st, lg V-st between last sm V-st and next 2-tr group, (sc, ch 1, sc) in next ch-1 sp, lg V-st in sp between next 2-tr group and next sm V-st, lg V-st between last sm V-st and next 3-dc group*; joining to bottom of First Row Second Motif (see Joining Diagram), 2 dc in next corner ch-5 sp, ch 2, drop lp from hook, insert hook from front to back through corresponding ch-5 sp on other Motif, pull dropped lp through, ch 2, 2 dc in same sp on this Motif, joining lg V-st in sp between next 3-dc group and next sm V-st, joining lg V-st between last sm V-st and next 2-tr group, sc in next ch-1 sp, drop lp from hook, insert hook from front to back through corresponding

ch-1 sp on other Motif, pull dropped lp through, sc in same ch-1 sp on this Motif, joining lg V-st in sp between next 2-tr group and next sm V-st, joining lg V-st between last sm V-st and next 3-dc group, 2 dc in next corner ch-5 sp, ch 2, drop lp from hook, insert hook from front to back through corresponding corner ch-5 sp on other Motif, pull dropped lp through, ch 2, 2 dc in same ch sp on this Motif; joining to side of last Motif made, joining lg V-st in sp between next 3-dc group and next sm V-st, joining lg V-st between last sm V-st and next 2-tr group, sc in next ch-1 sp, drop lp from hook, insert hook from front to back through corresponding ch-1 sp on last Motif, pull dropped lp through, sc in same ch-1 sp on this Motif, joining lg V-st in sp between next 2-tr group and next sm V-st, joining lg V-st between last sm V-st and next 3-dc group, 2 dc in next corner ch sp, ch 2, drop lp from hook, insert hook from front to back through corresponding corner ch-5 sp on last Motif, pull dropped lp through, ch 2, 2 dc in same ch sp on this Motif; repeat between **, join with sl st in top of ch-3, fasten off.

Work Second Motif 3 more times for a total of 5 Motifs.

Work Second Row 5 more times for a total of 7 rows.

BORDER
Working around entire outer edge, join off-white with sl st in corner ch-5 sp before one short end, ch 3, 6 dc in same sp, ◊*[skip next st, sc in sp between next 2 sts (3 dc in next ch sp, sc in sp between next 2 sts) 5 times], 3 dc in ch sp before next joining, sc in next joining, 3 dc in ch sp after joining*; repeat between ** 3 more times; repeat between [ ], 7 dc in next corner ch sp; repeat between ** 6 times; repeat between [ ]◊, 7 dc in next corner ch sp; repeat between ◊◊, join with sl st in top of ch-3, fasten off. ❦

JOINING DIAGRAM

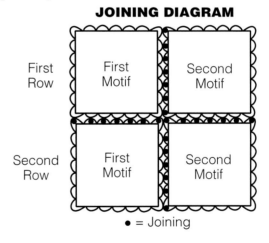

● = Joining

Poinsettia Delight
Continued from page 91

Holding Blocks right sides together, matching sts, with green, sew together through **front lps** in 4 rows of 5 Blocks each.

POINSETTIA (make 20)
Rnd 1: With red; *for **petal,** (ch 10, sc in 2nd ch from hook, hdc in next ch, dc in next ch, tr in each of next 3 chs, dc in next ch, hdc in next ch, sc in next ch); repeat from * 4 more times, join with sl st in first ch of first petal (5 petals).

Rnd 2: Working on opposite side of ch on first petal, ch 1, *sc in first 9 chs, sc in end of row, sc in last 9 sts; working on next petal; repeat from * around, join with sl st in first sc, fasten off.

Rnd 3: Join green with sl st in any st, ch 1, (sl st in next st, ch 1) around, join with sl st in first sl st, fasten off.

To **attach Poinsettia to center of Block,** holding wrong side of Poinsettia to right side of Block, with yellow, using French Knots (see page159), embroider 9 sts around center of Poinsettia through Block, embroider 3 more sts to fill center.

Repeat on remaining Blocks.

Continued on next page

Poinsettia Delight

Continued from page 149

BORDER

Rnd 1: Working around entire outer edge, join green with sl st in any center corner st, ch 3, 2 dc in same st, dc in each st and in each seam around with 3 dc in each center corner st, join with sl st in top of ch-3.

Rnds 2-3: Ch 3, dc in each st around with 3 dc in each center corner st, join. At end of last rnd, fasten off.❧

GRAPH

Each square on Graph equals 1 sc.

☐ = Off-white ■ = Green

Sweet Dreams

Continued from page 97

pink, yellow and lt. green, repeat rows 2-7 consecutively, ending with row 2. At end of last row, **do not** turn or fasten off.

BORDER

Rnd 1: Working around outer edge, ch 1, 3 sc in first corner, 2 sc in end of each row and sc in each st around with 3 sc in each corner, join with sl st in first sc, **turn.**

Rnds 2-3: Ch 1, sc in each st around with 3 sc in each center corner st, join, **turn.** At end of last rnd, fasten off.

Rnd 4: Join variegated with sc in any st, sc in each st around with 3 sc in each center corner st, join, **turn,** fasten off.

Rnd 5: Join white with sc in any st, sc in each st around with 3 sc in each center corner st, join, **turn.**

Rnds 6-7: Repeat rnds 2 and 3.

FRINGE

For **each Fringe,** cut 2 strands white each 10" long. With both strands held together, fold in half, insert hook in st, draw fold through, draw fold through st, draw all loose ends through fold, tighten, trim.

Fringe in each st around entire outer edge of Afghan.❧

Baby Stars

Continued from page 99

sp on this Motif, sc in next ch-1 sp, 3 dc in next ch-2 sp, sc in joining sc between last Motif on this row and adjoining Motif on last row, 3 dc in same sp on this Motif, sc in next ch-1 sp, 3 dc in next ch-2 sp, sc in joining sc between last Motif and next Motif on last row, 3 dc in same sp on this Motif, sc in next ch-1 sp, *(3 dc, ch 1, 3 dc) in next ch-2 sp, sc in next ch-1 sp; repeat from * around, join, fasten off.

Repeat Second Row 4 more times for a total of 6 rows.

SEVENTH ROW
First Motif

Rnds 1-2: Repeat same rnds of First Row First Motif on page 99.

Rnd 3: Join yellow with sl st in any ch-2 sp, ch 3, 2 dc in same sp; joining to last row made, sc in 4th ch-2 sp on First Motif of last row, 3 dc in same sp on this Motif, sc in joining sc between First Motif and Next Motif on last row, 3 dc in same sp on this Motif, sc in next ch-1 sp, 3 dc in next ch-2 sp on this Motif, sc in joining sc between last Motif and Next Motif on last row, 3 dc in same sp on this Motif, sc in next ch-1 sp, *(3 dc, ch 1, 3 dc) in next ch-2 sp, sc in next ch-1 sp; repeat from * around, join, fasten off.

ASSEMBLY DIAGRAM

Second Row

First Row

First Motif →

Next Motif →

Next Motif

Work same as Second Row Next Motif on page 99.

Working number of Motifs on each Row according to Assembly Diagram, repeat Second Row 4 more times for a total of 11 rows.❧

Double Delight

Continued from page 101

around with 3 sc in each center corner st, join, fasten off.

Rnd 3: With pink, repeat rnd 2, **do not** fasten off.

Rnd 4: Working this rnd in **front lps** only, sl st in each st around, join with sl st in first sl st, fasten off.

Rnd 5: Working in **front lps** of rnd 1, join pink with sl st in any st, sl st in each st around, join, fasten off.

Rnd 6: Working in **front lps** of rnd 2, join white with sl st in any st, sl st in each st around, join, fasten off.

LITTLE BOY BLUE

SIZE: 34" x 41½".

MATERIALS: Worsted-weight yarn — 25 oz. lt. blue and 2 oz. white; J crochet hook or size needed to obtain gauge.

GAUGE: 3 hdc = 1"; 3 hdc rows = 2¼".

SKILL LEVEL: ☆☆ Average

AFGHAN

Row 1: With lt. blue, ch 120, hdc in 3rd ch from hook, hdc in each ch across, turn (119 hdc).

NOTE: *Beginning ch-2 is used and counted as first st of each row.*

Row 2: Ch 2, hdc in each st across, turn.

Row 3: Ch 3, skip next st, hdc in next st, (ch 1, skip next st, hdc in next st) across, turn (60 hdc, 59 ch-1 sps).

Row 4: Ch 2, hdc in each st and in each ch-1 sp across, turn (119 hdc).

NOTE: *For **cross stitch (cr st)**, skip next st, hdc in next st; working over last st, hdc in skipped st.*

Row 5: Ch 2, cr st across, turn (59 cr sts, 1 hdc).

Rows 6-76: Repeat rows 2-5 consecutively, ending with row 4.

Row 77: Ch 1, sc in each st across, turn, **do not** fasten off.

BORDER

Rnd 1: Working around outer edge, ch 1, 3 sc in first st, sc in each st across to last st, 3 sc in last st; working in ends of rows, skip first row, (2 sc in next row, sc in each of next 2 rows) across to last row, skip last row; working on opposite side of starting ch, 3 sc in first ch, sc in each ch across to last ch, 3 sc in last ch; working in ends of rows, skip first row, (sc in each of next 2 rows, 2 sc in next row) across to last row, skip last row, join with sl st in first sc, fasten off.

Rnd 2: Working this rnd in **back lps** only, join white with sc in any center corner st, 2 sc in same st, sc in each st around with 3 sc in each center corner st, join, fasten off.

Rnd 3: With lt. blue, repeat rnd 2, **do not** fasten off.

Rnd 4: Working this rnd in **front lps** only, sl st in each st around, join with sl st in first sl st, fasten off.

Rnd 5: Working in **front lps** of rnd 1, join lt. blue with sl st in any st, sl st in each st around, join, fasten off.

Rnd 6: Working in **front lps** of rnd 2, join white with sl st in any st, sl st in each st around, join, fasten off.🐦

Pastel Puzzle

Continued from page 103

this Motif, ch 1, sl st in next corner ch sp on other Motif, ch 1, 3 dc in ring on this Motif, ch 1; joining to side of last Motif on this row, sl st in corresponding corner ch sp on other Motif, ch 1, 3 dc in ring on this Motif, ch 3, join with sl st in top of ch-3, fasten off.

With color indicated on Color Diagram, repeat Second Motif 28 more times for a total of 30 Motifs.

With colors indicated on Color Diagram, repeat Second Row 28 more times for a total of 30 rows.

EDGING

Working around entire outer edge, join white with sc in any corner ch sp, ch 3, sc in same sp, *[ch 1, skip next st, sc in next st, ch 1, skip next st, (sc in next ch sp, ch 1, skip next joining seam, sc in next ch sp, ch 1, skip next st, sc in next st, ch 1, skip next st) across] to next corner ch sp, (sc, ch 3, sc) in next corner ch sp; repeat from * 2 more times; repeat between [ ], join with sl st in first sc, fasten off.🐦

JOINING DIAGRAM

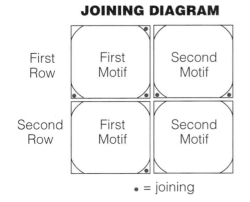

• = joining

COLOR DIAGRAM

☐ = White   ▦ = Pink   ▨ = Lt. green

Butterfly Kisses

Continued from page 105

2 dc around next ch-3, 2 dc around next picot) 38 times, join with sl st in top of ch-3 (798 dc).

Rnds 2-4: Ch 3, dc in each st around with 3 dc in each center corner st, join, ending with 822 dc in last rnd.

Rnd 5: Ch 3, dc in each st around with 2 dc in each of center 3 sts on each corner, join (834).

Rnd 6: Ch 3, dc in each st around with 2 dc in each of center 2 sts on each corner, join (842).

Rnds 7-9: Ch 3, dc in each st around with 2 dc in each of center 4 sts on each corner, join, ending with 890 dc in last rnd.

Rnd 10: Ch 1, sc in first st, ch 6, beg picot, (dc in same sc, picot) 4 times, skip next 4 sts, *sc in next st, ch 6, beg picot, (dc in same sc, picot) 4 times, skip next 4 sts; repeat from * around, join with sl st in first sc, fasten off.

BUTTERFLY (make 12)
Wings

NOTE: *Use No. 10 steel hook and size-20 crochet cotton unless otherwise stated.*

With yellow; for **first Wing,** *ch 7, sl st in 4th ch from hook, skip next 2 chs, dc in last ch, picot, (dc in same ch as last dc, picot) 3 times*; working in end of Wing, 2 sl sts across last dc; for **second Wing,** repeat between **, fasten off.

Body

With brown, ch 13, sl st in 2nd ch from hook, sl st in each of next 2 chs, sc in each of next 3 chs, hdc in next ch, dc in next ch leaving last 4 chs unworked; for **antennae,** ch 4, fasten off.

Sew Wings to center of Body.

LONG STEM & LEAVES (make 8)

With green, ch 17, sl st in 4th ch from hook, ch 4, sl st in same ch, ch 9, sl st in 4th ch from hook, ch 7, sl st in 4th ch from hook, ch 10, fasten off.

SHORT STEM & LEAVES (make 8)

With green, ch 9, sl st in 4th ch from hook, ch 4, sl st in same ch, ch 4, fasten off.

LEAF (make 16)

With green, ch 4, sl st in 4th ch from hook, ch 3, sl st in same ch, fasten off.

FLOWER (make 32 variegated pink and 8 variegated lavender)

Ch 2, sl st in 2nd ch from hook, ch 3, (sl st in same ch, ch 3) 5 times, join with sl st in first sl st, fasten off.

For **Flower center,** with yellow, embroider French Knot (see page 159) in center of each Flower.

Sew Stems, Leaves, Flowers and Butterflies in each corner of Border according to Assembly Diagram.❦

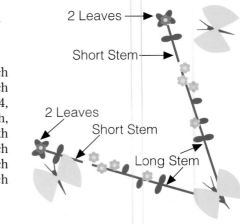

ASSEMBLY DIAGRAM

2 Leaves
Short Stem
2 Leaves
Short Stem
Long Stem

Zigzag Adventures

Continued from page 107

across each edge between corner ch-2 sps).

NOTE: *For **front post stitch (fp,** see page 159), yo, insert hook from front to back around post of next st, draw lp through, (yo, draw through 2 lps on hook) 2 times.*

Rnd 3: Ch 3, dc in next st, *fp around each of next 2 sts, (dc in each of next 2 sts, fp around each of next 2 sts) across to next corner ch sp, (2 dc, ch 2, 2 dc) in next corner ch sp; repeat from * 3 more times, fp around each of last 2 sts, join (114 sts across each edge between corner ch-2 sps).

Rnd 4: Ch 3, dc in next st, *(fp around each of next 2 sts, dc in each of next 2 sts) across to next corner ch sp, (2 dc, ch 2, 2 dc) in next corner ch sp, dc in each of next 2 sts; repeat from * 3 more times, fp around each of last 2 sts, join (118 sts across each edge between corner ch-2 sps).

Rnd 5: Ch 3, dc in next st, *fp around each of next 2 sts, (dc in each of next 2 sts, fp around each of next 2 sts) across to next corner ch sp, (2 dc, ch 2, 2 dc) in next corner ch sp; repeat from * 3 more times, fp around each of next 2 sts, dc in each of next 2 sts, fp around each of last 2 sts, join (122 sts across each edge between corner ch-2 sps).

Rnd 6: Ch 3, dc in next st, (fp around each of next 2 sts, dc in each of next 2 sts) across to next corner ch sp, *[(2 dc, ch 2, 2 dc) in next corner ch sp], dc in each of next 2 sts, (fp around each of next 2 sts, dc in each of next 2 sts) across to next corner ch sp; repeat from * 2 more times; repeat between [ ], (dc in each of next 2 sts, fp around each of next 2 sts) across, join, fasten off (126 sts across each edge between corner ch-2 sps).

Rnd 7: Join variegated with sl st in first st, ch 3, dc in next st, *[fp around each of next 2 sts, (dc in each of next 2 sts, fp around each of next 2 sts) across] to next corner ch sp, (2 dc, ch 2, 2 dc) in next corner ch sp; repeat from * 2 more times; repeat between [ ], join, fasten off (130 sts across each edge between corner ch-2 sps).

Rnd 8: Join white with sl st in first st, repeat rnd 6 (134 sts across each edge between corner ch-2 sps).

Rnd 9: Repeat rnd 7 (138 sts across each edge between corner ch-2 sps).

Rnd 10: Join white with sl st in first st, ch 3, dc in next st, (fp around each of next 2 sts, dc in each of next 2 sts) across to next corner ch sp, *[(2 dc, ch 1, 2 dc) in next corner ch sp], dc in each of next 2 sts, (fp around each of next 2 sts, dc in each of next 2 sts) across to next corner ch sp; repeat from * 2 more times; repeat between [ ], (dc in each of next 2 sts, dc fp around each of next 2 sts) across, join (142 sts across each edge between corner ch-1 sps).

Rnd 11: Working this rnd in **back lps** only, sl st in each st around with 2 sl sts in each corner ch-1 sp, join with sl st in first sl st, fasten off.❦

Interlaced Images

Continued from page 113

working behind next ch sp, 2 dc in next skipped st on row before last, sc in last st, fasten off (190 sts).

Row 6: Join med. gray with sl st in first st, ch 3, dc in each st across, fasten off.

Row 7: With med. gray, repeat row 2.

Rows 8-9: With dk. gray, repeat rows 3 and 4.

Rows 10-12: With lt. gray, repeat rows 5, 6 and 2.

Rows 13-14: With med. gray, repeat rows 3 and 4.

Rows 15-16: With dk. gray, repeat rows 5 and 6.

Rows 17-121: Repeat rows 2-16 consecutively. At end of last row, **do not** fasten off.

Row 122: Working from left to right, ch 1, **reverse sc** (see page 158) in each st across, fasten off.

Row 123: Working in starting ch on opposite side of row 1, join dk. gray with sl st in first ch, ch 1, reverse sc in each ch across, fasten off.

FRINGE

For **each Fringe,** cut one strand of each color each 14" long. Holding all three strands together, fold in half, insert hook in end of row, draw fold through, draw all loose ends through fold including 7"-long strand, tighten. Trim ends.

Fringe in end of each row on each short end of Afghan.❦

Morning's Glow

Continued from page 115

corner ch sp on one Block, *[ch 1, sc in corresponding corner ch sp on other Block, (ch 1, sc in next st on this Block, ch 1, sc in next st on other Block) across to next corner ch sp, ch 1, sc in next corner ch sp on this Block, ch 1, sc in next corner ch sp on other Block]; holding two more Blocks next to last two Blocks worked, sc in first corner ch sp on next Block; repeat from * 9 more times; repeat between [ ], fasten off (2 rows of 11 Blocks each). Repeat with remaining Blocks, making a total of 8 rows with 11 Blocks each. Join remaining edges in same manner.

BORDER

Rnd 1: Working around entire outer edge, join brown with sc in any corner ch sp, 2 sc in same sp, sc in each st and 2 sc in each joining ch sp around with 3 sc in each corner ch sp, join with sl st in first sc.

Rnd 2: Ch 2, 3 hdc in next st, hdc in each st around with 3 hdc in each center corner st, join with sl st in top of ch-2.

Rnd 3: Working from left to right, ch 1, **reverse sc** (see page 158) in each st around, join with sl st in first sc, fasten off. ❦

Peaceful Surroundings

Continued from page 117

across each side between ch sps).

Rnd 4: Join green fleck with sl st in any ch sp, ch 3, (dc, ch 2, 2 dc) in same sp, dc in **back lp** of next 13 sts, *(2 dc, ch 2, 2 dc) in next ch sp, dc in **back lp** of next 13 sts; repeat from * around, join, fasten off (17 sts across each side between ch sps).

Holding two Squares wrong sides together, matching sts, with green fleck, sew together through **back lps** across one side. Repeat until all Squares are joined end to end.

Edging

Row 1: Join navy fleck in corner ch sp before one long edge, ch 3, *[dc in each of next 3 sts, tr fp around next st, (dc in next st, tr fp around next st) 5 times, dc in each of next 3 sts, dc in next ch sp], tr last ch sp and next ch sp tog, dc in same ch sp; repeat from * 10 more times; repeat between [ ] leaving remaining sts unworked, **do not** turn, fasten off (239 sts).

Row 2: Join burgundy fleck with sl st in first st, ch 3, dc in each of next 2 sts, *tr fp around next st, (dc in next st, dtr fp around next st on last rnd of Square, dc in next st on last row, tr fp around next st) 3 times, dc in each of next 3 sts], tr fp around next st, dc in each of next 3 sts; repeat from * 10 more times; repeat between [ ], **do not** turn, fasten off.

Row 3: Join green with sl st in first st, ch 3, dc in each of next 2 sts, *tr fp around next st, (dc in next st, tr fp around next st) 6 times, dc in each of next 3 sts], tr fp around next st, dc in each of next 3 sts; repeat from * 10 more times; repeat between [ ], fasten off.

Work Edging across one long edge of 2 Strips and across both long edges of 4 Strips.

Holding Strips wrong sides together, matching sts of Edging, working through both thicknesses, with burgundy fleck, sc together according to Assembly Diagram.

BORDER

Rnd 1: Working around entire outer edge, join navy fleck with sl st in corner ch sp before one short end, ch 3, (dc, ch 2, 2 dc) in same sp; work following steps to finish rnd:

Step A: *[dc in each of next 3 sts, tr fp around next st, (dc in next st, tr fp around next st) 5 times, dc in each of next 3 sts], dc in next ch sp, tr last ch sp and end of next row tog, dc in same row, 2 dc in end of next row, dc in end of next row; skipping seam in between, tr last row and next row on next Strip tog, dc in same row, 2 dc in end of next row, dc in end of next row, tr same row and next ch sp tog, dc in same ch sp; repeat from * 4 more times; repeat between [ ];

Step B: (2 dc, ch 2, 2 dc) in next corner ch sp, *[dc in each of next 3 sts, tr fp around next st, (dc in next st, tr fp around next st) 5 times, dc in each of next 3 sts], dc in next ch sp, tr last ch sp and next ch sp tog, dc in same ch

ASSEMBLY DIAGRAM

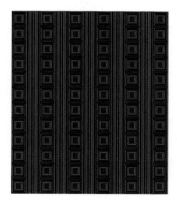

Continued on next page

Peaceful Surroundings

Continued from page 153

sp; repeat from * 10 more times; repeat between [ ];

Step C: (2 dc, ch 2, 2 dc) in next corner ch sp; repeat Step A;

Step D: Repeat Step B, join with sl st in top of ch-3, fasten off (171 sts across each short end between ch sps, 241 sts across each long edge between ch sps).

Rnd 2: Join burgundy fleck with sl st in first ch sp, ch 3, (dc, ch 2, 2 dc) in same sp; work following steps to finish rnd:

Step A: Dc in next 4 sts, *[tr fp around next st, (dc in next st, dtr fp around next st on rnd before last, dc in next st, tr around next st) 3 times], dc in each of next 3 sts, tr fp around next st, (dc in next 4 sts, tr fp around next st) 2 times, dc in each of next 3 sts; repeat from * 4 more times; repeat between [ ], dc in next 4 sts;

Step B: (2 dc, ch 2, 2 dc) in next corner ch sp, dc in next 4 sts, tr fp around next st, (dc in next st, dtr fp around next st on rnd before last, dc in next st on last rnd, tr fp around next st) 3 times, *(dc in each of next 3 sts, tr fp around next st) 2 times, (dc in next st, dtr fp around next st on rnd before last, dc in next st on last rnd, tr fp around next st) 3 times; repeat from * 10 more

times, dc in next 4 sts;

Step C: (2 dc, ch 2, 2 dc) in next corner ch sp; repeat step A;

Step D: Repeat step B, join, fasten off.

Rnd 3: Join green fleck with sl st in first corner ch sp, ch 3, (dc, ch 2, 2 dc) in same sp; work following steps to finish rnd:

Step A: Dc in next 6 sts, tr fp around next st, (dc in next st, tr fp around next st) 6 times, *dc in each of next 3 sts, tr fp around next st, (dc in next 4 sts, tr fp around next st) 2 times, dc in each of next 3 sts, tr fp around next st, (dc in next st, tr fp around next st) 6 times; repeat from * 4 more times, dc in next 6 sts;

Step B: (2 dc, ch 2, 2 dc) in next corner ch sp, dc in next 6 sts, tr fp around next st, (dc in next st, tr fp around next st) 6 times, *(dc in each of next 3 sts, tr fp around next st) 2 times, (dc in next st, tr fp around next st) 6 times; repeat from * 10 more times, dc in next 6 sts;

Step C: (2 dc, ch 2, 2 dc) in next corner ch sp; repeat Step A;

Step D: Repeat step B, join, fasten off.

Rnd 4: Join burgundy fleck with sc in first corner ch sp, 2 sc in same sp, sc in each st around with 3 sc in each corner ch sp, join with sl st in first sc, fasten off. ❧

Revelations

Continued from page 121

ch-1 sp) 2 times], shell in ch sp of next shell; repeat from * 2 more times; repeat between [ ], join, **turn,** fasten off (12 pc, 8 3-dc groups, 4 shells).

Rnd 3: Join rust with sc in ch sp of any shell, 2 sc in same sp, sc in each st around with 3 sc in ch sp of each shell, join with sl st in first sc, **turn** (17 sc across each side between center corner sts).

Rnd 4: Ch 3, 5 dc in next st, dc in each st around with 5 dc in each center corner st, join with sl st in top of ch-3, **turn** (21 dc across each side between center corner sts).

Rnd 5: Ch 1, sc in each st around with 3 sc in each center corner st, join with sl st in first sc, fasten off (23 sc across each side between center corner sts).

Holding Blocks wrong sides together, matching sts, with rust, sew together in 6 rows of 7 Blocks each.

EDGING

Rnd 1: Working around entire outer edge, join variegated with sc in center corner st before one short end, 2 sc in same st, sc in each st around skipping seams with 3 sc in each center corner st, join with sl st in first sc (150 sc across each short end between center corner sts, 175 sc across each long

edge between center corner sts).

Rnd 2: Sl st in next st, ch 3, 2 dc in same st, *ch 1, skip next 2 sts, (dc in next st, ch 1, skip next st) across to next center corner st, 3 dc in next st, ch 1, skip next st, (dc in next st, ch 1, skip next st) across* to next center corner st, 3 dc in next st; repeat between **, join with sl st in top of ch-3.

Rnd 3: Ch 1, sc in first st, (ch 3, sc in next st) 2 times, (ch 3, sc in next ch sp) across to next 3-dc corner, *(ch 3, sc in next st) 3 times, (ch 3, sc in next ch sp) across to next 3-dc corner; repeat from * around; to **join,** ch 1, hdc in first sc.

Rnds 4-5: Ch 1, sc around joining hdc, (ch 3, sc in next ch sp) around, join as before.

Rnd 6: Ch 1, 2 sc around joining hdc, 3 sc in each ch sp around, sc in joining ch-1 sp of last rnd, join with sl st in first sc, fasten off. ❧

MOTIF JOINING DIAGRAM

• = Joining

Timeless Treasure

Continued from page 127

2 sts, dc in next 8 sts, dc-bp around each of next 2 sts, (dc in next 4 sts, hdc in next 23 sts, dc in next 4 sts, dc-bp

around each of next 2 sts, dc in next 8 sts, dc-bp around each of next 2 sts) 6 times, dc in last 5 sts, turn.

Row 8: Ch 3, dc in each of next 2 sts, back twist, dc in next 8 sts, front twist, *dc in next 5 sts, pc in next st, (dc in each of next 3 sts, pc in next st) 4 times, dc in next 5 sts, back twist, dc in next 8 sts, front twist; repeat from * 5 more times, dc in each of last 3 sts, turn.

Row 9: Ch 3, dc in each of next 2 sts, dc-bp around each of next 2 sts, dc in next 12 sts, dc-bp around each of next 2 sts, (dc in each of next 2 sts, hdc in next 23 sts, dc in each of next 2 sts, dc-bp around each of next 2 sts, dc in next 12 sts, dc-bp around each of next 2 sts) 6 times, dc in each of last 3 sts, turn.

Row 10: Ch 3, dc in each of next 2 sts, dc-fp around each of next 2 sts, dc in next 12 sts, dc-fp around each of next 2 sts, *dc in each of next 3 sts, (pc in next st, dc in each of next 3 sts) 6 times, dc-fp around each of next 2 sts, dc in next 12 sts, dc-fp around each of next 2 sts; repeat from * 5 more times, dc in each of last 3 sts, turn.

Row 11: Ch 3, dc in each of next 2 sts, dc-bp around each of next 2 sts, dc in next 12 sts, dc-bp around each of next 2 sts, (dc in each of next 2 sts, hdc in next 23 sts, dc in each of next 2 sts, dc–bp around each of next 2 sts, dc in next 12 sts, dc-bp around each of next 2 sts) 6 times, dc in each of last 3 sts, turn.

Row 12: Ch 3, dc in each of next 2 sts, front twist, dc in next 8 sts, back twist, *dc in next 5 sts, pc in next st, (dc in each of next 3 sts, pc in next st) 4 times, dc in next 5 sts, front twist, dc in next 8 sts, back twist; repeat from * 5 more times, dc in each of last 3 sts, turn.

Row 13: Ch 3, dc in next 4 sts, dc-bp around each of next 2 sts, dc in next 8 sts, dc-bp around each of next 2 sts, (dc in next 4 sts, hdc in next 23 sts, dc in next 4 sts, dc-bp around each of next 2 sts, dc in next 8 sts, dc-bp around each of next 2 sts) 6 times, dc in last 5 sts, turn.

Row 14: Ch 3, dc in next 4 sts, front twist, dc in next 4 sts, back twist, *dc in next 5 sts, pc in next st, (dc in each of next 3 sts, pc in next st) 5 times, dc in next 5 sts, front twist, dc in next 4 sts, back twist; repeat from * 5 more times, dc in last 5 sts, turn.

Row 15: Ch 3, dc in next 6 sts, dc-bp around each of next 2 sts, dc in next 4 sts, dc-bp around each of next 2 sts, (dc in next 6 sts, hdc in next 23 sts, dc in next 6 sts, dc-bp around each of next 2 sts, dc in next 4 sts, dc-bp around each of next 2 sts) 6 times, dc in last 7 sts, turn.

Row 16: Ch 3, dc in next 6 sts, front twist, back twist, *dc in next 9 sts, pc in next st, (dc in each of next 3 sts, pc in next st) 4 times, dc in next 9 sts, front twist, back twist; repeat from * 5 more times, dc in last 7 sts, turn.

Row 17: Ch 3, dc in next 8 sts, dc-bp around next 4 sts, (dc in next 8 sts, hdc in next 23 sts, dc in next 8 sts, dc-bp around next 4 sts) 6 times, dc in last 9 sts, turn.

Rows 18-194: Repeat rows 2-17 consecutively, ending with row 2. At end of last row, **do not** turn.

Rnd 195: Working in rnds, ch 3, 2 dc in top of last dc made; (working in ends of rows, skip first row, 2 dc in end

of each row across to last row, skip last row); working in starting ch on opposite side of row 1, 3 dc in first ch, dc in each ch across with 3 sc in last ch; repeat between ( ); working in sts across last row, 3 dc in first st, dc in each st across, join with sl st in top of ch-3 (280 dc across each short end between center corner sts, 386 dc across each long edge between center corner sts).

***NOTE:** For **treble cluster (cl),** *yo 2 times, insert hook in same st, yo, draw lp through, (yo, draw through 2 lps on hook) 2 times; repeat from *, yo, draw through all 3 lps on hook.*

Rnd 196: (Ch 4, 2 cl) in same st, (sl st, ch 4, 2 cl) in each of next 2 sts, [skip next 2 sts, *(sl st, ch 4, 2 cl) in next st, skip next 2 sts*; repeat between ** across to next 3-dc corner, (sl st, ch 4, 2 cl) in each of next 3 sts, skip next 2 sts; repeat between ** across to next 3-dc corner], (sl st, ch 4, 2 cl) in next 3 sts; repeat between [ ], join with sl st in joining sl st on last rnd, fasten off.

ROSE (make 24)

Row 1: With No. 12 steel hook and pink, ch 23, sc in 5th ch from hook, (ch 2, skip next ch, sc in next ch) across, turn (10 ch sps).

Row 2: Ch 1, (sc, 5 dc, sc) in each ch sp across, fasten off. Roll into rose shape; tack together at bottom.

For **stem,** with No. 12 steel hook and green, (ch 8, sl st in 5th ch from hook) 2 times, ch 13, sl st in 5th ch from hook, ch 5, sl st in same ch, ch 10, sl st in 5th ch from hook, ch 5, sl st in same ch, fasten off.

ROSEBUD (make 84)

With No. 12 steel hook and pink, ch 5, sl st in 5th ch from hook to form loop, ch 1, (sc, 5 dc, sc) in loop, join with sl st in first sc, fasten off.

For **stem,** with No. 12 steel hook and green, (ch 8, sl st in 5th ch from hook) 2 times, (ch 10, sl st in 5th ch from hook, ch 5, sl st in same ch) 2 times, fasten off.

FINISHING

Sew one Rosebud between 2 top ch-5 lps of each Rose stem. Working vertically, starting with first column of diamond shapes on Afghan, sew one Rose stem to center of every other diamond beginning with 2nd diamond. Sew one Rose to center of each stem. Repeat on every other column of diamonds across Afghan.

Sew one Rosebud between 2 top ch-5 lps of each Rosebud stem. Starting with 2nd column of diamond shapes on Afghan, sew one Rosebud stem to center of every other diamond beginning with first diamond. Repeat on every other column of diamonds across Afghan. ❦

Enduring Love

Continued from page 129

across to next corner ch sp, *(3 dc, ch 2, 3 dc) in next corner ch sp, 2 dc in next ch sp, (3 dc in next ch sp, 2 dc in next ch sp) across to next corner ch sp; repeat from * around, join with sl st in top of ch-3, fasten off (28 dc across each side between corner ch sps).

Holding Blocks wrong sides together, matching sts, with winter white, sew together through **back lps** in 5 rows of 7 Blocks each.

BORDER

Rnd 1: Working around entire outer edge, join med. rose with sc in any corner ch sp, sc in each st and in each seam around with 3 sc in each corner ch sp, join with sl st in first sc, fasten off (146 sc across each short end between center corner sc, 204 sc across each long edge between center corner sc).

Rnd 2: Join winter white with sc in any center corner st, ch 3, skip next 2 sts, (sc in next st, ch 3, skip next st) across to next center corner st, *(sc, ch 3, sc) in next st, ch 3, skip next 2 sts, (sc in next st, ch 3, skip next st) across to next center corner st; repeat from * around, join.

Continued on next page

Enduring Love

Continued from page 155

Rnds 3-4: Sl st in first ch sp, ch 1, (sc, ch 3, sc) in same sp, ch 3, (sc in next ch sp, ch 3) across to next corner ch sp, *(sc, ch 3, sc) in next ch sp, ch 3, (sc in next ch sp, ch 3) across to next corner ch sp; repeat from * around, join. At end of last rnd, fasten off.

Rnd 5: Join green with sc in any corner ch sp, (ch 3, sc) in same sp, ch 3, *(sc, ch 3, sc) in next ch sp, ch 3; repeat from * around, join, fasten off.❦

Sunshine & Roses

Instructions on page 131

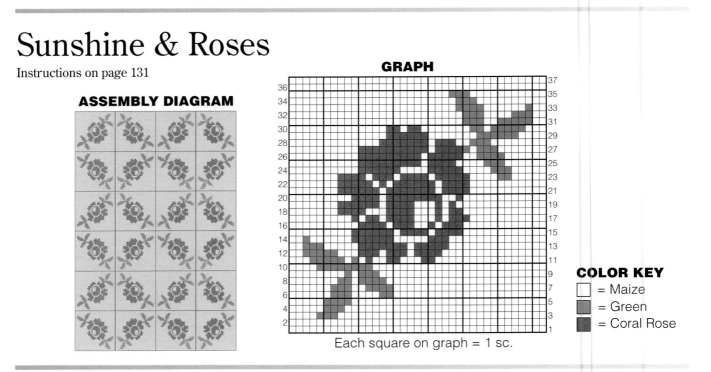

ASSEMBLY DIAGRAM

GRAPH

Each square on graph = 1 sc.

COLOR KEY
☐ = Maize
▨ = Green
▦ = Coral Rose

Endless Romance

Continued from page 133

across, join, ending with 6 V-sts across each side between corner ch-3 sps in last rnd.

Rnd 10: Ch 1, sc in each dc and in each ch-1 sp around with 3 sc in each corner ch-3 sp, join with sl st in first sc, fasten off (25 sc across each side between center corner sts).

Holding Large Squares wrong sides together, matching sts, with black, sew together through **back lps** according to Assembly Diagram.

SMALL SQUARE (make 24)

Rnd 1: With black, ch 4, sl st in first ch to form ring, beg V-st in ring, ch 3, (V-st in ring, ch 3) 3 times, join with sl st in 3rd ch of ch-4 (4 V-sts, 4 ch-3 sps).

Rnd 2: Sl st in next ch-1 sp, sl st in next st, sl st in next ch-3 sp, beg V-st, (ch 3, V-st) in same sp, ch 1, skip next V-st, *(V-st, ch 3, V-st) in next ch-3 sp, ch 1, skip next V-st; repeat from * around, join (8 V-sts, 4 ch-3 sps, 4 ch-1 sps).

Rnd 3: Ch 1, sc in each dc and in each ch-1 sp around with 3 sc in each corner ch-3 sp, join with sl st in first sc, fasten off (9 sc across each side between center corner sc).

Holding Squares wrong sides together, matching sts, with black, sew Small Squares to sps between Large Squares through **back lps** according to Assembly Diagram.

TASSEL (make 22)

For **each Tassel,** cut 30 strands red each 12" long. Tie sep-arate strand red tightly around middle of all strands; fold strands in half. Wrap separate strand several times around folded strands 2" from top of fold, secure and hide ends inside Tassel. Trim ends.

Tie one Tassel to each point of Large Squares and Small Squares on each short end of Afghan.❦

ASSEMBLY DIAGRAM

For More Information

Sometimes even the most experienced needle-crafters can find themselves having trouble following instructions. If you have difficulty completing your project, write to:

Afghan Romance Editors
The Needlecraft Shop
23 Old Pecan Road, Big Sandy, Texas 75755

General Instructions

Yarn & Hooks

Always use the weight of yarn specified in the pattern so you can be assured of achieving the proper gauge. It is best to purchase extra of each color needed to allow for differences in tension and dyes.

The hook size stated in the pattern is to be used as a guide. Always work a swatch of the stitch pattern with the suggested hook size. If you find your gauge is smaller or larger than what is specified, choose a different size hook.

Gauge

Gauge is measured by counting the number of rows or stitches per inch. Each of the patterns featured in this book will have a gauge listed. Gauge for some small motifs or flowers is given as an overall measurement. Proper gauge must be attained for the project to come out the size stated, and to prevent ruffling and puckering.

Make a swatch in the stitch indicated in the gauge section of the instructions. Lay the swatch flat and measure the stitches. If you have more stitches per inch than specified in the pattern, your gauge is too tight and you need a larger hook. Fewer stitches per inch indicates a gauge that is too loose. In this case, choose a smaller hook size. Next, check the number of rows. If necessary, adjust your row gauge slightly by pulling the loops down a little tighter on your hook, or by pulling the loops up slightly to extend them.

Once you've attained the proper gauge, you're ready to start your project. Remember to check your gauge periodically to avoid problems later.

Pattern Repeat Symbols

Written crochet instructions typically include symbols such as parentheses, asterisks and brackets. In some patterns a diamond or bullet (dot) may be added.

( ) Parentheses enclose instructions which are to be worked again later or the number of times indicated after the parentheses. For example, "(2 dc in next st, skip next st) 5 times" means to follow the instructions within the parentheses a total of five times. If no number appears after the parentheses, you will be instructed when to repeat further into the pattern. Parentheses may also be used to enclose a group of stitches which should be worked in one space or stitch. For example, "(2 dc, ch 2, 2 dc) in next st" means to work all the stitches within the parentheses in the next stitch.

* Asterisks may be used alone or in pairs, usually in combination with parentheses. If used in pairs, the instructions enclosed within asterisks will be followed by instructions for repeating. These repeat instructions may appear later in the pattern or immediately after the last asterisk. For example, "*Dc in next 4 sts, (2 dc, ch 2, 2 dc) in corner sp*, dc in next 4 sts; repeat between ** 2 more times" means to work through the instructions up to the word "repeat," then repeat only the instructions that are enclosed within the asterisks twice.

If used alone an asterisk marks the beginning of instructions which are to be repeated. Work through the instructions from the beginning, then repeat only the portion after the * up to the word "repeat"; then follow any remaining instructions. If a number of times is given, work through the instructions one time, repeat the number of times stated, then follow the remainder of the instructions.

[ ] Brackets, ◊ diamonds and • bullets are used in the same manner as asterisks. Follow the specific instructions given when repeating.

Finishing

Patterns that require assembly will suggest a tapestry needle in the materials. This should be a #16, #18 or #26 blunt-tipped tapestry needle. When stitching pieces together, be careful to keep the seams flat so pieces do not pucker.

Hiding loose ends is never a fun task, but if done correctly, may mean the difference between an item looking great for years or one that quickly shows signs of wear. Always leave 6-8" of yarn when beginning or ending. Thread the loose end into your tapestry needle and carefully weave through the back of several stitches. Then, weave in the opposite direction, going through different strands. Gently pull the end and clip, allowing the end to pull up under the stitches.

If your project needs blocking, a light steam pressing works well. Lay your project on a large table or on the floor, depending on the size, shaping and smoothing by hand as much as possible. Adjust your steam iron to the permanent press setting, then hold slightly above the stitches, allowing the steam to penetrate the thread. Do not rest the iron on the item. Gently pull and smooth the stitches into shape, spray lightly with starch and allow to dry completely.

Stiffening

There are many liquid products on the market made specifically for stiffening doilies and other soft items. For best results, carefully read the manufacturer's instructions on the product you select before beginning.

Forms for shaping can be many things. Styrofoam® shapes and plastic margarine tubs work well for items such as bowls and baskets. Glass or plastic drinking glasses are used for vase-type items. If you cannot find an item with the dimensions given in the pattern to use as a form, any similarly sized item can be shaped by adding layers of plastic wrap. Place the dry crochet piece over the form to check the fit, remembering that it will stretch when wet.

For shaping flat pieces, corrugated cardboard, Styrofoam® or a cutting board designed for sewing may be used. Be sure to cover all surfaces of forms or blocking board with clear plastic wrap, securing with cellophane tape.

If you have not used fabric stiffener before, you may wish to practice on a small swatch before stiffening the actual item. For proper saturation when using conventional stiffeners, work liquid thoroughly into the crochet piece and let stand for about 15 minutes. Then, squeeze out excess stiffener and blot with paper towels. Continue to blot while shaping to remove as much stiffener as possible. Stretch over form, shape and pin with rust-proof pins; allow to dry, then unpin.

Stitch Guide

Chain (ch)
Yo, draw hook through lp.

Slip Stitch (sl st)
Insert hook in st, yo, draw through st and lp on hook.

Treble Crochet (tr)
Yo 2 times, insert hook in st (a), yo, draw lp through (b), (yo, draw through 2 lps on hook) 3 times (c, d and e).

a

b

c

d

e

Single Crochet (sc)
Insert hook in st (a), yo, draw lp through, yo, draw through both lps on hook (b).

a   b

Double Crochet (dc)
Yo, insert hook in st (a), yo, draw lp through (b), (yo, draw through 2 lps on hook) 2 times (c and d).

a   b

c   d

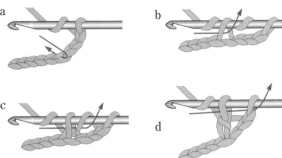

Double Treble Crochet (dtr)
Yo 3 times, insert hook in st (a), yo, draw lp through (b), (yo, draw through 2 lps on hook) 4 times (c, d, e and f).

a   b
c   d
e   f

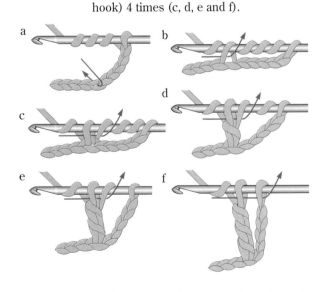

Half Double Crochet (hdc)
Yo, insert hook in st (a), yo, draw lp through (b), yo, draw through all 3 lps on hook (c).

a
b
c

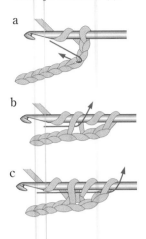

Front Loop (a)/ Back Loop (b)
(front lp/back lp)

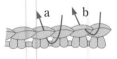

Reverse Single Crochet (reverse sc)
Working from left to right, insert hook in next st to the right (a), yo, draw through st, complete as sc (b).

a

b

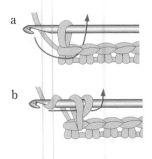

The patterns in this book are written using American crochet stitch terminology. For our international customers, hook sizes, stitches and yarn definitions should be converted as follows:

US	= UK
sl st (slip stitch)	= sc (single crochet)
sc (single crochet)	= dc (double crochet)
hdc (half double crochet)	= htr (half treble crochet)
dc (double crochet)	= tr (treble crochet)
tr (treble crochet)	= dtr (double treble crochet)
dtr (double treble crochet)	= ttr (triple treble crochet)
skip	= miss

Thread/Yarns
Bedspread Weight = No.10 Cotton or Virtuoso
Sport Weight = 4 Ply or thin DK
Worsted Weight = Thick DK or Aran

Measurements
1" = 2.54 cm
1 yd. = .9144 m
1 oz. = 28.35 g

But, as with all patterns, test your gauge (tension) to be sure.

Crochet Hooks

Metric	US	Metric	US
.60mm	14	3.00mm	D/3
.75mm	12	3.50mm	E/4
1.00mm	10	4.00mm	F/5
1.50mm	6	4.50mm	G/6
1.75mm	5	5.00mm	H/8
2.00mm	B/1	5.50mm	I/9
2.50mm	C/2	6.00mm	J/10

Double Love Knot Illustration

Step 1:

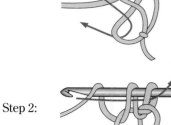

Step 2:

Step 3:

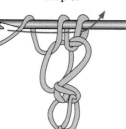

Step 4:

Step 5:

Completed
Double Love Knot

Single Crochet Color Change
(sc color change)
Drop first color; yo with 2nd color,
draw through last 2 lps of st.

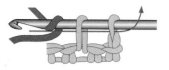

Double Crochet Color Change
(dc color change)
Drop first color; yo with 2nd color,
draw through last 2 lps of st.

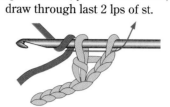

Single Crochet
next 2 stitches
together
(sc next 2 sts tog)
Draw up lp in each of
next 2 sts, yo, draw
through all 3 lps on hook.

Half Double Crochet
next 2 stitches together
(hdc next 2 sts tog)
(Yo, insert hook in next st,
yo, draw lp through) 2
times, yo, draw through
all 5 lps on hook.

Front Post/Back Post Stitches (fp/bp)
Yo, insert hook from front to back (a) or back to
front (b) around post of st on indicated row;
complete as stated in pattern.

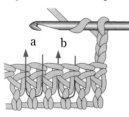

a   b

French Knot

Double Crochet next 2 stitches together
(dc next 2 sts tog)
(Yo, insert hook in next st, yo, draw lp through,
yo, draw through 2 lps on hook) 2 times, yo,
draw through all 3 lps on hook.

Standard Stitch Abbreviations

ch(s) . . . . chain(s)
dc . . . . double crochet
dtr . . . . double treble crochet
hdc . . . . half double crochet
lp(s) . . . . loop(s)
rnd(s) . . . . round(s)
sc . . . . single crochet
sl st . . . . slip stitch
sp(s) . . . . space(s)
st(s) . . . . stitch(es)
tog . . . . together
tr . . . . treble crochet
tr tr/ttr . . . . triple treble crochet
yo . . . . yarn over

Skill Level Requirements:

★ **Easy** — Requires knowledge of basic skills only;
great for beginners or anyone who wants quick
results.

★ ★ **Average** — Requires some experience; very
comfortable for accomplished stitchers, yet suitable for beginners wishing to expand their abili-
ties.

★ ★ ★ **Advanced** — Requires a high level of skill in
all areas; average stitchers may find some areas
of these patterns difficult, though still workable.

★ ★ ★ ★ **Challenging** — Requires advanced skills
in both technique and comprehension, as well
as a daring spirit; some areas may present difficulty for even the most accomplished stitchers.

Index

Acknowledgments

Our sincere thanks and appreciation to the following companies and persons for graciously providing their products, time, personal items and/or locations for use in producing this book.

Yarn Companies

Caron International
Wintuk – Endless Romance

Coats & Clark
Patons Canadiana – Regal Bows, Revelations
Patons Decor – Faithful Friends, Tailors Fancy, Picture Perfect, Love's Devotion, Royal Treatment, Enduring Love, Christmas Fever
Red Heart Baby Sport – Baby Stars, Zigzag Adventures
Red Heart Classic – Contradiction, Country Communion, Daffodil Garden, Warm & Welcome, Sunshine & Roses
Red Heart Jeweltone – Inlaid Amethyst, Grandiloquence, Picot Paradox
Red Heart Sport – Poinsettia Delight
Red Heart Super Saver – Sculpted Sapphires, Rave Reviews, Petunia Potluck, Symphony in Violet, Sweet Impressions, Kitten Soft, Solid Comfort, Morning's Glow

Lion Brand
Chenille Sensations – Yuletide Rose
Homespun – Reflections
Jiffy – Mountain Sunrise, Yuletide Rose, Interlaced Images

Spinrite
Bernat Berella 4 – Spring Melody, Grandma's Favorite, Eternal Blooms, Anticipation, Circles of Love, Musical Days, Chorus of Lace

East Texas Photography Locations and Credits

Locations: Arp — James & Mary Barnett, Eddy & Jacki Calicutt; Kilgore — Craig & Jan Jaynes; Lindale — Dale Miller; Longview — *Stitches 'n Stuff*, Sue Childress & Frances Hughes, owners; Mineola — *Noble Manor Bed & Breakfast*, Rick & Shirley Gordon, owners; Overton — Terry & Jill Waggoner; Tyler — *Encore*, Diane Stewart, owner; Bill & Ruth Whitaker.
Special Prop Help: *Broadway Florist of Big Sandy*, Dale Miller, owner; *Encore*, Diane Stewart, owner; *The Needlecraft Outlet*, Tammie Godfrey, manager; Teri Currington; Jennifer McClain; Jean & Shawn Schrecengost.
Models: *Corinne Hamilton Thornburg*, Fran Rohus; *Clarice Hamilton*, Donna Robertson; *Eustace "Milt" Hamilton*, L.D. McClain; *Tyler*, Nick Cornelison; *Preston*, Henry Hardee; *Ashley*, Diana Kordsmeier.